Intelligence and Espion

Intelligence and Espionage: Secrets and Spies provides a global introduction to the role of intelligence – a key, but sometimes controversial, aspect of ensuring national security. Separating fact from fiction, the book draws on past examples to explore the use and misuse of intelligence, examine why failures take place and address important ethical issues over its use.

Divided into two parts, the book adopts a thematic approach to the topic, guiding the reader through the collection and analysis of information and its use by policymakers, before looking at intelligence sharing. Lomas and Murphy also explore the important associated activities of counter-intelligence and the use of covert action, to influence foreign countries and individuals. Topics covered include human and signals intelligence, the Cuban Missile Crisis, intelligence and Stalin, Trump and the US intelligence community, and the Soviet Bloc. This analysis is supplemented by a comprehensive documents section, containing newly released documents, including material from Edward Snowden's leaks of classified material.

Supported by images, a comprehensive chronology, glossary, and 'who's who' of key figures, *Intelligence and Espionage* is an invaluable resource for anyone interested in the role of intelligence in policymaking, international relations and diplomacy, warfighting and politics to the present day.

Dr Daniel W.B. Lomas, Lecturer in International History at the University of Salford, UK, specialises in the post-1945 British intelligence community. His first book, *Intelligence, Security and the Attlee Governments, 1945–51*, was published in December 2016. He has written for *History Today, BBC History Magazine* and the History of Government Blog.

Dr Christopher J. Murphy is Lecturer in Intelligence Studies at the University of Salford, UK, researching the history of British intelligence in the Twentieth Century. Dr Murphy has published extensively on the history of the British Special Operations Executive (SOE) and intelligence historiography.

Introduction to the series

History is the narrative constructed by historians from traces left by the past. Historical enquiry is often driven by contemporary issues and, in consequence, historical narratives are constantly reconsidered, reconstructed and reshaped. The fact that different historians have different perspectives on issues means that there is often controversy and no universally agreed version of past events. *Seminar Studies* was designed to bridge the gap between current research and debate, and the broad, popular general surveys that often date rapidly.

The volumes in the series are written by historians who are not only familiar with the latest research and current debates concerning their topic, but who have themselves contributed to our understanding of the subject. The books are intended to provide the reader with a clear introduction to a major topic in history. They provide both a narrative of events and a critical analysis of contemporary interpretations. They include the kinds of tools generally omitted from specialist monographs: a chronology of events, a glossary of terms and brief biographies of 'who's who'. They also include bibliographical essays in order to guide students to the literature on various aspects of the subject. Students and teachers alike will find that the selection of documents will stimulate the discussion and offer insight into the raw materials used by historians in their attempt to understand the past.

Clive Emsley and Gordon Martel
Series Editors

Intelligence and Espionage

Secrets and Spies

Daniel W.B. Lomas and
Christopher J. Murphy

Routledge
Taylor & Francis Group
LONDON AND NEW YORK

First published 2019
by Routledge
2 Park Square, Milton Park, Abingdon, Oxon OX14 4RN

and by Routledge
52 Vanderbilt Avenue, New York, NY 10017

Routledge is an imprint of the Taylor & Francis Group, an informa business

British Library Cataloguing-in-Publication Data
A catalogue record for this book is available from the British Library

Library of Congress Cataloging-in-Publication Data
Names: Lomas, Daniel W. B., author. | Murphy, Christopher J. (Christopher John), 1976- author.
Title: Intelligence and espionage : secrets and spies / Daniel W.B. Lomas and Christopher J. Murphy.
Description: Abingdon, Oxon ; New York, NY : Routledge, 2019. | Includes bibliographical references. |
Identifiers: LCCN 2018044908 (print) | LCCN 2018048075 (ebook) | ISBN 9780429021978 (Ebook) | ISBN 9781138303126 (hardback : alk. paper) | ISBN 9781138303133 (pbk. : alk. paper) | ISBN 9780429021978 (ebk)
Subjects: LCSH: Intelligence service. | Espionage. | Spies.
Classification: LCC JF1525.I6 (ebook) | LCC JF1525.I6 L65 2019 (print) | DDC 327.12–dc23
LC record available at https://lccn.loc.gov/2018044908

ISBN: 978-1-138-30312-6 (hbk)
ISBN: 978-1-138-30313-3 (pbk)
ISBN: 978-0-429-02197-8 (ebk)

Typeset in Sabon
by Swales & Willis Ltd

Contents

Figures

Chronology

February 1855	British War Department creates a Topographical and Statistical Department. Later split into two, the Statistical Department became the Intelligence Branch.
June 1866	Following an attempt on his life during the previous month, Prussian Chancellor Otto von Bismark orders the creation of a Political Police organisation, later to become the Central Intelligence Bureau.
June 1871	The French military undergoes a major reorganisation, which includes the creation of the Deuxieme Bureau, responsible for the analysis of intelligence.
July 1908	The US Federal Bureau of Investigation (**FBI**) is created.
October 1909	Britain sets up a Secret Service Bureau (SSB) split into foreign and domestic sections. The domestic arm would become the Security Service (**MI5**) and the foreign section the Secret Intelligence Service (**SIS** or **MI6**).
January 1917	Codebreakers in Britain's Room 40 intercept a telegram from German Foreign Minister Arthur Zimmerman to the Mexican government proposing a German–Mexican alliance, should the United States enter the First World War. The telegram is used as a pretext for the US declaration of war on Germany on 6 April.
December 1917	The Cheka (short for **Chrezvychayneyye komissii** or the 'All-Russian Extraordinary Commission for Combating Counter-Revolution, Sabotage and Speculation') is formed as the first Soviet intelligence and security agency.
January 1921	The Abwehr, a German military intelligence organisation, focusing on counter-espionage organisation, but expanding into foreign intelligence operations, is formed.
October 1924	The so-called Zinoviev Letter – a forged document reportedly from the head of the Communist

	International Grigory Zinoviev – leaked by members of the British intelligence community to the right-wing press in an attempt to undermine Britain's first Labour Government.
June 1931	American cryptologist Herbert O. Yardley publishes *The American Black Chamber* revealing the work of the US Cipher Bureau, America's first peacetime codebreaking organisation.
November 1931	German cipher officer Hans-Thilo Schmidt (codenamed *Asché*) provides French intelligence with details of Germany's Enigma cipher machine.
September 1932	Polish mathematician and cryptologist Marian Adam Rejewski begins work trying to break the Enigma machine. Rejewski – helped by colleagues Jerzy Różycki and Henryk Zygalski – would provide the first breaks laying the groundwork for Allied wartime codebreaking.
October 1937	Soviet intelligence officer Walter Krivitsky defects, offering Western intelligence access to secrets on Stalinist Russia.
August 1940	Leon Trotsky assassinated by Spanish-born Soviet NKVD agent Ramón Mercader.
May 1941	Sailors from the Royal Navy's *HMS Bulldog* capture the Enigma machine and codebooks from German submarine U-110 commanded by *Kapitänleutnant* Fritz-Julius Lemp.
December 1941	Imperial Japanese Navy (IJN) aircraft attack the US Pacific Fleet based at Pearl Harbor, Hawaii.
September 1945	Soviet cipher clerk Igor Gouzenko defects to Canada, providing evidence of a major spy ring including Canadian, US and British agents.
March 1946	British and US officials sign the 'British-American Communication Intelligence Agreement' (or BRUSA) setting out future transatlantic communications intelligence collaboration.
September 1947	Central Intelligence Agency (**CIA**) is formed after the passing of the 1947 National Security Act.
March 1949	Australia's domestic security agency the Australian Security Intelligence Organisation (**ASIO**) is formed.
December 1949	**Mossad** (*HaMossad leModi'in uleTafkidim Meyuḥadim*), the national intelligence service of Israel, is formed.
February 1950	East Germany's Ministry of State Security, popularly known as the Stasi, is formed.

November 1952	The US signals-intelligence organisation the National Security Agency (**NSA**) is formed.
December 1952	Markus Wolf appointed head of East Germany's foreign intelligence service, the HVA (*Hauptverwaltung Aufklärung*), part of the Stasi.
April 1953	Former intelligence officer Ian Fleming publishes the first James Bond novel *Casino Royale*, fictionalising the work of Britain's SIS. Fleming's literary depiction of intelligence continues to shape popular understanding of the subject.
August 1953	Britain's SIS and America's CIA overthrow the Iranian government of Mohammed Mossadeq in Operation BOOT/AJAX.
March 1954	Soviet **KGB** (*Komitet Gosudarstvennoy Bezopasnosti* or Committee for State Security) set up. It was the successor of the Cheka, NKGB, NKVD and MGB.
April 1954	Intelligence officer Vladimir Petrov defects to Australia. Petrov gave the Australian Security Intelligence Organisation (ASIO) important details on Soviet operations.
March 1955	The Berlin Tunnel (Operation Stopwatch/Gold), a 1,476 foot long tunnel constructed by British and US intelligence between East and West Berlin, goes into operation.
April 1956	Germany's foreign intelligence agency the Federal Intelligence Service (*Bundesnachrichtendienst* or **BND**) formed out of the post-war Gehlen Organisation.
May 1960	American U-2 spy plane shot down in Soviet air space. Pilot Francis Gary Powers is captured and later released in a spy swap in February 1962.
August 1960	First successful recovery of film from spy satellite Discoverer 14 used in the CIA's CORONA programme. The first film covered 1,650,000 square miles of Soviet territory, giving a wide range of intelligence on Soviet nuclear and technological development.
August 1961	KGB assassin Bogdan Shashinsky defects to West Germany admitting to the deaths of Ukrainian nationalists Lev Rebet and Stephan Bandera.
October 1962	An American U-2 spy plane provides photographic evidence of Soviet medium-range ballistic missiles (MRBMs) on Cuba, sparking the Cuban Missile Crisis.
January 1963	Former SIS officer Harold Adrian Russell 'Kim' Philby defects to the Soviet Union. Philby was a member of the 'Cambridge Five' and a KGB mole.

November 1963	Soviet Union establishes a signals-intelligence facility at Lourdes, Cuba.
August 1966	Iraqi pilot Munir Redfa defects to Israel in a MiG-21 Soviet fighter plane, allowing the West an insight into Soviet technology.
January 1968	North Korea captures the spy ship *USS Pueblo*.
September 1971	The British government expels 105 Soviet diplomats suspected of spying in Operation FOOT.
October 1973	Israeli analysts and policymakers surprised by a coalition of Arab states led by Egypt and Syria in the Yom Kippur (or October) War.
January 1975	US Senate votes to set up a bipartisan committee under Senator Frank Church to probe abuses by the CIA.
May 1975	CIA officer Philip Agee publishes *Inside the Company: CIA Diary*, identifying around 250 officers, front companies and foreign agents working for the United States.
September 1978	Dissident writer Georgi Markov assassinated in London by Bulgarian secret service using a poisoned pellet deployed from an umbrella.
July 1985	KGB officer Oleg Gordievsky defects from the Soviet Union. Gordievsky had been an SIS agent from 1974 to 1985.
July 1985	Officers from France's external intelligence agency the *Direction Générale de la Sécurité Extérieure* (General Directorate for External Security) sink the Greenpeace ship *Rainbow Warrior* in the port of Auckland, New Zealand.
July 1987	Former MI5 officer Peter Wright publishes *Spycatcher: The Candid Autobiography of a Senior Intelligence Officer*, a book banned by Britain's Conservative Government, resulting in legal action.
March 1988	GRU (Glavnoye razvedyvatel'noye upravleniye) Major-General Dmitri Fyodorovich Polyakov executed having been found guilty of spying for US intelligence. Polyakov had been recruited by the FBI while serving at the UN in New York in 1961.
February 1994	CIA officer Aldrich Ames arrested and charged with spying for the Soviet KGB and Russian **SVR** (Sluzhba vneshney razvedki).
February 2001	FBI agent Robert Hanssen charged with spying for Russia. Hanssen spied for the KGB and SVR for 22 years.
September 2001	Al-Qaeda terrorists in a series of coordinated attacks using hijacked passenger planes strike the World Trade

	Center in New York, the Pentagon in Washington, and crash a fourth airplane in rural Pennsylvania, killing almost 3,000 and injuring 6,000 people.
September 2002	British government publishes a report based on the reports of the Joint Intelligence Committee to justify the invasion of Iraq.
November 2005	Journalist Dana Priest reveals that the CIA have been holding and interrogating suspected Al-Qaeda operatives at 'black sites' in Afghanistan, Thailand and Eastern Europe.
November 2006	Former **FSB** (Federal'naya sluzhba bezopasnosti Rossiyskoy Federatsii) officer Alexander Litvinenko murdered in London by Russian agents using a dose of radioactive polonium-210.
July 2009	Former Boeing employee Dongfan 'Greg' Chung found guilty of committing economic espionage for the People's Republic of China, and sentenced to 15 years and nine months in prison.
May 2011	US Navy Seals from Seal Team 6, using CIA intelligence, kill Al-Qaeda leader Osama bin Laden.
May 2013	US intelligence whistle-blower Edward Snowden leaves the United States bound for Hong Kong. Within days, Snowden leaks details of sensitive NSA and GCHQ surveillance programmes, widely reported in Western media.
December 2014	Senate Select Committee on Intelligence publishes a 525-page summary of a still-classified document on the CIA's 'enhanced interrogation' programme, concluding that the use of torture was 'not an effective means of obtaining accurate information'.
October 2016	US Department of Homeland Security and Director of National Intelligence issue a joint statement that Russia was trying to interfere in the US Presidential Election by stealing sensitive information and manipulating the media.
May 2017	*New York Times* reports that Chinese intelligence had killed or arrested 18 to 20 CIA agents between 2010 and 2012, crippling US HUMINT in the country.
May 2017	FBI Director James Comey sacked by President Donald Trump.
March 2018	Former FSB double agent Sergei Skripal and his daughter Yulia poisoned using a suspected 'nerve agent' in Salisbury.

Who's who

Allende, Salvador (Salvador Allende Gossens) (1908–1973): Marxist President of Chile from November 1970 to September 1973. Allende unsuccessfully ran for President in 1952, 1958 and 1964. His rise was a cause of concern in the White House, with the CIA tasked with undermining Allende. In September 1973, Allende's government collapsed amid a military coup. Allende committed suicide having vowed not to resign.

Ames, Aldrich Hazen (1941–): Former CIA officer turned KGB mole. Ames joined the CIA in 1962, after graduating from George Washington University, and was first posted to Turkey. Postings to Washington, New York and Mexico City followed, before a return to CIA headquarters as a counterintelligence officer. Due to financial difficulties, Ames approached the KGB promising to sell classified information. During his career as a KGB mole, Ames provided the details of Western agents and passed an estimated 10–15,000 documents before his arrest in 1994. Ames is currently serving a life sentence without the possibility of parole.

Angleton, James Jesus (1917–1987): CIA Director of Counterintelligence sacked in December 1974. Angleton started his career with the OSS, later joining the CIA. He became convinced that Western intelligence was penetrated by the KGB, using testimony provided by defector Anatoli Golitsyn. Angleton's growing paranoia handicapped Western intelligence, turning away genuine defectors and starting a series of destructive witch-hunts, before he was removed by DCI Bill Colby.

Belhaj, Abdel Hakim (1966–): Libyan dissident and member of the Libyan Islamic Fighting Group who, along with his wife, Fatima Boudchar, was kidnapped and illegally rendered by the CIA from Kuala Kumpur following an SIS tipoff in 2004. Documents found in 2011 led to claims of SIS's 'complicity' in torture, resulting in legal action. In May 2018, the UK government issued an apology to Belhaj and Boudchar.

Blake, George (born George Behar) (1922–): Born in Rotterdam, Blake became a British national through his father. Living in the Netherlands at the time of the German invasion, he escaped to Britain in 1943, changing his name to Blake. In 1944, he was recruited to SIS and, after a crash-course in Russian, was posed to the British Legation in Seoul where he was captured at the start of the Korean War (1950–1953). Shortly before his release, Blake was recruited by the KGB and betrayed SIS operations in Germany, notably the Berlin Tunnel operation, before his arrest in 1961, being sentenced to a record 42 years in prison. In October 1966 he escaped to Moscow where he still lives today.

Chung, Dongfan 'Greg' (1936–): Born in China, Chung came to the US in the 1960s, becoming naturalised shortly afterwards. An aerospace engineer working for Boeing, he was found guilty of spying for the PRC in the first ever trial under the Economic Espionage Act and sentenced to 15 years for spying in 2010.

Dulles, Allen Welsh (1893–1969): First civilian and longest serving Director of Central Intelligence of the Central Intelligence Agency, 1953–1961. As DCI Dulles saw expansion of the CIA and oversaw coups in Iran (1953) and Guatemala (1954) but was forced to resign by President John F. Kennedy following the failure of the CIA-sponsored Bay of Pigs invasion in 1961.

Fuchs, Emil Julius Klaus (1911–1988): German-born physicist, naturalised as a British subject in 1942, recruited by Soviet intelligence. Working on British atomic research (codenamed 'Tube Alloys'), Fuchs was sent to the US to assist the wartime Manhattan Project and handed the Soviet Union information on the atomic bomb. Fuchs was identified by American codebreakers working on the VENONA programme and confessed to interrogators that he was Soviet spy, and was sentenced to 14 years in prison. He was released in 1959 and emigrated to the German Democratic Republic.

Gordievsky, Oleg Antonovich (1938–): Career KGB officer recruited as an SIS agent while serving under diplomatic cover as a press attaché in Copenhagen in 1974. Assigned to the Soviet Embassy in London in 1982, Gordievsky gave the British details of Soviet operations in the UK and beyond, also providing the British government with a unique insight into Soviet foreign policy, especially fears of a nuclear confrontation in the early 80s. Recalled to Moscow, Gordievsky defected to the West in July 1985.

Gouzenko, Igor Sergeyevich (1919–1982): Soviet cipher clerk working for military intelligence (GRU) in the Soviet Embassy, Ottawa, who defected to the West in September 1945 – three days after the Second World War had formally ended. Gouzenko provided the first real evidence of Soviet spying on their wartime allies, leading to an international counterintelligence investigation and resulting in the arrest of Soviet agents on both sides of the Atlantic, most notably the British scientist Alan Nunn May. Gouzenko remained in Canada, dying in 1982.

Hanssen, Robert Philip (1944–): FBI counterintelligence agent serving 15 consecutive life sentences having spied for the Soviet Union and Russian Federation until his arrest in 2001. Hanssen joined the FBI in 1976, approaching the GRU three years later. In 1985, he gave the KGB the names of FBI agents inside the Soviet Embassy in Washington. During his long career, he compromised NSA/FBI bugging operations, tradecraft with his case described by the FBI as 'possibly the worst intelligence disaster in U.S. history'.

Helms, Richard McGarrah (1913–2002): Director of Central Intelligence, 1966–1973.

Litvinenko, Alexander Valterovich (1962–2006): FSB defector and naturalised British subject poisoned using radioactive polonium-210 in 2006; most likely, a public inquiry concluded, on the orders of Russian President Vladimir Putin.

Marwan, Ashraf (1944–2007): Egyptian billionaire, son-in-law of former President Gamal Abdel Nasser and Mossad agent. As Nasser's son-in-law and a close advisor to his successor, Anwar Sadat, Marwan (codenamed 'The Angel') provided the Israelis with high-level strategic information before the Yom Kippur War in 1973. On the eve of the Egyptian attack, Marwan told the Israelis the attack 'would start tomorrow' allowing for a partial mobilisation. Marwan remained a Mossad asset until 1998, with his identity leaked in 2002. Marwan died in 2007, falling from his fifth floor apartment in central London.

Mohamed, Binyam (1978–): Ethiopian national and UK resident who travelled to Afghanistan in 2001, seized in Pakistan a year later as a suspected enemy combatant and rendered to Morocco by the CIA, before being transferred to the US Guantanamo Bay facility. While detailed in Pakistan and Morocco, Mohamed was 'tortured in medieval ways'. MI5 officers were later found to be complicit in his treatment, leading to a significant financial settlement.

Penkovsky, Oleg Vladimirovich (1919–1963): Colonel in Soviet Military Intelligence (GRU), Penkovsky served as military attaché in Ankara, Turkey, and volunteered to spy for the US in 1960 but was turned down as a likely provocation. Penkovsky was recruited by SIS and jointly run by a SIS/CIA team, codenamed HERO. During his eighteen-month career, Penkovsky provided information on Soviet nuclear weapons and decision-making. Arrested in October 1962, he was convicted of spying, and executed.

Philby, Harold Adrian Russell ('Kim') (1912–1988): Born 1 January 1912 in the Punjab to Harry St John Bridger Philby and his wife, Dora, Philby was educated at Westminster and Trinity College, Cambridge. In 1933 he travelled to Vienna where he met Alice 'Litzi' Friedman who persuaded Philby to become a Soviet agent. The following year, now in London, Philby was approached by the Soviet NKVD to penetrate 'the bourgeois institutions'. Philby started his career as a journalist but joined SIS in July 1940, rising through the service. He was appointed head of SIS's anti-communist Section IX in 1944, head of station Turkey (1946) and Washington (1949) but forced out of SIS in 1951 having come under suspicion for helping fellow spies (and friends) Guy Burgess and Donald Maclean defect in 1951. Philby returned to journalism and defected to Moscow in January 1963, passing away in May 1988.

Pollard, Jonathan (1954–): US naval intelligence analyst convicted of providing top-secret information to Israeli spies. Refused political asylum at the Israeli Embassy in Washington, Pollard was arrested by the FBI and later sentenced to life imprisonment. He was released in 2015.

Powers, Francis Gary (1929–1977): US Air Force and CIA pilot shot down in his U-2 spy plane over Soviet territory. Sentenced to ten years in prison, Powers was released after less than two in a well-publicised spy swap on the Glienicke Bridge, Berlin. He was killed in a helicopter accident in 1977.

Scappaticci, Freddie (1946–): Former double agent and head of the Provisional Irish Republican Army's Internal (PIRA) Security Unit or 'Nutting Squad' codenamed Stakeknife, run by the British Army's Force Research Unit (FRU). Stakeknife gave the security forces 'the crown jewels' on the PIRA. Stakeknife has also attracted considerable controversy; FRU handlers turned a blind eye to Stakeknife's work for the 'Nutting Squad' in order to protect his identity, resulting in up to 40 deaths.

Snowden, Edward Joseph (1983–): Computer professional, former CIA employee and contactor working for the NSA, responsible for disclosing thousands of classified US and 'Five Eyes' community documents to journalists in June 2013. Snowden's reports of mass surveillance by the NSA, GCHQ and other organisations were published in *The Guardian, The Washington Post, Der Spiegel* and others, promoting considerable debate over privacy and accountability. Considered a whistle-blower by some, DCI James Clapper said the leaks had done 'huge, grave damage' to US intelligence. He currently resides in Russia.

White, Sir Dick Goldsmith (1906–1993): British intelligence officer and the first to become both Director General of the Security Service (MI5) (1953–1956) and Chief of SIS (1956–1968). White also served as Intelligence Coordinator in the Cabinet Office.

Vassall, William John Christopher (1924–1996): British Admiralty clerk compromised by a homosexual 'honey trap' while working at the British Embassy in Moscow in 1954. Photographed in compromising positions with other men, Vassall was blackmailed into spying for the KGB and on his return to London gave the Soviets information on British radar, torpedoes and anti-submarine warfare. Vassall was identified as a Soviet spy after the defection of Anatoli Golitsyn and was imprisoned in October 1962. He was released ten years later.

Walsingham, Sir Francis (1532–1590): English diplomat and statesmen who served as Elizabeth I's principal secretary from 1573–1590. A committed Protestant, Walsingham ran an extensive intelligence network protecting the Elizabethan state from those wanting to install a Catholic monarchy, using codebreaking, agents and propaganda.

Wolf, Markus Johannes 'Mischa' (1923–2006): Head of the Main Directorate for Reconnaissance (*Hauptverwaltung Aufklärung*), the foreign intelligence arm of East Germany's Ministry for State Security (**MfS** or **Stasi**).

Part I

Analysis

Introduction

What is 'intelligence'? Theoretical approaches

Before we can begin our study, it is necessary to have some understanding of what is meant by the word 'intelligence'. Despite the fact that it has been the subject of academic study for some 70 years, there continues to be debate and disagreement over what it means. As Warner (2002:n.p.) has observed, the word tends to be 'defined anew by each author who addresses it, and these definitions rarely refer to one another or build off what has been written before'. Others question whether it is possible to pin down a precise definition, or whether this will remain elusive – 'It is like the term "news"', Kahn (2001:79) argues. 'Though all but impossible to define, every journalist knows what it is: when something newsworthy is said in a court of a legislative hearing, all the reporters start taking notes'.

Perhaps the first thing many people will think of when it comes to intelligence is informed by popular culture; a secret agent, engaged in a battle with a (usually foreign) foe. The agent manages to defeat the enemy and thereby saves the world as we know it, perhaps enjoying a vodka martini or two along the way. Unfortunately, this is not a very useful starting point! Hollywood's fictional spies tend to have a licence to kill, while real-life intelligence activity is primarily concerned with the acquisition of information – likely secret – without the knowledge of its owner. Who is responsible for collecting this information? Here again, the popular image of the secret agent falls short; for example, a Caucasian British agent, despatched from London to Beijing, is likely going to draw immediate attention to themselves simply on account of their physical appearance, even if they speak fluent Mandarin. In such cases it would be more useful to approach a commercial traveller who has legitimate business interests in China, and ask them to carry out the illicit information gathering alongside the main purpose of their visit. Yet even this would have its limitations; unless it concerned the company with which they were dealing, how would the traveller access the information, which is likely secret and held in a secure location? Ultimately, the most valuable secret agent, or spy, is a national of the country that is being targeted, who works in, or otherwise has access to, the organisation that holds the desired information, and who can be persuaded, through one or more of a variety of means, to betray the trust of that organisation – indeed, betray their own country – and to collect and pass on the desired information to an intelligence officer, likely working under diplomatic cover in the embassy of the country interested in collecting the information, or otherwise residing in the country covertly. Rather than a Walther PPK, as Herman has observed, 'the most dangerous of an agent's weapons is uncontrolled access to a Xerox copier' (Herman, 1996:65), although it is hard to imagine a photocopier playing a starring role in a Hollywood spy blockbuster. Today, access to such machines has likely been supplanted by access to an organisation's computer network, and the ability to extract information from this onto pen drives that are increasingly large in terms of memory yet increasingly small in terms of their physical size, and thereby easily secreted about one's person.

Another challenge facing any definition of intelligence concerns the question of what sort of material needs to be collected in order to be considered intelligence: *must* it consist of secrets – that is, information that one country does not want another country to know – that have been collected secretly? Some would argue that intelligence has to be derived from secret sources, otherwise it isn't *really* intelligence, but information. Where does that leave material that has been gathered from non-secret sources, known as OSINT (open source intelligence)? Further, is there any guarantee that secret information gathered by covert means will automatically be more reliable than that which can be found in the public domain? The fact that someone considers certain information worthy of protecting would suggest that this is likely to be the case, but is its accuracy always guaranteed? The danger, then, is that secret information collected secretly may end up being imbued with a credibility that may not, in fact, be justified. Johnson (2017) offers an answer to this conundrum by suggesting that intelligence is actually a mix of both open *and* secret information, in which the 'secret component' need not necessarily be particularly high. Somewhere in the region of 90 per cent of the intelligence reports provided to decision makers in the United States is actually based on *non-secret* material. However, the remaining 10 per cent – the secret 'nugget' – can be absolutely vital, providing a specific context within which the remaining non-secret information can be interpreted (Johnson, 2017:46–7).

As illustrated above, it is immediately apparent that intelligence activity involves a lot of people; those who want the information and those who are responsible for gathering it. As such, a useful definition of intelligence could be that which considers its 'life cycle'; that is, the process whereby policymakers – intelligence 'consumers', or customers, ask for information (their 'requirements'), which the intelligence agency then proceeds to collect through the most appropriate means, be that secret or open source. Once gathered, the information is then processed (it may need to be translated, for example) and analysed as quickly as possible, before being passed to the policymakers, as requested. Taken together, this series of actions is known as the Intelligence Cycle. Yet while such an overview of the process may appear to offer a reasonable definition of intelligence, when looked at in greater detail this is also problematic, its simplicity perhaps constituting its greatest weakness. For example, intelligence agencies collect a vast amount of information on a wide array of subjects, so they are unlikely to have to start from scratch every time they are asked for something new. In addition, some would question whether policymakers actually have a sufficiently good grasp of what intelligence agencies are capable of to make achievable requests in the first place!

For others, such as Arthur S. Hulnik, the Intelligence Cycle is problematic because it ignores both counterintelligence and covert action. This criticism takes us to another aspect of the definitional debate. Counterintelligence involves the specific targeting of enemy intelligence organisations, alongside preventative measures to stop such enemies from targeting one's own organisation. Covert action, meanwhile, involves carrying out certain types of offensive secretly, thereby allowing those who ordered them to deny their involvement – that is, plausible deniability. Is it appropriate to describe such activities – for example, destabilising a country's economy – as 'intelligence'? For Herman, intelligence consists of 'information and information gathering' (Herman, 2004:342). As such, there is no place for them in his definition. Rather, he regards them as 'associated activities'. In order to consider covert action and counterintelligence as part of intelligence, a definition must take a step back, and to consider intelligence as a set of interconnected 'missions', where they sit alongside the gathering and analysis of information. This helps us to understand why the world's most well-known, fictional secret agent is considered to work in intelligence. James Bond clearly works for the British Secret Intelligence Service, MI6; we know this because the real-life headquarters of the organisation are seen (being blown up, on one occasion) on screen. But would this be accurate in the real world? The answer to this question ultimately depends upon the definition of 'intelligence' adopted. If our definition of gathering intelligence involves working quietly and unobtrusively at a target organisation, copying secret documents with a digital camera or copying sensitive files onto a pen drive, then Bond doesn't really fit the bill (it's hard to imagine a film showing Bond engaged in such work for 90 minutes being a box office smash). He's far more likely to be seen in some kind of physical altercation with an enemy thug, blowing up an enemy's subterranean secret base or assassinating a target. These sorts of activities would place Bond more comfortably under the heading of covert action rather than intelligence. However, if covert action is itself considered as one of the intelligence 'missions', and conducted by an intelligence agency on account of their expertise in acting secretly, then while Bond may not be a spy his activities could indeed be considered to fall under the wider remit of intelligence.

There are a number of further issues that may be considered when trying to define intelligence. For example, is a *globally* accepted definition of intelligence actually possible, or is a nationally accepted definition the best that can be hoped for? Through a comparative study of how intelligence is perceived in the United Kingdom and the United States, Davies concluded that the different usage of the word in a UK as opposed to a US context was so great that 'transatlantic dialogue on the subject ... has tended to be conducted at cross-purposes' (Davies, 2002:62). In the US, he notes that intelligence 'tends to refer to "finished" intelligence', while in the UK intelligence 'tends to refer more narrowly to those kinds of information not available from the "normal product" of departmental activity'. As such, he suggests that we should ask 'How do different countries and institutions define intelligence?'

A definition of intelligence also needs to take into account the nature of the political regime under which it functions. As Andrew (2004:176) has observed, it is important to differentiate 'between the roles of intelligence communities in authoritarian and democratic regimes', arguing that during the Cold War 'there was a fundamental asymmetry between intelligence operations in East and West. Similarities in intelligence vocabulary disguised basic differences of function'. Intelligence agencies operating under authoritarian rule tend to serve as a means of upholding the regime, acting as an instrument of repression that will engage in surveillance of members of the general public who are considered a threat. In addition to playing this role, such intelligence agencies will also participate in 'reinforcing the regime's misconceptions of the outside world': few members of authoritarian intelligence communities would be so bold as to challenge the views of their political leadership, regardless of their own intelligence assessments – to do so could cost them their lives (Andrew, 2004:177).

Finally, does intelligence have to be a state-backed activity, focussed upon issues of *national* security, and securing *national* advantage? Recently, greater attention has turned to the use of intelligence by non-state actors, including terrorist groups and the corporate world of big business. It is certainly possible for non-state actors to replicate, in many respects, the intelligence process as seen in the Intelligence Cycle, but ultimately they are limited to open source material that has not been acquired through covert means; only state intelligence agencies are able to 'legally' break the law; should a big business engage in similar tactics, then it could be argued that, rather than 'doing' intelligence, what they are actually doing is breaking the law. Luca De Pra, a coach from Genoa FC, found himself suspended from his job in September 2013 when he was caught spying on a rival football team, in full Rambo gear, in the run up to a derby match (*Observer*, 2013:n.p.). In 2001, Proctor and Gamble agreed to pay its rival Unilever somewhere in the region of $10 million in order to settle a case of corporate espionage (Barnes, 2001:n.p.) which had seen Unilever's rubbish stolen in the hope of discovering details of a new brand of shampoo (Hulnick, 2002:566).

Having begun with a very narrow definition of intelligence as the gathering of information, our discussion has continued to become increasingly broad, first considering a larger process within which such collection sits (the Intelligence Cycle), then expanding to an even wider definition around a series of activities that are linked by their secretive, covert nature, which sees counterintelligence and covert action placed alongside the collection and analysis of information. Complicating matters further are the questions of whether the information gathered needs to be 'secret' in order to constitute intelligence, how intelligence is defined at a national level, itself likely influenced by the political regime of the country concerned, and finally whether intelligence has to be a state-based activity, or whether it can be conducted by non-state actors. Ultimately, perhaps it is best to suggest, as Gill and Phythian do, that intelligence is 'an umbrella term' (2006:19) that can encompass all of the above, which 'renders precise definition problematic' – if not indeed impossible.

Global intelligence: a brief history

There is nothing remotely new about the concept of gathering information on an enemy or rival. 'The spy', Phillip Knightley (1986:3) writes, 'is as old as history'. Indeed, Khan goes so far as to argue that intelligence is intrinsically biological:

> Every animal, even a protozoan, must have a mechanism to perceive stimuli, such as noxious chemicals, and to judge whether they are good or bad for it. At that level intelligence is like breathing: essential to survival, but not to dominance.
>
> (Kahn, 2001:79–80)

As such, it is unsurprising that activity that would today be classed as intelligence has been in evidence in recorded human history for thousands of years. Even when found in what we know of ancient civilisations, such information gathering can be broadly divided into serving one of two main functions: the pursuit of knowledge about things 'external', particularly foreign enemies, their military strength and plans; and things 'internal', such as dissidence and dissatisfaction of citizens at home, which could challenge the stability of the regime.

The Egyptian Pharaoh Ramesses II, who fought numerous battles and oversaw the successful expansion of the Egyptian empire, used prisoners of war to provide intelligence, beating them to reveal details of their military strength (Kahn, 2001:80). The sixth-century BC military tactician Sun Tzu pointed to the value of spies and the information they could provide. In *The Art of War*, he wrote: 'the reason the enlightened prince and the wise general conquer the enemy wherever they move and their achievements surpass those of ordinary men is foreknowledge' (Kahn, 2001:80). The Vedic literature of ancient India illustrates the use of intelligence as a means of supporting state security (Schaffer, 2018:598–610) Intelligence for internal security was also practised by the ancient Greeks, through the sycophants, while intelligence from abroad was gathered by ambassadors (Smith, 2004:35).

Spying can be found in evidence in the Old Testament of the Bible, in the book of Numbers, where the Lord instructed Moses to send his men 'on a mission to the land of the Canaan' (Knightley, 1986:3). Intelligence activity also played an important role during the early years of Islam, being used by the Prophet Muhammad (570–632 AD) to ensure the survival of the movement. He developed 'a network of informers, whereby he could cross-check and compare the bits and pieces of information in order to construct a larger picture'. In this way, the Prophet was able to keep appraised of both external developments and keep a watch of members of the group, fulfilling the dual role 'of head of intelligence and internal security in seeking to ensure that all his plans and activities were kept in absolute secrecy' (Suwaed and Kahana, 2018:180–1).

The Romans benefitted from intelligence in the form of intercepted communications prior to the Battle of the Metaurus River in Italy in 207BC; 'having intercepted a Cathaginian message', they 'were able to concentrate their forces, defeat Hasdrubal before his brother Hannibal could reinforce him, and become the chief power of the Western world' (Kahn, 2001:80). Later, 'Caesar's legions scouted their barbarian foes' (Kahn, 2001:80). The Romans also utilised intelligence in order to monitor dissent at home. As Smith notes, this task was originally the responsibility of the fire brigade (the speculators) before later passing to the corn merchants (the *frumentarii*), who 'were considered to have their ears close to the ground in the markets' (Smith, 2004:35–6).

British interest in intelligence activity can be seen from the turn of the fourteenth century, at which point King Edward II ordered 'the seizure of "all letters coming from or going to ports beyond the seas"' (Smith, 2004:36). It was not until the reign of Queen Elizabeth I that Britain developed what Smith describes as its 'first really effective intelligence service' under **Sir Francis Walsingham**, 'a man widely recognised as the father of the British secret services' (Smith, 2004:37). Walsingham's work was instrumental in foiling numerous conspiracies against Elizabeth, including the Babington plot. He also established networks to collect intelligence from Spain, which proved valuable in the defeat of the Armada.

Elsewhere, the practice of using spies to monitor the population continued.

> In Sixteenth Century India, the Great Mogul Akbar's security service comprised an army of 4,000 scavengers, pedlars and merchants. Their reports were relayed to the Mogul via a central council of advisers and analysts, which presented him with a daily intelligence summary.
>
> (Smith, 2004:36)

Meanwhile, spying was rife throughout renaissance Europe. As Stephen Alford has observed, 'Espionage was a thriving trade in the sixteenth century. In war-torn Europe spies did a healthy business of selling news and intelligence mostly for money, sometimes out of religious conviction, but often for both' (Alford, 2012:14). Indeed, in the monarchies of Italy and Spain in the sixteenth and seventeenth centuries we can see the prototypes of formalised intelligence activity. As Laurent (2013:301) notes, 'In the *Serenissima* Venice in the sixteenth century a modern intelligence service appeared', while in the early years of the seventeenth century 'an *Espio mayor* working directly for the Council of State was created to centralize all of the activities from Spanish spies and spy-rings'. Back in England, following the end of the Civil War Lord Protector Oliver Cromwell was 'kept well informed about royalist plots by a network of agents run by his secretary John Thurloe' – who, following the Restoration, 'offered his services to Charles II' (Andrew, 1985:1).

During the Napoleonic Wars (1803–1815), Britain's Duke of Wellington mastered the use of intelligence during his campaigns against the French on the Iberian Peninsula. Wellington's staff included George Scovell, an expert linguist and codebreaker responsible for running agents known as the Army Guides, who broke the codes of intercepted French letters providing vital to Wellington's victory over the French at the Battle of Vitoria in 1813. Added to his own sources, Wellington could also rely on the British government's networks of correspondents and agents reporting to Britain's ambassadors. But the use of intelligence remained ad hoc and unique to each campaign; when Britain sent an expeditionary force to the Crimea in 1854, commanders lacked basic information on the topography and even their Russian opponents (Davies, 2007).

The widespread emergence of intelligence *agencies* – formal, bureaucratic institutions in their own right, either civilian or military-based – is a more recent development. For Khan, 'The French and industrial revolutions begat new conditions. In shaping the modern world, they created modern intelligence' (Kahn, 2001:80). As Herman notes, the rise of the intelligence organisation was linked to military developments during the nineteenth century, which saw the creation of permanent staffs, among whose functions 'was the study of enemies and potential enemies' (Herman, 1996:16). Under pressure from a retired Indian Army major,

Thomas Best Jervis, the British War Department created a 'Topographical and Statistical Department' in February 1855 (Smith, 2004:50). In 1871 these two functions were split. The new Statistical Department was responsible for collecting 'all possible information relating to the strength, organisation, etc., of foreign armies; to keep themselves acquainted with the progress made by foreign countries in military art and science', and for maintaining this information in an easily accessible form. Within a matter of years, this was renamed the Intelligence Branch (Smith, 2004:50). In France and Germany, formal intelligence structures also emerged towards the end of the nineteenth century. Following defeat in the Franco-Prussian War, the French army was restructured, and the general staff organised into four bureaus, (Laurent, 2013:206), the second of which – the Deuxieme Bureau – dealt with intelligence. In Germany, following a failed assassination attempt on his life, the Prussian Chancellor, later Kaiser Wilhelm I, Otto von Bismark, employed Dr Wilhelm Stuber to create a German secret service which could 'protect the state and its leaders from threats both inside the country as well as abroad' (Shpiro, 2001:23). Stuber's organisation quickly found its way to the Foreign Office, where it became the Central Intelligence Bureau, and Stuber 'set about building a modern intelligence service that could collect political and military information for the new German Empire' (Shpiro, 2001:24). Watching on enviously, the following year the Military General Staff, led by General Helmuth von Moltke, established its own intelligence organisation, which soon became known as Section III B.

During the twentieth century, intelligence and security apparatus continued to develop around the globe, under both democratic and authoritarian regimes. Great Britain saw the creation of a Secret Service Bureau in 1909. Initially this was divided into two sections, which went on to form the basis of MI5 (more properly the Security Service) and MI6, otherwise known as SIS (Secret Intelligence Service). Professionally organised intelligence proved its value during the First World War. As Khan notes,

> At last the admirals and generals understood. Intelligence had made its influence clear to them in the way they knew best. Despite their reluctance to share power and glory with intelligence officers, they realized that to spurn intelligence might cost them a battle or even a war – and their jobs. They and their governments drew the appropriate conclusions. Britain, Germany, Italy, and the United States, none of which had had codebreaking agencies before the war, established them after it.
>
> (Kahn, 2001:83)

Shortly after, the UK also developed its signals intelligence capability through the formation of the Government Code and Cypher School (GC&CS), which would later become Government Communications

Headquarters (GCHQ). The United States came relatively late to the field of organised intelligence. While the Federal Bureau of Investigation (FBI), which dealt with espionage on American soil, had been established in 1908, and while its codebreaking capability had been developed during the First World War, it was only with the creation of the Central Intelligence Agency (CIA) in 1947, building on the precedent of the wartime Office of Strategic Services (OSS), that the US developed the capability to 'study foreign targets' (Herman, 1996:266).

The development of institutions primarily focussed upon internal intelligence gathering also took place during the nineteenth century. As Herman (1996:19) notes, secret policing emerged throughout Europe as a result of 'the widespread fear of repetitions of the French Revolution'. Predating developments in Germany by some 40 years, the Russian Third Section of the Imperial Chancery was one of the first. Established in 1826, this was succeeded by the Okhrana in 1881, which faced rising political terrorism and revolutionary activity, using such dubious methods as the use of agent provocateurs to collect their information. After the October Revolution the Bolsheviks established the 'Extraordinary Committee' or 'Cheka' (*Chrezvychayneyye komissii*) on 20 December 1917 to oppose counter-revolution. The new organisation borrowed the tradecraft and in some cases personnel of the old Okhrana, evolving into what became the KGB. Like its successor, the Cheka was the sword and shield of the Soviet state, uncovering plots (real or imagined) to defend the revolution from enemies of the state.

The British withdrawal from colonial rule during the second half of the twentieth century saw its imperial responsibility for intelligence and security affairs pass to a host of newly independent countries, particularly on the African continent. Here, intelligence expertise and advice proved to be one of the means employed by Britain in its efforts to maintain close ties with, and the ability to exert influence over, former colonial territories, something that was considered of particular importance in the context of the ongoing Cold War. This resulted in the emerge of intelligence and security structures which, to a greater or lesser degree, followed the British 'model', an approach which, it was hoped, would

> encourage the leaders of countries nearing independence to embrace a supposedly essential element of the British world intelligence community's creed: that intelligence gathering was to be carried out solely to preserve the interests of the state and not for political ends.
>
> (Murphy, 2002:140)

The British motivation here was not entirely altruistic; by supporting the development of such agencies in newly independent nations, important links were fostered, which in turn helped to secure Britain's own future intelligence interests.

As noted earlier, intelligence services are shaped by the political context within which they operate. While the monitoring of internal activity is a longstanding practice, when used by an authoritarian regime it will likely become part of the state's machinery of repression. The Cold War provides numerous examples of agencies that were focussed upon stamping out internal dissent throughout Eastern Europe, perhaps the most well-known being the Ministry for State Security (*Staatssicherheitsdienst*), popularly known as the Stasi, which formed an integral part of the Communist German Democratic Republic's ability to control the population. By the time of the collapse of the Berlin Wall in 1989, the Stasi had an estimated 100,000 full-time employees, mostly responsible for monitoring internal dissent. In the East German city of Rostock, the Stasi had 3,000 full-time employees for a population of 900,000 – one officer per 300 citizens, compared to one doctor per 400 inhabitants across the country (Childs and Popplewell, 1999:82). Stasi surveillance was supported by vast network of informants from across all areas of society, totalling over 170,000, including Communist Party members, journalists, factory workers, doctors, teachers and university lecturers, and even children. The Stasi could also rely on reports from government agencies, political parties, associations, companies, universities and cultural groups to protect the communist system.

Unsurprisingly, seismic changes therefore follow when such regimes collapse and turn towards democracy, as their intelligence agencies are required to undergo extensive reform. Such changes can be seen throughout Eastern Europe since 1989. Romania, for example, is considered to have successfully adapted its intelligence and security apparatus, which has been transformed from 'an instrument of communist dictatorship to being an effective intelligence community under democratic control' (Matei, 2007:629). Until the revolution in December 1989, which saw the death of the dictator Nicolae Ceausescu and his wife Elana, the intelligence and security machinery of the state, the Securitate, was 'ruthlessly effective' in supporting the regime. So-called enemies of the Ceausescu regime were harassed, imprisoned, and placed under surveillance at both home and work, resulting in 'a pervasive atmosphere of fear, intimidation, suspicion, and mistrust' (Matei, 2007:631). In the aftermath of the revolution, the Securitate was broken up into a new intelligence system which saw the development of several agencies. At the same time, the legacy of the past continued to be present due to continuity in 'infrastructure, logistics, and personnel (including some of the collaborators)' – something which did not sit well with the Romanian population, whose

> hostility toward the former Securitate officers, lack of confidence in the state institutions, the incomplete and dysfunctional legal framework and oversight, as well as the lack of transparency, shed a bad light on the intelligence agencies during the first years of transition.
>
> (Matei, 2007:632, 634)

Over time, the situation has improved. Legislation has been enacted, dealing with issues of democratic control and oversight, while steps have also been taken to address the past, with former Securitate officers dismissed and younger personnel recruited. The files of the now defunct Securitate itself have been opened up, allowing for the 'identification of current public officials who either collaborated with or were employed by the former Securitate during the Communist regime' (Matei, 2007:641).

Moving beyond Europe, such a process of intelligence democratisation continues to constitute a work in progress, even today. In the case of Chile, the legacy of the authoritarian past has proved more difficult to overcome. As we have seen elsewhere, the early twentieth century saw the creation of an intelligence organisation – in this case, Department of Reconnaissance and Information, renamed the Direccion de Inteligencia de Ejercito (DINE) in the mid-1960s. The military coup of September 1973, which saw the emergence of General Augusto Pinochet as President (a position he would hold until 1990), saw a change in intelligence function. Pinochet's rule was bolstered by the creation of the Department of National Intelligence (DINA), which proceeded to ruthlessly repress those considered to be enemies of the regime, making extensive use of informants – *soplones* (whisperers) – in its activities, which also involved torture and mass murder. By 1977 the reputation of the DINA was such that it was replaced by a new organisation, the National Information Centre (CNI), but beyond the change in name this simply continued the brutal work of its predecessor. The CNI was disbanded in February 1990, by which time Pinochet had been defeated at the ballot box and Chile had begun to turn back towards democracy. Both intelligence and military institutions were stained by the stigma of their association with the Pinochet era, compounded by the fact that old habits appeared to die hard: 'Pinochet-era practices plagued the intelligence sector during the first years after the transition to democracy. In 1992, the military intelligence spied on various center-right party members' (Matei and Garcia, 2017:361). Remarkably, between 1990–1993, following the disbanding of the CNI, Chile did not have a civilian intelligence organisation, while the Public Security and Information Directorate (DISPI), created in 1993 primarily as an organisation for intelligence analysis, only survived for some eight years before being disbanded. In October 2004 it was succeeded by the National Intelligence Agency (ANI). The legacy of the past continues to overshadow the present; as Matei and Garcia note, 'while the noxious DINA has de facto and de jure incrementally disappeared from the post-Pinochet Chile, its stigma has not faded away from citizens' minds and memories' (Matei and Garcia, 2017:361).

Established intelligence agencies in democratic systems have found themselves subject to increased scrutiny of their activities. In the United States, the late 1970s saw the emergence of congressional oversight bodies, following reports from the Church and Pike Committees that the CIA and other agencies had been spying on American citizens, conducting illegal wiretaps and cover-ups over covert activities overseas. Both the Select Committee on Intelligence (formed in 1976) and House Permanent Select Committee on Intelligence (formed in 1977) are responsible for reviewing intelligence activity and scrutinising budgets, while also receiving briefings or 'Presidential findings' on covert operations. The early 1980s also saw the creation of Canada's Security Intelligence Review Committee (SIRC), resulting from the McDonald Commission into illegal Royal Canadian Mounted Police activity, to guarantee that Canada's spy agencies use their powers 'legally and appropriately' (SIRC, 2006:n.p.). Formal oversight has been slower to take off elsewhere; despite pressure for parliamentary scrutiny in the 1980s, it was not until the 1994 Intelligence Services Act that an Intelligence and Security Committee (ISC) was finally set up in the UK, while New Zealand only formed their equivalent of the ISC in 1996. While in many respects such national oversight mechanisms may be considered to remain imperfect, they serve to reassure citizens that intelligence and security agencies are not beyond the law. Certainly, they reflect positively upon the place of intelligence within a democracy in contrast to their position in other parts of the world, where such agencies continue to serve a repressive function, acting as the strong arm of the regime. This much can be seen in relation to their role throughout much of the contemporary Arab world, where they represent 'symbols of a state's power to coerce its citizens and intimidate its enemies', and where the Arabic word for intelligence services – al-mukhabarat – 'evokes for many Arabs images of terror, torture and death' (Sirrs, 2010:1).

1 Gathering intelligence
Spies and signals

The gathering of information, be it through covert means without the knowledge of its owner, or through the use of non-secret sources, is the cornerstone of intelligence activity. The most well-known sources through which information is gathered are human intelligence (**HUMINT**) and technical intelligence (**TECHINT**), itself an umbrella term under which sit a number of particular means of collection, including signals intelligence (**SIGINT**) and imagery intelligence (**IMINT**). Alongside these covert means of collection sits open source intelligence (**OSINT**). This chapter provides an outline introduction to these various modes of collection, and considers their strengths and weaknesses.

1.1 Human intelligence (HUMINT)

Information obtained from people – human intelligence (HUMINT) – is the oldest means of gathering intelligence. People can be valuable sources of information on both an accidental and a conscious level. As Herman (1996:63) notes, useful knowledge may be gained from casual travellers on an ad hoc basis, as well as from long-serving agents, better known as spies. Developments in technology have aided the work of such agents; the days of having to copy papers by hand long gone. Cold War spy fiction has long pointed us to the key tools in the armoury of these agents, such as the miniature Minox camera, which allowed illicit photographs of sensitive documents to be made. The advent of photocopiers also aided in the duplication of material, while today the ability to download sensitive material onto a memory stick which can pass unobtrusively through security checks is perhaps the most valuable tool of all. In addition to the collection of physical material, personal observations based on, for example, attendance at secret meetings can also prove immensely valuable. This sort of information can be obtained through interviews with individuals – if friendly, or if not through interrogations, as in the case of prisoners of war.

The identities of long-serving agents will be kept secret – which is hardly surprising, as by 'consciously spying against their own countries' (Herman, 1996:63) they are committing an act of betrayal, if not treason, which if discovered may well be punishable by death. Even today, the British Secret Intelligence Service (SIS) refuses to release the names of those individuals who provided it with information over 100 years ago, believing that it is vital to maintain an unshakeable commitment to secrecy so as not to jeopardise the recruitment of future agents. The late Labour MP Robin Cook offered his support for this position during his time as Foreign Secretary, noting that

> Those who work with SIS overseas often risk their lives so that our lives may be safe. Their effectiveness and their lives depend on their identities and work remaining out of the public eye. Their ability to gather intelligence depends on the confidence that their sources have in the absolute trustworthiness and discretion of the service.
>
> (Cook, 1998:n.p.)

Some observers are sceptical of this argument, believing that such a 'blanket' of secrecy provides a useful smokescreen, behind which mistakes or other forms of dubious behaviour can be concealed. Nevertheless, it is a position that is unlikely to change. It is possible, however, to consider what motivates individuals to spy through what we know of spies who were, ultimately, discovered.

A whole host of possible motivations emerge when exploring why an individual consciously decides to spy against their own country, key amongst these being ideology, blackmail and greed. The 1917 Russian Revolution saw the growth of ideological espionage: spying fuelled by an individual's belief in a particular political creed. Ideology has proved capable of causing considerable damage, as can be seen in the case of the 'Atomic Spy' **Klaus Fuchs** (Figure 1.1). A German physicist and dedicated Communist, Fuchs fled Nazi rule for the UK in 1933, where he quickly found employment at Birmingham University, working alongside fellow German physicist Rudolph Peierls. Likely through his association with Peierls, Fuchs joined the Tube Alloys Project – the cover name for British research into the atomic bomb, before joining its US equivalent, the Manhattan Project. As a result of his political beliefs, Fuchs provided details of his work to the Soviet Union, which helped to expedite its own atomic programme, resulting in the appearance of a Soviet atomic bomb just four years after the American one [Document 1].

Ideology can, of course, work both ways, and hostility toward a regime can provide the motivation for spying against it. This can be seen in the case of Soviet military and intelligence officers who provided the CIA with information, or defected, when they could 'no longer in good conscience could remain loyal to the Soviet government' (Perry, 2006:225). This can be seen in the case of Pyotr Popov. A Soviet military intelligence officer, during the 1950s Popov provided the CIA with information 'apparently out of repugnance toward the KGB's treatment of Russian peasants' (Perry, 2006:225). This can also be seen in the case of **Oleg Gordievsky**, a KGB

Figure 1.1 Klaus Fuchs
Photo by © Hulton-Deutsch Collection/CORBIS/Corbis via Getty Images

Colonel who became disenchanted with his work following the Soviet invasion of Czechoslovakia in 1968. During a posting to Copenhagen, contact was made between Gordievsky and a British SIS officer. Over time, Gordievsky became an immensely valuable source; his usefulness 'soared' when he was posted to London in the early 1980s. Recalled to Moscow in 1985, a suspicious KGB told Gordievsky 'that he would never be allowed to serve abroad again'. He was subsequently smuggled out of the Soviet Union with SIS assistance, and returned to the UK (Urban, 1996:13) [Document 2].

An overdeveloped sense of patriotism may provide sufficient motivation to commit espionage. This can be seen in the more recent case of Greg Chung. A US citizen born in China, Chung was an engineer involved with the development and design of space shuttles for NASA. Such work was of great interest to China when its attention turned to the prospect of developing an Earth-orbiting space station. During a trip to China in the summer of 1985, Ching was asked by an official from the Chinese aviation ministry to provide information that would help advance Chinese plans. Out of a sense of loyalty to the country of his birth, Chung agreed, returning to the US with a list of questions which he proceeded to spend several months researching, resulting in the production of some 27 'book-length texts, most of them engineering manuals' from his employer (Bhattacharjee, 2014). Further information followed [Document 3]. Chung was put on trial in June 2009, the FBI having discovered a vast treasure trove of confidential material at his home. He was the first American to be convicted of committing economic espionage, and was sentenced to 15 years 9 months in prison.

In other cases, a degree of persuasion may be required – friendly or otherwise. Certain types of behaviour, if captured on camera or on film, may leave individuals open to blackmail, which sees them forced to commit espionage for fear of their own personal secrets being made public. Such operations, commonly known by the Russian term 'Kompromat', can be seen in evidence during the Cold War, and could prove to be particularly effective at a time when societal attitudes towards certain behaviour were less accepting than is the case today. In this context, homosexuality offered a useful means of exerting leverage on an individual. This can be seen in the case of the Admiralty clerk **John Vassall**, who was despatched to the British Embassy in Moscow in 1954. A gay man at a time when homosexuality was illegal in the UK, the KGB arranged for a sexual encounter – a honeytrap – to take place between Vassall and a number of other men, during which compromising photographs were taken. Unaware that he had been set up, Vassall was later presented with these images, and given a choice to either gather information for the Soviet Union, or to refuse and have the photographs released. As a result, Vassall proceeded to pass over sensitive material for a period of several years [Document 5].

Having been forced into spying, Vassall also accepted money from his Soviet handler, which allowed him to enjoy clothes and overseas holidays which would likely otherwise have been impossible on his civil service salary. Others have not needed to be forced into spying; greed, and the promise of hefty sums of money, can alone provide a sufficient inducement to make an individual betray the secrets they are privy to. This can be seen in the case of Aldrich 'Rick' Ames. Working for the CIA, Ames handed over details of some 100 operations and of 30 undercover agents in exchange for cash, which allowed him to enjoy a quality of life that, as with the case of Vassall, exceeded what may have been expected based on his government salary [Document 4].

Human intelligence may also be obtained through other means, such as interrogation. During the Second World War, high-ranking German POWs were used as HUMINT sources by the Combined Detailed Interrogation Centre United Kingdom (CSDIC(UK)), at a facility called Trent Park. Here, the rooms in which prisoners were held had been fitted with covert recording equipment, which captured their conversations, some of which were guided through the use of 'stool pigeons', or members of staff. Thousands of such conversations were recorded during the war, which involved the collective effort of an extensive team of stenographers, transcribers, interpreters and technicians.

1.2 Signals intelligence (SIGINT)

While human intelligence represents the oldest form of intelligence collection, since the early years of the twentieth century, developments in technology have quickly been recognised for their intelligence gathering potential. Signals intelligence (SIGINT) is one such type of technical intelligence (TECHINT), which involves the collection, processing and exploitation of signals transmitted via technical means. The best-known type of SIGINT is communications intelligence (**COMINT**), which involves the interception of messages that use the human voice or other language-based means, such as Morse code or, more recently, SMS messaging and electronic mail. While it does not have its origins in technology – communications, in the form of letters between individuals, have been intercepted for hundreds of years – technological developments during the twentieth century have revolutionised what can be achieved here, in terms of intelligence collection.

The power of SIGINT was made apparent during the First World War. It can be seen, for example, playing a decisive role in the German victory at the Battle of Tennenberg. As Khan notes, German interception of a Russian order in August 1914

> told General Paul von Hindenburg and his deputy, General Erich Ludendorff, that they would have time to shift troops from a northern front in East Prussia, where the Russians were advancing slowly, to a southern one, where the Germans could outnumber them. The Germans made the move – and won the Battle of Tannenberg, starting Russia into ruin and revolution.
>
> (Kahn, 2001:82)

COMINT helped the German forces again in 1916 when the British 'fought to take the adjoining villages of Ovilliers and La Boiselle on the Somme. The British suffered casualties in the thousands. In a captured enemy dugout, they found a complete transcript of one of their operations orders. A brigade major had read it in full over a field telephone despite the protest of his subordinate that the procedure was dangerous' (Kahn, 2001:82–3). COMINT also helped the Allied forces; in 1917, British codebreakers revealed the Zimmerman telegram, described by Khan as 'the most important intelligence success in history' [Document 6]. The intercepted message from Arthur Zimmerman, Germany's foreign minister, 'promised Mexico her "lost territory" in Texas, New Mexico, and Arizona if she would join Germany in a war against America'. This 'helped bring the United States into the war' (Kahn, 2001:82).

The interception of enemy communications by technical means continued to reap enormous dividends during the Second World War; the interception and decoding of German messages sent using the supposedly unbreakable Enigma machine provided much valuable intelligence to the Allies, including information about the location of German submarines that were attacking merchant ships carrying resources vital to the war effort during the Battle of the Atlantic, shortening it by months (Kahn, 2001:83) (Figure 1.2). Much has been written about the success of the British codebreakers based at Bletchley Park. Allied codebreakers also enjoyed success breaking Axis diplomatic codes. Decrypted messages from the Japanese Ambassador to Berlin offered the Allies a valuable insight into the thoughts of Hitler's inner circle [Document 7].

1.3 Imagery intelligence (IMINT)

Imagery intelligence is another form of intelligence that has been revolutionised by developments in technology. In itself, there is little technical innately involved; in fact, as Herman notes, the observation of things constitutes a long-standing method of gathering information:

> Men have always watched for signs of the enemy on land or the departure of his ships from port, climbing hills or ships' masts to gain height. Balloons were first used in the wars of the 1870's, and again in the American Civil War, the Siege of Paris in 1870, and the Boer War.
>
> (Herman, 1996:72)

IMINT was revolutionised by the development of photography in the nineteenth century and the invention of the aeroplane in the early twentieth. Taken together, these saw the emergence of a valuable new resource: aerial reconnaissance, which was used during both the First and Second World Wars. From 1914, the aeroplane combined with reliable photographic equipment allowed both sides to take vertical aerial images for accurate map-making, intelligence gathering and verifying the accuracy of artillery bombardments. On the battlefields of the First World War, the accuracy of artillery could mean the difference between success and failure.

Figure 1.2 Enigma machine
Photo by Richard Baker/In Pictures via Getty Images

In turn, the increasing effectiveness of early photo reconnaissance led to the development of new fighter aircraft as a counter-measure, developing aerial warfare. Photographic reconnaissance continued to be of importance during the Second World War, with IMINT giving the Allies' commanders important details of German positions, bombing accuracy and pinpointing targets. In the run-up to the D-Day landings, British and American aircraft extensively covered Western Europe, targeting landing beaches and communication lines to help the planning of the Allied liberation of Europe.

Imagery intelligence went on to be of particular value to the West during the early Cold War period, when the Western powers found it difficult to gather intelligence on the Soviet Union (Figure 1.3). A secretive, closed society made it difficult to gather intelligence from human sources, while

Figure 1.3 IMINT – 7 March 1968: squadron leader V A Robins examining photographs of a Soviet spy trawler taken by the RAF during a reconnaissance flight over the Atlantic

Photo by Central Press/Getty Images

strict security over the use of communications similarly limited the opportunities to gather SIGINT. This dearth of intelligence was, in turn, having a negative impact upon the quality of American intelligence assessments, which were effectively being made in the dark, using incomplete and dated information. As a later CIA publication would admit,

> half knowledge of the Soviet Union and uncertainty of its true power position posed tremendous problems for the United States. We were faced with the constant risk of exposing ourselves to enemy attack or of needlessly expending a great deal of money and effort on misdirected military preparations of our own.
>
> (Pedlow and Welzenbach, 1998:316)

The situation was eased somewhat by the collection of imagery intelligence, initially through the use of high-altitude aircraft – the U-2 – and later through satellites. The first U-2 mission was conducted in June 1956, with the first clandestine flights over the Soviet Union taking place the following month. These provided useful intelligence which allowed analysts to conclude that their previous estimates had been inaccurate, and to amend them accordingly. The launch of the first imagery reconnaissance satellite, CORONA, continued the work begun by the U-2 programme, with the associated technology developing rapidly during the 1960s (Figure 1.4). Even the first successful CORONA mission alone, in August 1960, 'yielded photo coverage of a greater area than the total produced by all of the U-2 missions over the Soviet Union' (Ruffner, 1995:24).

Following the shooting down of **Gary Powers**' U-2 mission in May 1960, such overflights of the Soviet Union ceased, but they continued to

Figure 1.4 IMINT – an example of a photograph taken from a spy satellite
Photo via Smith Collection/Gado/Getty Images

be used elsewhere. The U-2 programme continued to prove its value a few years later during the Cuban Missile Crisis – the 'most spectacular U-2 success', as Herman describes it, being when one such flight over Cuba resulted in over 900 photographs, taken in under ten minutes (six minutes), which 'revealed the presence of Soviet missiles' there (Herman, 1996:73–4). Developments in technology over the following decades have seen the capabilities of such satellites increase significantly, resulting in, for example, a 'dramatic improvement of resolution' (Herman, 1996:75).

1.4 Open source intelligence (OSINT)

Open source intelligence (OSINT) is derived from sources that are publicly available. It consists of non-secret material, such as newspapers, magazines, books and other printed material such as maps, alongside audio and audiovisual material, such as television, radio, CDs and DVDs. The fact that information is not classed as 'secret' does not necessarily mean that it is easily accessible; material may exist that is not published or widely distributed, but nevertheless remains legally available, if it can be tracked down. OSINT, therefore, can itself be divided into 'white' and 'grey' information. Some 80 per cent of intelligence material is estimated as being 'white' – i.e. easily available – while 9 per cent is 'grey', and the status of the remaining 11 per cent is contested. 'Grey' material contains a variety of publications such as company reports, working papers, yearbooks and academic dissertations which, while not secret, are not necessarily easy to come by for people outside of the originating organisation (Hribar, Podbregar and Ivanuša, 2014).

OSINT was widely exploited during the Cold War, much to the benefit of the Soviet Union. As Mercardo (2009:79) notes, the Soviets

> used technical information from open sources in the United States and other advanced industrial nations to monitor foreign developments and to save time and money on their own projects. The US aerospace publication *Aviation Week*, dubbed 'Aviation leak' for its scoops, was a perennial favorite.

The United States also made extensive use of OSINT during this period. It became 'a major part of all intelligence on the Soviet Union, China, and other adversaries'. By the late 1950s, a 'wealth of information' was being extrapolated from 'the increasing flow of books and periodicals from the Soviet Union' – so much so that, one observer observed a few years later, 'In aggregate, open sources probably furnish the greater part of all information used in the production of military intelligence on the Soviet Union' (Mercardo, 2009:79).

1.5 INTs in comparative perspective

The various forms of intelligence collection may be compared across a series of key criteria; cost, speed and reliability.

1.5.1 Cost

For some countries, the financial costs associated with various technical means of intelligence gathering may prove prohibitive; US intelligence had a budget estimated at between $26–30 billion during the 1990s (Johnson and Scheid, 1997:7), a considerable percentage of which was spent on technical intelligence methods; according to Herman (1996:40), by the mid-1990s some $4 billion was being spent on signals intelligence, while $7 billion was spent on satellite networks. In contrast, human intelligence may be considered far less expensive, even if the source is providing information for money, with some estimates putting the US spend on human intelligence at around 10 per cent of the total budget. Human sources can provide value for money, as in the case of the American CIA officer Aldrich Ames. Recruited by the Soviet Union in the mid-1980s, Ames proceeded to hand over details of both CIA operations and agents in exchange for cash, estimated by Taylor and Snow (1997:103) at somewhere in the region of $1,397,300. From a Soviet perspective, at least, this could certainly be considered to constitute money well spent. OSINT meanwhile, represents an even cheaper alternative, which can result in significant financial savings (Hribar, Podbregar and Ivanuša, 2014). As Hulnick notes, during the Cold War, while the United States 'was spending millions to try and observe its Soviet "enemy"', the Soviet Union itself spent 'relatively little' to watch the U.S. In the absence of spy planes and satellites, the Soviet Union 'was able to send its agents to military installations to attend "open houses," aircraft displays, and shipboard visits', while subscribing to such magazines as *Aviation Week* and *Popular Mechanics*, 'to learn all about the technology that was being used against them' (Hulnick, 2002:573).

1.5.2 Speed

Speed is a factor that separates technical intelligence from its human counterpart, and one which goes some way towards explaining the value that is gained from the costs involved. As Gill and Phythian note, signals intelligence may be considered 'the fastest source of current intelligence'. It is also more flexible than human intelligence. The target of a signals operation can be retargeted with relative ease; 'In contrast, the capacity of HUMINT to redirect its focus rapidly and effectively is hampered by the fact that sudden shifts in emphasis could require the time-consuming infiltration of new structures and the creation of new networks of informers' (Gill and Phythian, 2012:93). The development of human sources can be a slow process; as Herman notes, 'The identification and recruitment of potential agents takes a long time. Communications with their controllers are the most vulnerable point and have to be limited; their reporting is therefore slow, and usually excludes "real time" intelligence' (Herman, 1996:65). It is worth noting, however, that low-cost OSINT can sometimes have the edge when it comes to speed, through radio and television broadcasts. As a CIA officer once remarked,

> It is a well-known phenomenon in the field of intelligence that there often comes a time when public political activity proceeds at such a rapid and fulminating pace that secret intelligence, the work of agents, is overtaken by events publicly recorded.

Reports from technical or human intelligence sources are supplanted by real-time broadcast journalism (Mercardo, 2009:79).

The sheer volume of information that can be collected through various means can also prove challenging to deal with, and have an impact upon speed. Aldrich (2009:895) describes the efforts to process the unending flow of information from email, mobile phone communications and the like to 'trying to pour a glass of water with a fire-hose'. According to Aid and Wiebes, the US SIGINT organisation, the National Security Agency (NSA), was responsible for producing 400 reports a day in 1964, a figure which reached more than 1,000 by the end of the decade (Aid and Wiebes, 2001:9). At the same time, open source information grew during the 1960s to such an extent that, one intelligence insider observed, it 'both supported and threatened "to swamp" the Intelligence Community' (Mercardo, 2009:79). With so much material to process, opportunities to provide warnings of impending action can be missed; for example, in 1968 intelligence on the Czechoslovakian crisis did not reach policymakers in Washington DC until days after it had been intercepted (Aid and Wiebes, 2001:17); while more recently, in 2000, signals attention which warned of plans of a terrorist attack in the Middle East was not issued until after the USS Cole had been attacked (Aid, 2009b:91).

Is speed always best? While HUMINT may not always offer speed, it can compensate for this in other ways, particularly in terms of the nature of the information it can provide. As Herman (1996:65) notes, 'Documents have a comprehensiveness greater even than satellite photographs or deciphered telegrams, and a highly placed agent can provide additional oral explanations and background'. Able to penetrate the heart of a hostile state or organisation, human sources may provide information that is simply inaccessible via technical means, no matter how expensive or state-of-the-art they may be. This can be seen in the case of 'Stakeknife', a British source during the troubles in Northern Ireland, who was simultaneously deputy head of the Provisional IRA's internal security section.

Intelligence provided by Stakeknife allowed for important members of the PIRA to be arrested, or killed. The case also illustrates something of the differences in the degree of personal danger involved by the use of different collection methods. While any suspicion as to Stakeknife's true activities may have resulted in his death, the danger involved in the collection of OSINT by an intelligence officer sat in front of a PC in an office is negligible, as is the threat to those intercepting communications, hundreds of miles away from those who are having the conversation. It is difficult to overemphasise the danger that can be faced by human intelligence sources, whose actions can, ultimately, cost them their lives should they be uncovered. This much can be seen by the attrition rate faced by the CIA's Chinese agents during the 1950s; according to Aid and Wiebes, of 212 agents parachuted into China, 101 were killed while 111 were captured (Aid and Wiebes, 2001:5).

1.5.3 Reliability

Imagery intelligence is limited to recording that which can be seen. While IMINT can provide a valuable 'snapshot' of a geographical area, the picture can quickly change, while countermeasures can be taken to mislead the camera. As Johnson observes, the nuclear test conducted by India in 1998 was not anticipated by American intelligence, in no small part due the fact that India 'knew exactly when the satellite cameras would be passing over the nuclear testing facility', and camouflage could be used accordingly (Johnson, 2007:7). It may also take some time for the orbiting satellite to reach the position from which photographs can be taken. Yet Herman argues that it is 'difficult' to exaggerate the impact, in both practical and psychological terms, that the use of photographic satellites had upon US intelligence assessments of Soviet capabilities during the Cold War, allowing them to become more accurate and confident, with President Johnson himself stating that 'Before we had the photography our guesses were way off. We were doing things we didn't need to do. Because of satellites I know how many missiles the enemy has' (Herman, 1996:74). While it proved its value during the 1960s, IMINT was of far less use when Iranian student militants took American diplomats hostage inside the US embassy in Tehran during the Carter administration. US satellites could certainly provide photographs of Tehran, and of the embassy compound; but in order to plan a rescue mission, what was *really* needed was information about what was going on *inside* the building. As one of those involved later recalled:

> We had a zillion shots of the roof of the embassy and they were magnified a hundred times. We could tell you about the tiles; we could tell you about the grass and how many cars were parked there. Anything you wanted to know about the external aspects of the

> embassy we could tell you in infinite detail. We couldn't tell you shit about what was going on inside that building.
>
> (Johnson, 2007:8)

Communications intelligence, meanwhile, is similarly limited to that which can be overheard. While it may cause some inconvenience to the groups concerned, strict control over the use of electronic communications by a group can have a significant impact upon the ability of a rival to gather SIGINT about them. As Aid (2009b:52) notes, following a period during which American intelligence was able to effectively monitor the telephone communications of Osama bin Laden and his al-Qaida associates, around 1998–1999 bin Laden 'ceased using his satellite telephone to communicate with his subordinates and sympathizers outside of Afghanistan'. Even when a telephone conversation can be monitored, the intelligence value is limited by the accuracy of what is said; what Gill and Phythian refer to as the 'two idiots dilemma': 'Electronic intercepts are great, but you just don't know if you've got two idiots talking on the phone' (Gill and Phythian, 2006:94). It can also prove difficult to extract meaning from communications if those engaged in conversation take precautions, such as the use of code words. While in the months leading up to the 11 September 2001 terrorist attacks US intelligence intercepted 'an increasing volume of al-Qaeda messages which indicated that Osama bin Laden was planning a major operation against American targets', the use of 'codewords and double talk to disguise what they were talking about', combined with a lack of detailed specifics, limited the value of the intelligence (Aid, 2009b:54).

Human sources may exaggerate their knowledge in order to impress, or the pressure of spying may affect them psychologically, leading to alcohol or substance abuse and questions over their continued reliability. Human agents are also always at risk of discovery, and of consequently being 'turned' and becoming double agents. A lack of reliability can be seen in the case of 'Curveball': Rafid Ahmed Alwan al-Janabi, an Iraqi defector who claimed – falsely – that Saddam Hussein was following a secret biological weapons programme. His information fed directly into the intelligence assessments that were used by the US to justify the invasion of Iraq in 2003. The internet offers the opportunity for fake material to be disseminated to a wide audience, which may end up having a negative impact upon any OSINT collection effort. According to Hribar, Podbregar & Ivanuša, disinformation 'is hard to detect, and its effects can have serious consequences for the national security' (Hribar, Podbregar and Ivanuša, 2014:544). Hulnick, however, is less concerned, noting that questions over the reliability of OSINT have

> always been true, but over time, as with most other kinds of intelligence sources, analysts learn which sources to trust and which are

> likely to be incorrect, slanted, biased, propaganda, or disinformation ... The World Wide Web has led to the proliferation of individual sites that produce propaganda, misinformation, or disinformation. But professional intelligence analysts should have no trouble sorting wheat from chaff in Web databases.
>
> (Hulnick, 2002:568)

Prejudice on the part of those who use intelligence can also end up having an impact upon what is perceived as reliable. OSINT has been described as 'the lifeblood of intelligence' (Hulnick, 2002:566). Given that it makes up an estimated 80 per cent of US intelligence, this is hardly an exaggeration. Yet paradoxically, it is 'not in great demand by consumers'. There can be a bias on the part of policymakers in favour of 'intelligence from secret agents and technical sources – materials they can't read in *The New York Times*' (Hulnick, 2002:573). Covert methods of collection are certainly more challenging, carry a higher risk and cost more than the collection of OSINT; yet do such characteristics automatically make them more reliable? The covert mode of collection can certainly give the impression that the material is more valuable than that collected from open sources, but there is a danger here of conflating collection with quality and reliability – a trap that, according to Hulnick, policymakers and other intelligence consumers have a habit of falling into, placing a greater value on material collected covertly to that gathered via open sources (Hulnick, 2002).

1.6 Intelligence collection: ethical considerations

Irrespective of the method whereby intelligence is collected, it is an area of activity that is not without ethical considerations. Due to its openly accessible nature, OSINT may be considered to represent the most ethically sound means of intelligence collection. As Hribar, Podbregar and Ivanuša (2014:530) note, OSINT 'does not violate human rights', and may arguably be considered as 'the only fully legal method'. Beyond this, ethical questions begin to emerge. Herman argues that the practice of 'pure' intelligence – that is, the gathering of information quietly and unobtrusively, should offer little by way of moral or ethical consideration, constituting 'information and information gathering, not doing things to people; no-one gets hurt by it, at least not directly' (Herman, 2004:342). While it is difficult to argue with the overall point that intelligence is about gathering information, the means whereby that information is gathered can be more of a cause for concern than Herman suggests. One of HUMINT's key strengths – the ability to get close to the source of power in a hostile state or organisation – can also present a difficult ethical dilemma; people in such positions may well have committed crimes themselves – and may need to continue to do so while providing intelligence, in order not to arouse suspicion surrounding their activities. The issue was addressed by the CIA during the 1990s, when the Director of Central Intelligence, John Deutch, ruled that individuals who had violated human rights could no longer be recruited, following claims that a CIA 'asset' had killed an American citizen and the husband of another American citizen (Johnson 2010a:314). However, the so-called 'Deutch rules' were ultimately abandoned in 2002. Human intelligence can also be gathered through coercive means – such as torture. As Bellaby notes, torture 'is an issue at the forefront of the debate regarding what standards should be expected from a state and its intelligence agencies' (Bellaby, 2010:94).

There are further issues that go beyond HUMINT into the technical sphere, where 'the growing ability and tendency of intelligence and security services to intercept, monitor, and retain personal data in an increasingly computer-centred world' is a matter of concern (Bellaby, 2010:94). **Edward Snowden**'s flight to Hong Kong and disclosure of the treasure trove of digital files handed to journalists led to worldwide outrage from privacy groups, campaigners and even governments over surveillance in the internet age, in the face of claims from the agencies themselves that such methods were necessary to protect national security. The CEO of London-based Index of Censorship, Kirsty Hughes, argued that the TEMPORA programme disclosed by Snowden 'is unacceptable – it both invades privacy and threatens freedom of expression' [Document 8]. A European Parliament investigation found that bulk data collection undermined trust between citizens and government, the rule of law, and online security, ruling there was little 'justification for untargeted, secret and sometimes even illegal mass surveillance programmes' (European Parliament Draft Report, 2013:17).

For many, Snowden's disclosures served as a reminder that modern-day collection techniques may undermine the very freedoms that Western intelligence agencies are supposed to protect. Unsurprisingly, for those who work in the intelligence community Snowden undermined security and should be viewed as a traitor, especially after leaving to live in Moscow. NSA Director Keith Alexander said the leaks 'caused significant and irreversible damage to our nation's security ... the irresponsible release of classified information about these programs will have a long-term detrimental impact on the intelligence community's ability to detect future attacks'. The fine line between security and privacy is one of those ethical issues that practitioners, policymakers, and individuals are presented with in the digital age, and there are no easy answers.

2 Intelligence analysis

Analysis, the 'thinking part' of the process whereby information is transformed into finished intelligence, is a key part of the intelligence cycle. Indeed, for all the importance of collection, analysis may be considered the cornerstone of the whole process. Raw information rarely speaks for itself; it needs to be analysed to extract meaning. Without providing such insight, the rest of the intelligence process is effectively rendered useless – there is little point in 'collecting data to sit idle, untouched, and unanalyzed forever' (Lefebvre, 2004). Yet in contrast to the huge sums of money poured into new and increasingly sophisticated collection systems, only a small amount of money is actually spent on analysis. The US 9/11 Commission noted that the FBI's analytical systems were 'woefully inadequate', lacking effective systems to 'know what it knew' (Gill and Phythian, 2006:84). It is at the analytical stage that the intelligence process often fails. For the former CIA officer Richards J. Heuer, major intelligence failures are caused by 'failures of analysis, not failures of collection' (Heuer, 1999:65). The nature of analysis means that some surprise 'is inevitable' (Heuer, 2005:76). History is littered with major 'intelligence failures'. The Japanese attack on Pearl Harbor (1941), North Korean invasion of the South (1950), the Egyptian/Syrian attack on Israel during Yom Kippur (1973), the Soviet invasion of Afghanistan (1979) and the 9/11 attacks in Washington and New York (2001), all took intelligence agencies by surprise.

Before an analyst can set to work, information needs to be processed. Raw intelligence doesn't always arrive in a ready-to-use format. Satellite images need to be closely scrutinised, signals need to be decoded and possibly translated, and open source information sifted and selected, so they can be used [Document 9]. Raw material needs to be separated into the 'wheat' and 'chaff' – what's useful, what's not – or what Roberta Wohstetter famously referred to as the 'signals' and 'noise', with useful material extracted and the rest discarded (Wohlstetter, 1962:228). This is increasingly challenging as intelligence agencies are ever more overloaded with information. One former head of America's National Security Agency (NSA) compared the flow of raw intelligence to 'a firehose held to the mouth' (Johnson, 2010:19). Another, asked about potential issues facing the US intelligence community, said: 'I have three major problems: processing, processing, and processing' (Johnson, 2010:19). In 1971, the Schlesinger Report into the US intelligence community found that analysts were often 'swamped with data' (Schlesinger Report, 1971:11). In the digital age, the situation is even worse. The information universe is bigger than anything 'we can touch, feel, or see' (Olcott, 2012:104). Intelligence officers are, as the 9/11 Commission reported, 'drowning in information and trying to decide what is important' (9/11 Commission Report, 2004:355). Every day, the NSA receives some 4 million telephone, fax and email intercepts (Johnson, 2017:57). Of these, it is able to report on just 1 per cent (Aid, 2009a:304). Overall, it is claimed that 90 per cent of what is collected by the US intelligence community is never studied (Johnson, 2017:58). In Britain, the situation is similar; according to Edward Snowden, GCHQ receives access to 50 billion events – details of incoming and outgoing phone and email traffic – thanks to exploitation of fibre optic cables. Yet only a tiny fraction of this material is ever used (Corera, 2016:337).

It is the job of the analyst to piece together the processed information from a variety of sources into 'descriptions, explanations, and judgments' for those who need to use it (Lefebvre, 2004:236). Essentially, they are aiming, writes Sherman Kent, to provide 'a close approximation of the truth' (Johnson, 2017:66), however difficult that is. In reality, analysis is an art not a science. The collected information never provides the 'full story' and is 'sporadic and patchy' (HC 898 (Butler Report), 2004:14) [Document 10]. Even a good analyst would be undermined if there was little, if any, information to go off. Despite extensive IMINT of North Korea, it is difficult, for example, for intelligence analysts to accurately forecast their underground nuclear programme, thanks to the lack of HUMINT or, in the absence of UN monitors, OSINT. Former CIA Director Robert Gates talked about 'secrets' – things knowable through intelligence collection – and 'mysteries' – things where there is no clear-cut answer. An enemy's secrets are knowable: information on Eastern Bloc military formations during the Cold War, or China's growing military capability in the Asia-Pacific region may be discovered, with time and effort. Predicting how an individual leader will react is much more difficult and prone to guesswork as 'leaders do not know what they are going to do or have not worked out their problems' (Herman, 1996:103). As a result, many of the Joint Intelligence Committee's assessments of Soviet Cold War intentions were guesswork based on speeches, the number of Soviet Bloc tanks and economic information, given the absence of hard intelligence on policy from inside the Kremlin. Similarly, the intentions of Kim Jong-un's North Korea – behind the rhetoric, missile tests and diplomatic brinksmanship – are unknown, thanks to the closed nature of the system. Speeches, defector reports and other sources can only go so far in explaining their policy to the outside world. The job of the analyst, then, is to bridge the gap between the known and unknown based on the information available, however limited that is. Analysts need to draw on all the information available – all-source analysis, drawing on what is already known from open sources (OSINT) before turning to secret sources to write their assessments (Bruce and George, 2014:70).

Intelligence reports can take two forms: short-term and long-term assessments. Short-term assessments deal with issues of an immediate concern, while long-term assessments forecast issues that could be a problem in future. Short-term assessments dominate analytical output; policymakers – the President or Prime Minister – need up-to-date advice to deal with issues now, rather than in the future (Johnson, 2010:21). Since 1964, American Presidents have been provided every morning with the Presidential Daily Brief (**PDB**) – the 'Holy Grail of the nation's secrets' – summarising the most important information from across the US intelligence community [Document 11].

Long-term forecasts are important, if less pressing. Pieces on such matters as long-term energy security and transnational crime may come second to more pressing issues on terrorism or the interests and intentions of a particular state. When looking at long-term issues, analysts need to communicate uncertainty to readers, providing best guesses about what may happen. This results in the use of what Lowenthal (2009:131) refers to as 'weasel words'; 'maybe' and 'perhaps', along with phrases such as 'on the one hand' often appear in assessments. Other phrases such as 'we believe', 'we assess' or 'we think' appear to show policymakers where judgement has been used. As such, policymakers unfamiliar with intelligence products may be inclined to add greater weight to the intelligence than they normally would. In 2002, the **JIC** – despite the 'limited' intelligence available – judged that the Iraqi Dictator Saddam Hussein 'has a chemical and biological weapons capability and ... is prepared to use it', giving a level of apparent certainty where there was none [Document 12].

Given the complicated nature of analysis, analysts face significant problems in trying to get to 'the truth'. In addition to the challenges outlined above, analysts also have to deal with certain psychological issues. The mindset of the analyst can be a problem. Few analysts start with a 'blank mind'. They have certain views shaped by their education, political views and general life experience which can unintentionally shape their assessments. Working with incomplete information, analysts may turn to their own personal views. Mindsets can be quick to form and resistant to new information, with analysts reluctant to change their individual viewpoints (Heuer, 2005:85).

One of the biggest problems is mirror imaging, where analysts tend to think of other leaders and countries behaving in the way they would. During the Cold War, for example, some US analysts tended to explain Soviet policy through American eyes, rather than understand the unique motivations of the Kremlin. Britain's analysts, too, suffered this problem.

A 1982 review of the JIC found that the committee struggled to think how the Soviets would, instead believing that Moscow would react in the same way as London and not as a 'one-party' state, 'heavily under the influence of a single leader' (Goodman, 2007:531). In 1999, India's intelligence services were surprised by a Pakistani intrusion into the Kargil district of the disputed Kashmir region. Indian intelligence officers deceived themselves into thinking an intrusion was unlikely because, in their view, it was irrational and went against the growing détente between India and Pakistan (Chaudhuri, 2013:188–9). Analysts sometimes become so absorbed by their subject that they are also prone to clientism (or 'clientisis') and become apologists for the state they are supposed to be impartially analysing. Teams of analysts can also reinforce each other's assessments, unquestioningly arriving at the same conclusion. This is called 'groupthink'. During the lead up to the Iraq invasion in 2003, intelligence communities on both sides of the Atlantic collectively presumed that Iraq had significant stockpiles of weapons of mass destruction (**WMD**) – an assessment that proved to be false.

There are also significant organisational issues. Despite its importance, analysis may come second to the collection process. One SIS officer told the Chilcot Inquiry that his service's focus on agent running led to analytical issues: 'within SIS, the reporting role had always, if you like, had a second class position, as against the agent recruitment and agent running role'. Culturally, processing and analysing agent reports was 'not a good place to be for one's career or quite at the sort of front line of SIS work' (SIS-5, 2010:n.p.). Analysts may come from the same social backgrounds. Analysts recruited from 'Ivy League' universities – a traditional recruiting ground for the US intelligence community – may think and act the same way, undermining the ability to 'think outside of the box'. To some extent, analysts are also prisoner of the system they work in. In the Soviet Union, analysts in the KGB were constrained by 'ideologically based stereotypes and conspiracy theories' (Andrew and Gordievsky, 1990:535). While having some of the best HUMINT sources available to any intelligence agency, the Soviets wrongly believed at one point the 'Cambridge Five' – Philby, Maclean, Burgess, Blunt and Cairncross – were British plants, misleading the Soviets, rather than the genuine thing (Andrew and Elkner, 2003:81). These distortions remained part of the Soviet analytical process throughout the Cold War.

In democracies too, analysts may find themselves pressured into distorting intelligence to fit a policymaker's political agenda. In Britain, this can be seen in the government's attitude towards intelligence before the invasion of Iraq in 2003. Seeking to justify claims that Iraq's weapons of mass destruction posed a threat, and coming under political and public pressure for supporting evidence, the government tasked intelligence officials to create a watertight case for military action. While the chair of the JIC persistently denied giving in to pressure from Downing Street, the subsequent inquiry led by Sir John Chilcot found that the JIC, along with other parts of the intelligence community, failed to consider the 'hypothesis that Iraq might not have chemical, biological or nuclear weapons or programmes' (Chilcot, 2016:76). Prime Minister Tony Blair's claims that the intelligence was authoritative and established beyond doubt, a claim deceptively linked to the JIC, were seemingly unchallenged. Intelligence had been politicised without resistance from officials.

2.1 Signals and noise: Pearl Harbor

The Japanese surprise attack on the US Pacific Fleet's base at Pearl Harbor in December 1941 stands out as one of the most notable examples of intelligence failure. By the end of 7 December, a Japanese taskforce had crippled US naval power in the Pacific, at least in the short term, sinking or heavily damaging eight battleships, three light cruisers, three destroyers, and over 180 aircraft. Tragically, 2,403 personnel were killed, and over 1,400 injured. It was, as President Roosevelt told Congress a day later, a 'date which will live in infamy'. Simultaneously, Japanese forces launched attacks on British, Netherlands and US possessions in the Far East, from Hong Kong and Singapore to the Dutch East Indies and the Philippines, extending Japanese influence in the region and sparking the Pacific War. The scale and completeness of the surprise has been the subject of historical controversy. It has been suggested that Britain's spies misled their American counterparts, withholding vital information and tricking a then isolationist US into fighting the Second World War (Rusbridger and Nave, 1991). In reality, the truth is more mundane: it was an intelligence failure.

By 1941, America's analysts faced an uphill task in identifying where Japan would strike in the Pacific. Since 1937, Japan had been fighting a war with neighbouring China, remaining neutral from the fighting in Europe. Japanese attempts to extend their influence northwards had been dealt a considerable blow by their defeat by the Red Army at the Battles of Khalkhin Gol, and, with operations in China at a stalemate – draining Japan's already dwindling supplies of rubber, tin and oil – the Japanese leadership was forced to look southwards to the increasingly vulnerable colonies of France, the Netherlands and Britain for important raw materials. In July 1941, Japan's leaders decided to push south into French Indochina and Thailand, even if this meant war (Mawdsley, 2009:203). Despite Tokyo initially favouring a diplomatic solution to the crisis, on 5 November 1941 they decided to use force; a naval task force would be sent to cripple the US fleet at Pearl Harbor, preventing the US from intervening in assaults on European and American colonial possessions elsewhere in the Asia-Pacific region. Yet US analysts were in the dark about Tokyo's decision for war. While American codebreakers were able to read Japan's high-level diplomatic traffic, given the codename MAGIC, as well as some naval communications (JN-25), signals intelligence gave away little, if any, detail of the plan. The US lacked sources that would give an accurate view of Japan's intentions.

Tight security and an absence of HUMINT sources effectively left US intelligence blind. MAGIC gave vague warnings of danger as far wide as the Panama Canal, America's west coast, US possessions in the Philippines, and the Hawaiian Islands. Intercepted signals in July 1941 even suggested that the Japanese military were 'keenly watching developments' in eastern Siberia to combat the 'Communist menace'. There was 'a good deal of evidence ... to support all the wrong interpretations', concludes Wohlstetter (1962:392). As a result, analysts wrongly believed Japan would first strike against 'the South China coast or ... French Indo-China', interpreting naval and military movements in the region as part of a push southwards, rather than a threat to US interests. In November, analysts warned that Thailand and Southern China remained the most likely targets of any future attack (Wohlstetter, 1962:392). Meanwhile, the Japanese taskforce remained undetected thanks to tight signals security.

Reports by analysts which suggested that the US base at Pearl Harbor would be the target of a Japanese attack were quickly ruled out. There was some intelligence that the US Pacific Fleet could be a target, but this was drowned out by the wider 'noise'. At the start of 1941, the US Ambassador to Tokyo reported rumours from Peruvian diplomats that Japan intended to attack Pearl Harbor. On 15 November, the Japanese consulate in Honolulu was told to report on the position of US ships in Pearl Harbor, while decrypts ordered Japan's diplomatic missions to destroy cypher machines after receiving a coded message disguised as a weather report. With hindsight it is easy to identify the relevant 'signals' pointing to Hawaii, yet analysts had to cope with fragmented information. For analysts, there were also a number of reasons why Japan wouldn't attack US interests. Growing shortages of raw materials thanks to the US embargo and the perceived weakness of the Japanese army were used as evidence to support the view that Tokyo would embark on limited operations (Ford, 2010). The consistent downplaying of Japanese military capability based on racial stereotypes and observations of Japanese operations in China was another factor. It made little sense for Japan's leaders to commit 'national hara-kiri' against a stronger power (Kahn, 1991:n.p.), while the strength of a reinforced US Pacific Fleet, protected by extensive fortifications and aircraft, was considered a significant deterrent, resulting in overconfidence. There was also too much reliance on America's codebreakers. While detailed, SIGINT gave only a partial picture of Japanese intentions. Intercepted messages to Japan's Washington Embassy showed a gradual deterioration in US–Japanese relations, suggesting the situation was 'very grave'. By December, the Japanese foreign ministry told the Berlin Embassy that war with the 'Anglo-Saxon nations ... may come quicker than anyone dreams' and on 6 December – a day before the attack on Pearl Harbor – Tokyo started to send the US ambassador a fourteen part message, leading analysts to believe a break in diplomatic relations was to be expected. As before, US analysts pointed to a Japanese attack in the Southern Pacific. The lack of precise intelligence and the range of misleading information meant that analysts were unable to separate the 'signals' from the wider 'noise'. On 7 December, the US Pacific Fleet was caught unawares.

2.2 A flawed concept: the Yom Kippur War

The outbreak of the Yom Kippur War of October 1973 between Israel and a coalition of Arab states led by Egypt and Syria stands out as a case of analytical failure. The surprise Arab attack on Yom Kippur, the Jewish Day of Atonement, had significant political and military implications, weakening Israeli Prime Minister Golda Meir's position and denting Israel's image as the dominant military power in the region. The Israeli intelligence community was taken completely by surprise by Egyptian and Syrian forces. In a short period of time, 90,000 Egyptian troops, 850 tanks, and 11,000 vehicles had crossed the Suez Canal, breaching the 'Bar Lev' defence line – a series of bunkers and trenches to protect Israeli-occupied Sinai – inflicting significant losses on the Israeli defenders. In the north, too, there were setbacks; Syrian forces took significant portions of the Golan Heights, before the situation was saved by the Israeli Defence Forces (IDF). In the opening phase of the war, over 700 Israeli soldiers were killed, a significant number of tanks destroyed and the Israeli Air Force lost thirty aircraft (Bar-Joseph, 2005:225). In the end, Israeli mobilisation and superior fighting ability turned the tables, and, by the end of the conflict, over 15,000 Arabs and 2,500 Israelis had been killed (Bregman, 2016:147–8). The initial reverses sparked controversy and led to the formation of a commission, led by Shimon Agranat, to look into the causes of the disaster. As it turned out, Israeli intelligence had all the information it needed to assess an attack was likely, yet drew the wrong conclusions. The failure stemmed from faulty analysis.

Israeli political and military leaders wrongly assumed that their Arab neighbours were too weak to launch an attack, based on past experience and knowledge of Israeli's military might. In 1967, Israel had launched pre-emptive strikes against Egypt, Syria and Jordan. Outstanding intelligence allowed the IDF to achieve surprise, wiping out the Egyptian air force on the ground and inflicting a series of defeats on numerically superior Arab forces within six days. Military success resulted in complacency. The head of Israeli military intelligence, Major General Eliahu Zeira, remained convinced that Egypt and its Arab allies would not attack Israel until it had 'assured aerial capability to attack deep inside Israeli airspace' to destroy the Israeli Air Force on the ground. The absence of advanced long-range Egyptian aircraft and Soviet-supplied Scud ballistic missiles convinced Zeira that an attack was highly unlikely. Any Egyptian preparations would also be quickly picked up by Israeli intelligence and the IDF would have significant warning of an 'all-out war' with the Arabs (Reinharz and Rabinovich, 2008:261). This misplaced confidence led to a rigid analytical framework called 'The Concept' (or 'The Conception'). Intelligence was used to support the view that Egypt would not attack until they had improved their air force – a decisive factor behind Israel's success in 1967 – and received Scud missiles which the Soviets were reluctant to provide. In June 1972, Zeira's predecessor, Major General Aharon Yariv, believed Israel's spies would give at least '36 hours' warning, while an overconfident Zeira told Israeli Prime Minister Golda Meir that military and political leaders would have 'several days' notice (Kahana, 2002:82). The Agranat Commission later concluded there was 'no basis for giving such an assurance' (Agranat Commission). Israeli political leaders, too, believed an attack was impossible. Defence Minister Moshe Dayan thought there would be no war for the 'coming ten years' (Walton, 2010:176). It also concluded that there has been a false sense of security; Israeli planning was based on 'mirror imaging' – guessing how Egypt would react, based on what Israel would do in a similar situation – rather than look at events from an Egyptian perspective. By 1972, Egypt's President Anwar el-Sadat concluded a limited war with Israel was possible. Rather than start a major war, which would fail – as the Israelis guessed – because of a lack of modern Soviet aircraft, Sadat gambled on a more limited operation to retake Sinai, under Israeli occupation since 1967, and inflict significant losses on the IDF. 'The idea of a limited war came from the fact that we did not have enough equipment to go into a general war', explained one Egyptian general (Bregman, 2016:116). The daring plan bypassed Israeli assumptions that Egypt would take time to prepare for a major conflict, giving Israel's spies adequate warning time.

Israel's excellent sources of information were used to support a flawed belief that Egypt and her Arab allies would not attack. In reality, Israeli HUMINT gave significant insights into Egyptian thinking. Mossad had several important sources: a general codenamed Koret (Hebrew for 'woodcutter'), a seaport worker in Alexandria and **Ashraf Marwan** ('the Angel') (Raviv and Melman, 2014:165–8). The son-in-law of former President Gamal Abdel Nassar, Marwan was part of Sadat's inner circle and was, one former insider revealed, the 'best agent any country ever had … a miraculous source' (Black and Morris, 1991:286). Marwan provided highly damaging order-of-battle information and, on the eve of the Egyptian attack, provided his handlers with an eleventh-hour warning, allowing for limited Israeli mobilisation. Another unlikely source was Jordan's King Hussein. In September, Hussein was flown to a safe house north of Tel Aviv to personally brief Golda Meir that there were growing signs from Cairo and Damascus that war was likely (Raviv and Melman, 2014:163). Israeli IMINT and COMINT also provided clues, as did visual reports from troops stationed on the Bar Lev line and the Golan. Yet Israeli spies remained unconvinced. Good intelligence was twisted to fit 'the Concept', rather than viewed as pointing to an impending attack. Egyptian preparations were dismissed as defensive measures or part of military exercises

(Sheffy, 2006:821). By October 1973, analysts were guilty of misreading the warning signs. On 4 October, Soviet military personnel and their families started to leave Egypt, confusing Israeli analysts. Was this part of a diplomatic spat with Moscow, or the start of something more sinister? Even reports of Egyptian tanks, bridging equipment and troops in the Canal Zone failed to prompt a significant response. As a result, on Saturday 6 October – the holiest day in the Jewish calendar – the Israeli military was largely unprepared with disastrous results. The post-war Agranat Commission singled out over-reliance on 'the Concept' as the major cause of the failure, its interim report leading to Zeira's removal.

2.3 Averting Armageddon: the Cuban Missile Crisis

Intelligence analysts played an important role in de-escalating one of the most dangerous episodes of the Cold War: the Cuban Missile Crisis of October 1962. The crisis in the Caribbean resulted from the growing imbalance in the nuclear arsenals of the United States and the Soviet Union. By the 1960s, the Soviet premier, Nikita Khrushchev, realised that the Soviet Union was falling far behind the US in the development and construction of medium- and intermediate-range ballistic missiles (MRBMs and IRBMs). To make matters worse, in the late 1950s the US government had also deployed its own MRBMs to Britain, Italy and Turkey, all aimed at the Soviet Union. Moscow felt increasingly vulnerable. Khrushchev was also aware that Moscow's ally, a revolutionary regime under Fidel Castro, in power since January 1959 on the island of Cuba – less than 100 miles off the US coastline – was in danger of being undermined by the Americans. Fearing that the Cuban revolution would be toppled, and concerned at the prospect of losing the nuclear arms race, Moscow's response was to deploy nuclear weapons to Cuba. 'Why not throw a hedgehog at Uncle Sam's pants', Khrushchev told advisors in April 1962 (Gaddis, 2007:75).

Despite often being hailed as an intelligence success, the crisis was preceded by a significant lapse by American intelligence. From January to October 1962, CIA analysts underestimated the desire of Khrushchev and his inner circle to deploy nuclear missiles to Cuba, interpreting this as a major provocation that the Kremlin would try to avoid (Zegart, 2012:n.p.). In August, despite evidence of a growing Soviet conventional military build-up, a CIA National Intelligence Estimate (NIE) failed to mention the possibility of nuclear weapons but pointed to the growing number of Soviet surface-to-air missile (SAM) sites (McAuliffe, 1992:35). A Special National Intelligence Estimate (SNIE), prepared in September, even raised the prospect of Soviet nuclear missiles being deployed to Cuba but dismissed this, concluding instead that such an event would 'indicate a far greater willingness [on the part of the Soviets] to increase the level of risk in US–Soviet relations' (McAuliffe, 1992:93). US analysts also discounted the presence of Soviet MRBMs or IRBMs because of Soviet deception measures and assurances that Soviet forces were contributing to the defence of Cuba. Intelligence reports suggesting the presence of missiles were therefore initially discounted, as they did not fit with the perceived intelligence picture. US analysts suffered from 'mirror imaging' and wishful thinking. At the top of the CIA there were concerns. Director of Central Intelligence (**DCI**) John McCone thought analysts needed to be more imaginative, believing (rightly as it turned out), that the deployment of Soviet SAMs was a defensive measure to protect possible MRBM sites. Analysts also began to receive evidence of suspected nuclear missile sites, requesting 'photographic confirmation' using U-2 high-altitude reconnaissance aircraft (Andrew, 1996:285). Photographic evidence of offensive missiles emerged on 14 October, following a U-2 overflight. The next day, analysts concluded that Soviet MRBMs on Cuba had a range of 700 to 1,000 miles, directly threatening the US's southern and eastern seaboard, and could be fully operational within weeks (McAuliffe, 1992:140–2). On 16 October, Kennedy was told of this development by his National Security Advisor McGeorge Bundy. The job of the analysts was now to provide information to assist Kennedy and his inner circle in deciding how to deal with the missiles. Despite their initial failure to anticipate the movement of offensive nuclear missiles, here US analysts performed well. In an NIE on 19 October, analysts believed use of military force would, through a series of miscalculations, 'escalate to general war'. The next day, a SNIE, while accurately predicting Soviet motives, echoed the grim assessment of the situation (McAuliffe, 1992:214). Faced with the evidence of Soviet MRBMs, Kennedy broadcast to the American people. 'Within the past week', he explained, 'unmistakable evidence has established the fact that a series of offensive missile sites is now in preparation'. With the warning that aggressive conduct may lead to war, Kennedy asked Khrushchev directly to deescalate and 'move the world back from the abyss of destruction' (Westad, 2017:306). Tensions were to reach a peak later that week; on 27 October – Black Saturday – with a U-2 shot down over Cuba, Khrushchev playing hard ball and more Soviet ships on their way to Cuba, things looked bleak. CIA analysts estimated that Soviet missile sites were 'fully operational' (McAuliffe, 1992:328). Yet that evening, there was a glimmer of hope. During talks with the Soviet Ambassador, 'Bobby' Kennedy offered to remove American missiles from Turkey if Khrushchev agreed to climb down over Cuba. Khrushchev accepted, signalling an end to the most dangerous period of the Cold War. The job of US analysts now turned to confirming the withdrawal of Soviet missiles. A CIA assessment on 29 October confirmed the absence of equipment at the missile sites, while further reports in November confirmed the withdrawal of Soviet IRBMs and MRBMs (McAuliffe, 1992:357). While the start of the crisis over Cuba marked a failure of US analysis, good intelligence and analysis helped to end it [Document 13].

Analysis is a vital stage of the intelligence process, but it is fraught with difficulties. With fragments of information in front of them, and likely aware of the gaps in their knowledge, analysts essentially have to give a best guess based on their expertise and judgement. This may be clouded by such factors as 'mirror imaging' and 'clientisis'. Analysts may also be under pressure to produce results, resulting in an environment in which they may end up drawing the wrong conclusions. Even where analysis is effective, it may end up being disregarded during the next stage of the intelligence cycle. Having been disseminated to policymakers, politicians or military commanders may ignore the analysis, should it fail to fit with their own perceptions and beliefs.

3 Intelligence and policy

Once analysed, intelligence needs to be passed to those who have the authority to use it – the policymakers. The role of policymaker is central to the whole intelligence process. For Sherman Kent, policymakers need information 'which is complete, which is accurate, which is delivered on time, and which is capable of serving as a basis for action' (Kent, 1966:5). Ideally, intelligence agencies need to provide policymakers with honest assessments that are free from any political bias. In turn, policymakers for their part need to use the information provided to improve their policies or help 'educate' themselves about problems on the horizon. The reality can be somewhat different. Uri Bar-Joseph observes that the relationship between policymaker and intelligence official is an 'ongoing obstacle race' where both sides often get irritated (Bar-Joseph, 1995:9). In part, this stems from their differing priorities. Intelligence officials strive to give policymakers unbiased assessments to improve the quality of their policies. Such information, however, is not always welcome. One former British intelligence head remarked that his job was to tell 'the Prime Minister what the Prime Minister does not want to know' (Andrew, 2004:179). In 1974, questioned by the Foreign Secretary about what his service did, the Chief of SIS replied: 'Our job, Secretary of State, is to bring you unwelcome news' (Hennessy, 2001:71). Policymakers might find that the intelligence advice goes against what they want to do and considerable tensions may follow as policymakers either ignore or twist ('politicise') the information to suit their own purposes. Tensions can also stem from the personality of the leader or the nature of the political system they are part of. In a democracy, differences of opinion are to be expected and can never be fully resolved. In authoritarian regimes – Stalin's Soviet Union or Hitler's Germany – intelligence is often spun to fit the ideological beliefs of the system, supporting the one-party state. In a small number of extreme cases, intelligence agencies can even try to go against government policy and undermine it, using unauthorised leaks, briefings against politicians and other underhand tactics, feeling that national interests are being undermined.

For all the money spent on intelligence collection, one of the biggest problems in government is the non-use of intelligence by policymakers

(Betts, 2004:n.p.). In government most policymakers are driven by short-term issues and have to juggle a heavy workload. They want answers to immediate issues, writes Johnson. Relevance, then, is important. If intelligence fails to provide answers to the pressing issues facing policymakers it will often be ignored, regardless of the time and money spent on it. In the United States, an estimated 80–90 per cent of the analytical effort goes into 'current intelligence' – explaining 'what happened today and yesterday, and what is likely to happen tomorrow' (Johnson, 2017 citing Lowenthal). Perhaps the most famous example of 'current intelligence' is the President's Daily Brief (PDB) [Document 11], a short 'compilation of current intelligence items of ... significance to national policy concerns' (Richelson, 2012:409). The importance of this document was stressed by Bill Clinton, who during his time in the Oval Office noted that 'every morning I start my day with an intelligence report. The intelligence I receive informs just about every foreign policy decision we make' (Johnson, 2014:22). Intelligence also needs to be quick and easy to digest. While intelligence may be more exciting than, for example, local government finance, it is only one part of the complicated process of modern government with policymakers focusing on topics from foreign policy to defence, healthcare to the economy in a single day. Few leaders, then, have the time to focus entirely on intelligence; and, indeed, too much information (information overload) can often be counterproductive. In November 1940, Winston Churchill complained about 'the mass of stuff which reaches me in a single morning' (Hinsley, 1993:410). In the US, the PDB, while tailored to the needs of individual Presidents, has remained a relatively short document. Gerald Ford's PDB's were lengthy – running to twenty pages. By contrast, George W. Bush received six to eight items, each running to one or two pages in length (Richelson, 2012:409). Breaking with tradition, President Trump prefers an oral briefing from officials. Reading the PDB does not fit with his 'style of learning', one official revealed (Vinograd, 2018:n.p.).

Another important factor is the personality of the policymaker, which dictates how intelligence will be used. Ideally, they need to be open to new information. If too fixed in their views, they may ignore the latest intelligence. If a leader is too hesitant they may never be able to make a decision (Handel, 2004:5). A megalomaniac, unable to take advice that goes against their own preferred opinion, would likely make a poor intelligence consumer. At the other extreme, someone with little, if any, experience, believing intelligence to be completely correct and wholly reliable, would also be a poor consumer. Israeli Prime Minister Golda Meir believed that intelligence was fact, ignoring that consumers still need to read reports with healthy scepticism (Bar-Joseph, 1995:19). Policymakers may also have their own 'favourite INTs'. The excitement of spying makes HUMINT a firm favourite with some political leaders, while a fascination with new technology may lead to an obsession for TECHINT – IMINT or SIGINT – over more traditional forms of intelligence. On the other hand, a technophobe, unable to grasp TECHINT's sophisticated collection platforms, may be inclined to ignore this important source of intelligence (Gentry, 2018:3). President Eisenhower placed special emphasis on SIGINT and IMINT, while his successor, President John F. Kennedy, fascinated by HUMINT and CIA covert action, had little interest in SIGINT. British Prime Ministers have also had their preferred means of intelligence collection. Churchill's love for Bletchley Park and wartime SIGINT (his so-called 'golden eggs') has been well documented; others have preferred domestic security-intelligence (Gentry, 2018:7). The 'favourite INT' debate also underlines another important point. The romance often associated with spies and new technology may undermine faith in OSINT and non-secret sources of information.

Intelligence consumers also need to maintain a balance between 'intimacy and detachment' (Handel, 2004:5). Former FBI Director James Comey said the President and the Bureau 'must be at arm's length' (Comey, 2018:120). Intelligence and policy, writes Sir Percy Cradock, a former chair of the JIC, need to be 'close but distinct'. If too close, intelligence tells policymakers what they want to hear. But if too detached, intelligence is meaningless as it doesn't relate to real-world events. 'The best arrangement is intelligence in separate but adjoining rooms', Cradock suggests, 'with communicating doors and thin partition walls, as in cheap hotels' (Cradock, 2002:296). Leaders need to take a healthy interest in intelligence, but leave it to the professionals to provide expert analysis. Despite his passionate faith in intelligence, Churchill's 'insatiable appetite' for raw information – most notably the decrypts of Germany's Enigma machine – made him over-eager in trying to use intelligence, leading to arguments with the military. In the Middle East, intercepted messages from German commanders wanting more tanks, more men, more aircraft and fuel convinced Churchill that German forces were much weaker than they were, pressing British commanders to launch an offensive earlier than necessary. Churchill's inexperience, own interpretation of the evidence and a failure to grasp the situation on the ground clouded his judgement (Hinsley, 1993:418) [Document 14]. Labour's Harold Wilson – a passionate believer in domestic and foreign intelligence – grew paranoid that elements of MI5 were plotting to remove him. In the United States, Presidents have also experienced a rocky relationship with the CIA. President Lyndon Johnson unfavourably compared the agency to his cow, Bessie, who would swing a 'shit smeared tail' through a bucket of fresh milk, while Richard Nixon claimed the CIA were a bunch of 'Ivy League liberals' who had 'always opposed him politically' (Andrew, 1996:323, 350). George W. Bush was reportedly 'at war' with the CIA during the 2004 Presidential election, claiming they were guessing in their assessments of the Iraqi insurgency, while intelligence–policy relations have reached an all-time low under current President Donald J. Trump following claims of a series of leaks related to Russian involvement in the 2016 election campaign

(Lomas, 2017:n.p.). French politicians have also had difficult relationships with their intelligence agencies, often overlooking their work. In the 1960s, intelligence played no role in shaping President de Gaulle's foreign policy. Other leaders believed France's spies were 'inefficient, politicized, or both' (Porch, 1995:474). In Israel, too, there have been tensions. Public claims by Israeli Prime Minister Binyamin Netanyahu to the United Nations in 2012 that Iran was a year away from building a nuclear weapon were privately rejected by Mossad's Director Meir Dagan, believing they remained a number of years away (Raviv and Melman, 2014:18).

Policymakers may respond to intelligence officials by cutting them out of the picture altogether if they disbelieve the advice that's being provided to them. A breakdown of trust can be damaging for national security. In a small number of cases, intelligence officers – cut out from the decision-making process altogether – can even reveal their frustrations by trying to influence government policy by underhand methods. Here intelligence officers may think 'they know better than their political masters' leading, writes Bar-Joseph, to the manipulation of information, conspiracy and unauthorised leakages to the media (Bar-Joseph, 1995:13). The history of British intelligence is littered with stories of plots. In the 1920s, members of the intelligence community – a 'very, very incestuous circle, an elite network' (Norton-Taylor, 1999:n.p.) of officials who often went to the same schools, shared the same beliefs, being politically conservative and had extensive contacts with the press – undermined government policy at several times. Most notably, Britain's first Labour Government was embarrassed by sensitive leaks in 1924, leading to claims that British intelligence forced the government from power. More recently in the US, President Trump's administration has found itself the victim of a series of sensitive leaks – described by Trump himself on Twitter as 'un-American' by disgruntled members of the intelligence community.

The influence of intelligence can also change depending on the political system. In a liberal democracy, intelligence officials can usually tell 'truth to power' – even if it is unwelcome and perhaps ignored. By contrast, in authoritarian or totalitarian systems, telling 'truth to power' can be a risky business. Intelligence is intimately connected with the one-party state, protecting it from all forms of internal dissent, while reinforcing misconceptions of the outside world in line with the political views of the regime (Andrew, 2004:179). The KGB was the 'Sword and Shield' of the Soviet system, while the East German Ministry for State Security (*Ministerium für Staatssicherheit*) – the Stasi – had around 100,000 full-time employees and an extensive informer network – larger even than Hitler's infamous Gestapo – that pitted teacher against student, friend against friend and husband against wife to protect the ruling Socialist Unity Party (SED) (Childs and Popplewell, 1999:82–111). Stalin's Russia, Saddam Hussain's Iraq and Kim Il-sung's North Korea have all relied on their internal security organs to retain power. In China, the PRC's intelligence apparatus agencies – the civilian Ministry of State Security (**MSS**), combining domestic and foreign activities, and the People's Liberation Army's Second and Third Departments (respectively running HUMINT and SIGINT) – is inevitably linked to foreign policy decision-making, economic development and crackdowns on internal political dissent (Eftimiades, 2014:191). China's policymakers have often blamed internal dissent on foreign influence, a long tradition in Chinese politics, shaped by events from the mid-nineteenth century (Eftimiades, 1994). While undoubtedly successful in stealing western technology, China's intelligence analysis, as in other authoritarian systems, may have suffered because of Beijing's paranoia towards internal dissent and foreign policy. During Mao Zedong's leadership, few, if any, intelligence officials were willing to challenge his often paranoid judgements: ' ... we were terrified of saying something wrong', one member of the Politburo wrote (Short, 1999). By the 1950s, Chinese intelligence became a tool for internal security, rather than to speak 'truth to power'. Ironically, during China's 'Cultural Revolution' – a decade long upheaval that killed and imprisoned millions – many intelligence officers were branded 'renegade and traitor' and imprisoned or executed at the hands of the regime (Chambers, 2012:34). In 1967, the head of China's Central Investigation Department (CID) – a predecessor for the Ministry of State Security – Kong Yuan and his deputy, Zou Dapeng, were purged and many officers sent to re-education camps in the countryside (Guo, 2014:358). Similarly, throughout the Cold War, Soviet intelligence was consistently guilty of political manipulation, providing the Kremlin with 'intelligence to please'. During Stalin's time, his belief in conspiracy – especially a non-existent wartime British plot to undermine the Soviet Union – tarnished some of the best intelligence from the 'Cambridge Five'. Reports from Anthony Blunt and **Kim Philby** were disbelieved as 'disinformation' (Andrew and Elkner, 2003:81). By the 1980s, fears that an assertive United States under President Ronald Reagan was actively preparing for a nuclear attack on the Soviets resulted in Operation RYAN, a KGB operation to look for impending signs of war. KGB officers were sent to count the number of cars and lighted windows in government buildings, unusual working hours and changes in military routine, placing a huge burden on Soviet intelligence in the West, despite evidence that talk of nuclear war was largely rhetoric. RYAN became a self-fulfilling prophecy as, rather than challenging the Kremlin's conspiratorial hypothesis, intelligence was found to support it (Andrew and Gordievsky, 1990:496).

3.1 Ideology: Hitler and Stalin

The damaging influence of ideology on intelligence in an authoritarian regime can be seen in Hitler's Germany. As Fuhrer from 1933, Adolf Hitler relied on his own intuition and personal judgement. Early foreign policy achievements that breached the Treaty of Versailles, such as rearmament and the remilitarisation of the Rhineland in 1935, against the judgement of his generals, confirmed for Hitler his own infallibility and strengthened his 'all-consuming egomania'. Further successes strengthened this; Germany's unification with Austria (the *Anschluss*), the Sudetenland and, finally, annexation of Czechoslovakia in March 1939, proved Hitler correct that Britain and France, divided over how to respond to Nazi aggression and unwilling to go to war in the short term, would be unable to do anything militarily. As with the Rhineland, success only underlined dependence on his 'own will' (Kershaw, 2009:512). Even the gross miscalculation over Britain and France's determination to defend Polish sovereignty – something Hitler believed they would never do based on past experience, leading to the start of a European war in August 1939 – failed to dent his egomania and overreliance on judgement alone. In November 1939, Hitler revealed to some 200 senior members of the German armed forces that 'Providence has had the last word and has brought me success' (Noakes and Pridham, 1998:155). Germany's lightning victories over Norway and France and the Low Countries in the spring and summer of 1940 further enhanced this view. Only Britain – which Hitler believed would have to sue for peace – stood in his way in the West. The Soviet Union became the next target. German military planning for the invasion, codenamed Operation Barbarossa, was based on wishful thinking, faulty intelligence and was tainted by Nazi ideology. Initial estimates suggested the Soviet Union had only 171 large formations. By June 1941, on the eve of the operation, German intelligence listed over 200 (Kahn, 1980:441). Hitler and the German military also underestimated the fighting capacity of the Red Army. Stalin's purge of the Soviet officer corps, heavy losses in the 'Winter War' of 1939–1940 and contempt for Slavs and Bolshevism generally, resulted in a gross underestimation. 'You have only to kick in the door', said Hitler confidently, 'and the whole rotten structure will come crashing down'. The German attack on 22 June 1941 achieved near-tactical surprise. In a short space of time, three German army groups had surrounded the Red Army's forward units and advanced deep into Soviet territory. Almost half of the Red Army's Western Army Group was destroyed and 3,300 tanks destroyed or severely damaged. In early July, Hitler optimistically told his propaganda minister Joseph Goebbels that two-thirds of the Soviet armed forces had been destroyed, while Franz Halder, Chief of the German General Staff, wrote in his diary that the campaign 'will be won within a fortnight' (Hartman, 2013:49). Yet there had been a significant intelligence failure; Halder complained: 'At the start of the war we had counted on about 200 enemy divisions. We have now counted 360'. Both Hitler and the German military had seriously miscalculated the strength of the Red Army and the Soviet political system. Though further stunning advances were made – Soviet losses between June and September 1941 were over 2 million – there would be no immediate end to the war in the East. The 1941 campaign cost the German armed forces over 300,000 fatalities – more than the number between September 1939 and May 1941. Halder bleakly admitted: 'We will not again have ... the army we had at our disposal in June 1941' (Mawdsley, 2007:117). With the initiative lost, Hitler's reliance on his own judgement and erratic use of intelligence backfired. Overreliance on judgement did little to cover over the serious flaws in German intelligence as the war dragged on.

Joseph Stalin's use of intelligence prior to Nazi Germany's invasion of the Soviet Union in June 1941 also highlights the limitations of intelligence in authoritarian regimes. Since 1939, the Soviet Union and Nazi Germany had been allies thanks to the Nazi–Soviet Pact, but Hitler increasingly set his sights on a showdown with Stalin. In July 1940, Hitler revealed to his generals that the Soviet Union would be his next target. While maintaining the pretence of an invasion of Britain in the West, the German armed forces were gradually turned eastwards to face the Soviets. By 1941, Soviet intelligence – the GRU (Soviet military intelligence) and NKGB (foreign intelligence) – had several important sources on German intentions in the East. In Berlin, Soviet intelligence had Harro Schulze-Boysen, a staff officer in the headquarters of the Luftwaffe (codenamed 'Starshina'), and an economist, Arvid Harnack ('Corsicanets'), while another significant source was the journalist Richard Sorge, who, as a confidant of Germany's Ambassador to Japan, had important insights into the German–Japanese alliance, and policy towards the Soviet Union. GRU intelligence also monitored the gradual build-up of German formations in the East, but the problem was how to interpret the information. Would Germany invade the Soviet Union or was the German military build-up part of a diplomatic war of nerves? Contrary to popular belief, the intelligence was often contradictory – it could be used to support both views. In June 1941, when presented with a range of intelligence by his senior military advisors, Semyon Timoshenko and Georgy Zhukov, on the likely German attack, Stalin threw the papers back at them: 'I have different documents' (Gorodetsky, 1999:296). Stalin was also highly suspicious of his intelligence advisors. His attitude to intelligence was described by his foreign minister, Molotov, who recalled being told: 'one can never trust the intelligence. One has to listen to them but then check on them ... one cannot count on the intelligence without a thorough and constant checking and double checking' (Andrew and Elkner, 2003:75). By the spring of 1941, Stalin had become convinced that Germany would not, in the short term, attack the Soviet Union, but would instead try and maintain the Nazi–Soviet Pact. When presented with information to the contrary that an attack was highly likely, provided by Schulze-Boysen, Stalin snapped, suggesting 'the "source" in the Staff of the German Air Force should be sent to his f****** mother! This is no source but a disinformer' (Gorodetsky, 1999:296). He dismissed a report from Richard Sorge that an attack would start on 22 June 1941 – the actual start of Operation Barbarossa – by saying: 'There's this b****** who's set up factories and brothels in

Japan ... Are you suggesting I should believe him too?' (Montefoire, 2004:360). Stalin's reluctance to read reports contradicting his own strongly held views shaped the intelligence process. For intelligence officials it was 'safer to say what Stalin wanted to hear or be silent ... Stalin got what he wanted. He alone had the right to an opinion' (Khlevniuk, 2015:188).

3.2 Conspiracy? The Wilson Plot

The history of the relationship between Britain's intelligence services and policymakers provides lessons about what can go wrong if trust breaks down. Leaks, manipulation of information and smears have all played a part, with the politically conservative establishment seen as anti-change. In 1920, the then Liberal Prime Minister David Lloyd George faced opposition to his policy of recognising Bolshevik Russia from inside the armed forces, intelligence officers and even members of his own Cabinet. Intelligence officers, supported by the Chief of the Imperial General Staff, Field-Marshall Sir Henry Wilson (who gave his name to the so-called 'Henry Wilson Plot') and Secretary of State for War Winston Churchill, supported leaks to wreck policy. By 1921, following a series of undisclosed leakages, Britain's ability to read Soviet diplomatic codes declined thanks to political sabotage (Bar-Joseph, 1995). But fears of rogue spies undermining government policy also sit in the long-term memory of the British Labour Party, thanks to repeated claims of dirty tricks. During the First World War, MI5 and Special Branch routinely watched Labour's James Ramsay MacDonald because of his anti-war speeches, while Labour MPs were critical of government surveillance at home (Lomas, 2016). But relations between Britain's spies and the Labour Party reached a low point following the 'Zinoviev Letter Affair', when leaks of a forged letter from Grigory Zinoviev, head of the Comintern, urging British communists to revolution, reached the national press during an election campaign. Members of the intelligence community, fearing a return of Ramsay MacDonald's Labour to Downing Street, were suspected of the leak.

The history of relations between the intelligence community and the Labour Party has also been dominated by the so-called 'Wilson Plot' and the reported attempts to undermine Prime Minister Harold Wilson in the 1970s. In 1974, Wilson entered Downing Street for his second tenure as Prime Minister but left mid-term in May 1976. Wilson himself fuelled fears of an intelligence community plot to destabilise his government. Having just left Downing Street, he invited two BBC journalists, Barrie Penrose and Roger Courtiour (referred to as Pencourt), to his house, telling them he was unsure about 'what was happening, fully, in security' during his years in office. MI5 contained 'very right-wing' staff who would have spread, he believed, stories of 'Number 10 and the Communist cell' – a false story suggesting that the KGB had infiltrated Downing Street (Penrose and Courtiour, 1978:9). The claims were certainly revelatory and marked one of the more unusual periods of intelligence–policymaker relations in Britain. Bizarrely, Wilson even referred to himself as the 'big fat spider in the corner of the room', telling the journalists to look for new sources. Wilson himself later retreated from the claims, suggesting they were invented by journalists of 'limited experience'. But the claims were believed by many in his own party. Labour left-winger Tony Benn noted in his diary his suspicion that 'our letters were being opened and our telephones bugged'. In reality, Wilson may have been, as his official biographer suggests, suffering from the long-term effects of ill-health. By the 1970s, he was becoming increasingly aware of his own mental fragility brought on by extreme tiredness and the onset of Alzheimer's disease. Unhealthily for a policymaker, he was also prone to conspiracy. Both the CIA and South African Bureau for State Security (referred to as **BOSS**) were targeting him and his inner circle, he claimed. Downing Street was also bugged, Wilson believed. The Cabinet room had a bug hidden behind a portrait of Gladstone, he claimed, while Wilson would only talk to other people in a lavatory – and even then the taps were turned on to drown out imaginary bugging devices (Ziegler, 1993:477). Wilson was also, surprisingly in light of the allegations, fixated by secrets. 'He was obsessed by intelligence', recalled one official. 'He was extremely interested in getting it – not only about the Russians ... but also information from the security forces about people in this country', he explained (Pimlott, 1992:706). Wilson's Home Secretary, Roy Jenkins, also wrote of his 'fascination with the cabalistic glamour of the Security Service'. For all his talk of MI5's alleged dirty tricks, however, Wilson wanted 'damaging material' on pro-Communist trade union leaders (Andrew, 2009:535). In 1966, during a national seaman's strike, Wilson even used MI5 reports as the basis of a key parliamentary speech.

The longevity of the so-called 'Wilson Plot' is down to the former MI5 officer Peter Wright, author of *Spycatcher* published in 1987. Among other damaging allegations, Wright claimed MI5 held a top-secret file on Wilson under the pseudonym 'Henry Worthington' and that officers planned to leak details to the press in a repeat of the Zinoviev Letter. 'Wilson's a bloody menace', said one officer. Wright claimed at least 'thirty officers' supported the leaks. 'We'll have him out', thought another (Wright, 1987:369). Yet Wright's testimony was misleading. Interviewed by BBC Panorama, Wright was forced to admit 'the maximum number was eight or nine. Very often it was only three'. Pressed further, Wright claimed only one other officer was serious about the plot. Even Wright admitted his memoir was 'unreliable'. Yet allegations persisted, thanks to Wright. In the 1990s, MI5's first female Director-General, Stella Rimington, tried to 'knock on the head' talk of a plot by inviting Labour's senior figures to her office. 'Though I tried my best to convince them that they were wrong', she recalled, 'I knew at the end of the exercise that further efforts would be fruitless' (Rimington, 2002:190). Suspicions ran too deep. Even the publication of an authorised history of MI5 failed to deal with the plot. Drawing on MI5's archive, Andrew confirmed the existence of a file on Wilson – named 'Norman John Worthington' – that had been opened thanks to Wilson's dubious friends, but little else. There was no plot, Andrew claimed. But redactions from the book undermined the argument, especially in the eyes of those who supported it: 'the "Wilson Plot" was true enough after all', wrote one reviewer (Leigh, 2009:n.p.). Claims about references to listening devices and bugs inside Downing Street, removed on the orders of the Cabinet Office, did little to end the 'Wilson Plot' conspiracy. Even now, despite evidence to the contrary, the view that MI5 plotted against Wilson and the Labour Party is deeply embedded in the party's psyche.

3.3 Trusting intelligence? The Iraq War

'In theory, intelligence work should be objective, autonomous, and free from political influence', writes the prominent Israeli academic Uri Bar-Joseph (Bar-Joseph, 1995:9). As discussed in the previous chapter, intelligence officers are meant to be far removed from the political rat race, offering impartial assessments based on the available information. They are not meant to push a favoured political agenda, even if, in reality, their assessments shape government policy. From the policymakers' side, if intelligence fails to support the desired policy of a President or Prime Minister it can often be manipulated to fit a desired goal. This is called intelligence 'politicisation'. The use of intelligence by the British government in September 2002 to support a joint US–UK invasion of Saddam Hussein's Iraq is one such example, showing what can go wrong if policymakers and intelligence officials work too closely together. Insufficient intelligence on Iraq's weapons of mass destruction (WMD) programme – the real impetus for the invasion, political meddling and false assumptions – plagued US/UK intelligence in the run-up to the invasion in March 2003. In part, the issue stemmed from the problem that intelligence was being produced to suit policy, not the other way around. As early as November 2001, George W. Bush's US administration had decided that Iraq was the next major battleground in the 'War on Terror'. In February 2002 SIS's Chief, Sir Richard Dearlove, reported that the US administration had already decided that 'containment' of Saddam's regime would not work (Chilcot, 2016:12). During a meeting in Downing Street, Dearlove elaborated, explaining that military action was 'inevitable' and that 'Bush wanted to remove Saddam, through military action, justified by the conjunction of terrorism and WMD'. Dearlove added: 'intelligence and facts were being fixed around the policy' (Downing Street Memo, 2002:n.p.). Despite agreeing that Iraq posed a long-term threat, the British government was divided on what to do next. There was little public support for a military operation leading to regime change, while the government remained divided over whether force was necessary. Yet there seemed to be little the British government could do to restrain Washington. Privately, Britain's Prime Minister, Tony Blair, told Bush, 'I will be with you, whatever'. Saddam's removal was, Blair believed, the 'right thing to do' (Chilcot, 2016:16–17). Despite pressing for a diplomatic solution through the UN, a military option was also on the table. Facing public and parliamentary opposition, Blair needed to urgently shape the debate. In September, the government took the unprecedented step of publishing its own assessment of Iraq's WMD, based on the available intelligence. The report was designed to 'make the case' for a robust response. 'The intelligence picture ... is extensive, detailed and authoritative', Blair told MPs. Iraq's WMD programme was 'up and running'. The intelligence gave an authoritative picture that Saddam had 'existing and active military plans for the use of chemical and biological weapons, which could be activated within 45 minutes', directly threatening British troops based in Cyprus – a claim that captured public and media attention [Document 15]. But the intelligence picture was flawed: 'more weight was placed on the intelligence than it could bear', Lord Butler's subsequent inquiry concluded (Butler, 2004:114). Intelligence on Iraqi WMD was far from conclusive. Butler's inquiry also found that SIS's sources provided gossip and even lies (Butler, 2004:151–2). Intelligence collection generally was aimed at proving that Iraq had WMD, rather than the opposite, while mindsets often fixed around Iraq's previous use of chemical weapons in the 1990s clouded judgement. The intelligence community were also coming under increasing pressure to support the government line. The problem was that the government's case for action published on 24 September 2002, while ultimately owned by the JIC, was shaped by political pressure, not by the actual intelligence. In their assessment on 9 September, the JIC admitted the intelligence was 'limited' with most of the paper based on 'judgement and assessment' (JIC, 2002:2). While wrongly assessing Iraq had WMD, the committee were clear they had little evidence on Saddam's aims. Words like 'could' and 'may' were used to mask uncertainty. But these caveats were removed from the final document handed to MPs. Emails released as part of the earlier Hutton Inquiry showed officials trying to create a watertight case: 'No. 10 ... want the document to be as strong as possible within the bounds of available intelligence. This is therefore a last (!) call for any items of intelligence that agencies think can and should be included', emailed one official (Phythian, 2008:96). The problem was that, rather than providing an unbiased intelligence assessment, the JIC's statements began to morph into a public relations exercise. Lord Butler's report concluded that, if intelligence was going to be used to support policy, the 'uses and limitations' of intelligence needed to be clearer (Butler, 2004:115). Without such caveats uncertainty suddenly became firm fact. Even the JIC's warnings on the incompleteness of the information were removed. In effect, the JIC's chairman had crumbled under political pressure. The JIC, whose job it is to tell truth to power, 'stepped outside its traditional role', said former JIC chair Sir Roderic Braithwaite. 'It was engulfed in the atmosphere of excitement which surrounds decision-making in a crisis', he explained. 'I suspect that if the JIC gets too close to issues then there is a temptation of providing intelligence to please'. In his foreword to the government case, Blair maintained the intelligence had established 'beyond doubt' that Iraq had WMD – a view, later investigations concluded, that was hard to support. Unfortunately for policymakers, the use of intelligence – later found to be incorrect – undermined the government's 'good faith and credibility' (Chilcot, 2016:75). For the JIC, the episode was unwelcome; the committee, never before put into the public spotlight, was projected into 'public controversy' (Butler, 2004:154) with long-term implications. In 2013, doubts were cast over JIC reports that it was 'highly likely' the Syrian regime used chemical weapons against regime opponents in a Damascus suburb (Syria: Reported Chemical Weapons Use, 2013:2).

3.4 A stormy relationship? Trump and the US intelligence community

Tensions between intelligence officials and the White House are by no means new. Lyndon Johnson, Richard Nixon and George W. Bush all disagreed with senior intelligence officials over policy. Yet the election of Donald J. Trump, controversial businessman and television personality, as the 45th President of the United States, marks a low point in the relationship. The example of President Trump's relationship with the intelligence community serves to highlight the pitfalls of poor intelligence–policy relations. Distrustful of their intelligence officials, policymakers can often marginalise or even ignore assessments that fail to fit their world view. Intelligence officials may respond with leaks to get their message across. Since 2016, President Trump has engaged in a very public battle with America's spies. Trump also shows the dangers of having a policymaker inexperienced in dealing with intelligence. While highlighting his extensive business credentials, Trump had no experience of government and is the first President in US history never to have served in elected office, the military or government before reaching the White House. Throughout the Presidential campaign, Trump proudly portrayed himself as the ultimate political outsider standing for the 'silent majority' and promising to 'drain the swamp' of Federal government in Washington. On foreign and domestic policy he had little, if any, knowledge of how the system works. In marked contrast to Eisenhower's extensive understanding of intelligence (see Andrew, 1996:199–256), Trump was also inexperienced in handling secret information. 'He's just new to this', explained one prominent Trump ally, following Trump's controversial sacking of FBI Director James Comey in May 2017 (Fox, 2017:n.p.). Headstrong, unable to take criticism and prone to endless Twitter rants often late into the night, Trump's personality was also as far away as you could get from Handel's image of the perfect policymaker, willing to be open-minded and take advice from intelligence officials, even if it went against their own personal views. Presented with the PDB, US intelligence's 'most important' product, Trump attacked the repetitive nature of the information: 'I don't have to be told – you know, I'm like a smart person' (Fox News, 2016:n.p.).

Trump's early exchanges with intelligence officials have been tense. Even before his first classified FBI briefing, Trump told Fox News he didn't trust America's spies. 'I mean, look what's happened over the last 10 years', he said, pointing to US policy in the Middle East. A month later, Trump revealed that, for all the 'respect' he gave those briefing him, he 'didn't learn anything' new (Gass, 2016:n.p.). In office, Trump has also displayed a stubborn unwillingness to learn from mistakes. Despite attacking his Presidential rival and Democratic nominee Hillary Clinton and officials for classified leaks, Trump himself leaked information provided by a 'Middle Eastern ally' (later confirmed to be Israel) about an Islamic State plot, later confirming the existence of a widely known, yet still officially classified, CIA programme to aid rebels fighting Syria's President Bashar Assad. The White House has also placed pressure on the CIA, according to insiders, to support Trump's attempts to revoke a multilateral agreement between Iran, the US and the European Union to contain Iran's nuclear programme (Borger, 2017:n.p.).

More controversial still has been Trump's response to allegations of Russian involvement in the 2016 US Presidential election. During the campaign, Russian hackers compromised the servers of the Democratic National Committee (DNC), leaking sensitive information to the websites DCLeaks.com and Wikileaks [Document 16]. By October, intelligence sources were 'confident' that Russia was behind the leaks, backing up the claims a few months later with a joint intelligence community assessment that Russian President Vladimir Putin ordered an 'influence campaign' to undermine Clinton in favour of Trump ('Assessing Russian Activities', 2017:i). In early 2018, intelligence officials also briefed the President-elect on separate claims from a private intelligence source that Russia had compromising sexual information on him, as well as unconfirmed reports of contacts between Trump's aides and Russian officials. Members of Trump's transitional team declared open war with the agency, releasing a statement: 'These are the same people who said Saddam Hussein had weapons of mass destruction'. Trump himself tweeted that America's spies were living in 'Nazi Germany' – a claim outgoing CIA Director John Brennan found 'outrageous'. In a bizarre speech to CIA officials, Trump even claimed the 'dishonest media' had worsened intelligence–policy relations – 'there is nobody that feels stronger about the intelligence community and the CIA than Donald Trump' – before criticising media coverage of his inauguration, standing in front of the CIA's memorial wall,

Figure 3.1 Donald Trump gives speech at CIA Headquarters, January 2017
Source: MANDEL NGAN/AFP/Getty Images

a speech that Trump later described as a 'win' (Figure 3.1). Intelligence–policy relations sank to a new low after the resignation of National Security Advisor Mike Flynn in February 2017, following a series of leaks disclosing discussions between Flynn and the Russian Ambassador to the US. This was the latest in a series of claims that members of Trump's inner circle had met Russian officials to influence the Presidential race. During the election, Trump's campaign manager, Paul Manafort, and his foreign policy advisor, Carter Page, were reported to have had close contact with the Russians. Following Flynn's resignation, Trump's Attorney General, Jeff Sessions, was revealed to have misled Senators over meetings with Russia's Ambassador to the US, while later claims were to involve Trump's son-in-law, Jared Kushner, and his son, Donald Trump Jnr. Trump's business contacts in Russia were also questioned. In March 2017, speaking to the House Intelligence Committee, FBI Director James Comey confirmed that his department was investigating links between the 'Trump campaign and the Russian government' (Full Transcript, 2017:n.p.). Comey's controversial sacking by President Trump – reportedly because he 'wasn't doing a good job' – just months later, mired the White House in further controversy, leading to a special investigation led by former FBI Director Robert Mueller into Russian interference and Trump's victory – a ticking time bomb for Trump and his inner circle.

The intelligence–policy relationship is vital to the whole process. While it may be argued that most intelligence failures happen at the analytical stage, the intelligence process can quickly be undone by a policymaker who ignores the advice they are being given – 'policy failure' can be just as prevalent as 'intelligence failure'. The intelligence–policy relationship is a careful balancing act between intimacy and detachment. A policymaker with an unhealthy appetite for spy stories and 'favourite INTs' can be just as damaging as someone unwilling to take the advice of their officials. Ideally, policymakers need to be open to new information, even if this upsets the most carefully laid out policies. They need to know the limitations of intelligence and realise that agencies are there to provide impartial advice, rather than toe the party line, yet the reality is much different. For their part, intelligence agencies need to stick to giving unbiased assessments and supporting policy when asked. In reality, however, intelligence can quickly become the 'subject, object and instrument of power politics' (Ransom quoted in Bar-Joseph, 1995:9). Intelligence assessments can easily go against a policymaker's preferred policy, leading to the intelligence being ignored, while policymakers may look elsewhere for the information they want or, worse still, politicise and twist assessments to suit their objectives. Relying on their own personal judgement they may even cut out officials out altogether, often with disastrous results. Examples from Britain, the United States and Israel show that agencies can turn against their political masters, leaking information and briefing against politicians if they're ignored, though this remains the exception rather than the norm. Intelligence politicisation remains a problem in all political systems, even if intelligence in undemocratic or totalitarian states has a tendency to reinforce the regime's view of the outside world. While certainly unwelcome and damaging to the intelligence process, these tensions are only a natural by-product of the roles of policymaker and intelligence advisor. Tensions are to be expected. The process remains, as Bar-Joseph observes, an 'ongoing obstacle race' (Bar-Joseph, 1995:9).

4 Intelligence liaison

The sharing of intelligence – intelligence liaison – is increasingly important in today's globalised world. Sir Stephen Lander, MI5's former Director-General, has observed that intelligence sharing is increasingly important as the twenty-first century becomes 'more competitive and complex' (Lander, 2004:483). A former chair of the JIC underlined the importance of intelligence sharing: 'Cooperation ... is a feature of almost all modern intelligence, overlaying the received picture of it as a secretive, exclusively "national" entity'. In short, liaison is now a 'multinational activity' (Herman, 1996:217). Intelligence liaison can exist in a variety of forms. It can be between one agency and another – bilateral exchanges – and restricted to one particular source. In some cases, countries may have agreements in place to share intelligence while others may be more improvised. At the other end of the scale, some sharing arrangements have similarities to large multinational organisations, wielding immense power and influence. The UKUSA or 'Five Eyes' countries – the United States, Britain, Canada, New Zealand and Australia – share extensive information on a wide range of subjects from signals intelligence to ocean surveillance.

While the sharing of intelligence is increasingly important, it is not a new phenomenon. Liaison became an important part of war and peace in the twentieth century. During the First World War, the sharing of captured German codebooks by Russia helped British Admiralty codebreakers crack the German naval code. Liaison continued to play a role during the inter-war years, in particular the British–French–Polish attack on Germany's Enigma machine. Intelligence liaison came into its own during the Second World War, with British–American intelligence exchanges laying the groundwork for further cooperation during the Cold War. The sharing of intelligence was also important to the Soviet Bloc; the KGB worked with allies from Cuba to Vietnam, the East Germans to Mongolia. While threats to national security have long transcended national borders, the global 'War on Terror' has placed an increased emphasis on intelligence sharing. In 2013 the Director of GCHQ, Sir Ian Lobban, talked of a 'global, agile, flexible array of intelligence and security capabilities, and therefore we need global partnerships'. For Britain, liaison has moved into non-traditional areas beyond the 'Anglo-Saxon' preserve of the UKUSA community, with trans-governmental organisations such as Europol (European Union Agency for Law Enforcement Cooperation) gaining prominence (Jeffreys-Jones, 2013:191–229). The UK's decision to leave the European Union taken in June 2016 certainly poses day-to-day challenges for UK and European security officials; Britain's continued involvement in Europol, participation in EU-wide OSINT research and European Arrest Warrant have an uncertain future. As partnerships in the Middle East, South Asia and Africa have become increasingly important, explained Sir John Sawers, when Chief of SIS,

> If there is a terrorist ... say a British extremist has gone to a foreign country and it is important for our security, in the UK, that an eye is kept on him ... It is the local partners that have the powers to do those things, so we have to work in partnership in order to be able to do things lawfully overseas.
>
> (ISC, 2013:n.p.)

Despite the advantages it offers, working with foreign intelligence partners can also prove controversial. Allegations of torture or working with corrupt or authoritarian regimes, for example, go against Western values of liberal democracy and human rights. The decision whether or not to work with foreign partners requires agencies to balance such risks against the potential benefits involved.

There is much to commend the sharing of intelligence. It is uneconomical, even downright impossible, for national agencies to do everything themselves – despite former NSA Director Keith Alexander's drive to 'collect it all' (Greenwald, 2015:95). The 200 staff in New Zealand's Security Intelligence Service are unable to compete with the staff and resources at the UK's disposal, while Britain's SIS, with its workforce of some 2,500, cannot possibly complete with the estimated 21,000 who work for the CIA. Even with its huge expenditure on technical and human intelligence, the US intelligence community relies on foreign agencies for a large amount of information. One US Defence Secretary explained: 'The United States has neither the opportunity nor the resources to unilaterally collect all the intelligence information we require' (Richelson, 2012:347). While dominant in technical intelligence methods, the US is weaker when running spies abroad due to cultural and language barriers. Trading technical intelligence with other local regional partners, or 'piggybacking' (Sims, 2006:203) agencies with the expertise to recruit and handle spies became a cost-effective way of accessing important information. America's allies in the Middle East are 'an invaluable source of intelligence ... They know the Islamic terrorist groups better than Americans ever can; they are able to penetrate them with agents and informers much more easily' (Ball, 2002:71). As a result, following al-Qaeda's 9/11 attacks in Washington and New York, the CIA's links with Egypt, Jordan and Algeria were significantly strengthened in terms of money, training and equipment, in return for human intelligence resources. Liaison extended beyond the Middle East. By 2009, the CIA had paid 'tens of millions of dollars' to Pakistan's **ISI** in return for the capture or killing of wanted militants. One CIA insider suggested the programme – that had led to 600–700 killed or captured suspects – had given 'big savings to [U.S.] taxpayers' (Miller, 2009:n.p.).

Training, new technical equipment and expertise are other cost-effective benefits. In the 1940s, Britain's Security Service helped reform Australian security, resulting in the formation of the Australian Intelligence Security Organisation (ASIO) (see Horner, 2014), while the KGB helped allies in the Eastern Bloc and elsewhere; KGB support for the Cuban *Dirección General de Inteligencia* resulted in what Moscow described as 'good working relations' (Andrew and Mitrokhin, 2006:91). Liaison can also be cost-effective in preventing unnecessary overlap and competition. Under the UKUSA system, the United States takes the lead in Latin America, Asia, Russia and parts of China, while Britain is responsible for parts of Europe, the former Soviet Bloc and Africa. Canada, New Zealand and Australia focus on parts of the Pacific (Richelson, 2012:349). Geography can be another important factor. During the Cold War, Norway's proximity to the Soviet Union made it an important partner for US and UK signals intelligence agencies to monitor Soviet movements (Riste, 1999:228). Exploiting geographical advantages gave Norway 'predominantly US-equipped and principally US-financed' technology that it would not have otherwise had (Herman, 2001:142–3). West Germany, Turkey, Japan, the UK itself, as well as Britain's overseas territories – especially Hong Kong – were important in providing ports, airfields and secure facilities for monitoring equipment, spy planes and ships. Similarly, Soviet intelligence maintained technical facilities in Cuba, Vietnam, Yemen and other sites of importance for monitoring the US and its allies. Geography remains important today; sitting at the heart of a global submarine cable network, Britain's access to fibre-optic cables through GCHQ Bude allows the organisation to exploit up to 25 per cent of the world's internet traffic, making it a valuable ally for the NSA (Marks, 2013:n.p.). As a result, the US government provided GCHQ with an estimated £100 million to upgrade systems and infrastructure (Hopkins and Borger, 2013:n.p.). GCHQ and NSA liaison with Oman also allows the exploitation of cables carrying internet communications passing through the Persian/Arabian Gulf (Campbell, 2014:n.p.).

For all its merits, sharing intelligence also carries with it significant risks that need to be taken into consideration. While modern intelligence requires liaison, intelligence retains a significant element of national self-interest. In October 2017, the head of Germany's Federal Intelligence Service (BND or *Bundesnachrichtendienst*) rejected the idea of a 'European intelligence service' – a proposal floated by French President Emmanuel

Macron. Any new EU-wide agency would 'create bureaucratic double structures ... [lowering] our efficiency profoundly', he warned (Kaleta, 2017:n.p.). Agencies may also become too dependent on allies for their information. In the 1980s, an estimated 90 per cent of the UKUSA budget was provided by the US. Canadian, Australian and New Zealand agencies contributed a mere 2 per cent. In 1985, a New Zealand ban on nuclear-capable warships provoked a fierce response from Washington, leading to a reduction in intelligence sharing. Canada experienced similar treatment following an initial refusal to provide warships to support US-led operations during the 1990 Gulf War (Aldrich, 2010:n.p.). In Britain, too, reliance on US money and knowhow could be seen to have a negative impact; one GCHQ insider revealed the 'requirements from our friends across the water often had to be met first under the special relationship' (Urban, 1996:59). Another area of concern is trust; there are even limits to what will be shared between the UK and the US. One former senior UK official remarked that intelligence sharing on the Soviet Bloc was near total, while restrictions were placed on areas such as Cuba and South America where 'commercial matters were concerned' (Urban, 1996:60). A breakdown in trust may even lead to outright animosity. The CIA's relationship with the ISI worsened considerably because of suspicions of extensive collusion with Taliban and other militant groups. In December 2009, Secretary of State Clinton warned US embassies that ISI officials maintained ties to 'a wide array of extremist organizations'. For their part, the ISI treated the CIA station in Islamabad as a 'hostile intelligence presence', despite supposedly being on the same side (Aid, 2012:106).

By sharing intelligence, agencies also lose control of how information is used, or who actually uses it, with some handed to third parties. This has often led to claims that intelligence agencies have broken ethical boundaries by sharing intelligence with allies which has been used to capture and fly individuals to another state, where they have been subjected to torture and other forms of inhumane treatment. Britain's sharing of intelligence with the CIA leading to the illegal rendering of terrorism suspects post-9/11 has led to claims of 'complicity' in torture. The UK's sharing of information with allied agencies who have then gone on to render or even kill using drone strikes has resulted in controversy. This is not just restricted to the UK; Australian SIGINT supported US drone strikes, leading to calls for greater transparency. 'It is perfectly reasonable for the Australian public to want to know what exactly is going on here', said the Melbourne-based Human Rights Law Centre (Dorling, 2014:n.p.), following claims that Australia's Lone Pine SIGINT facility played a leading role in supporting US policy. Setting the ethical parameters over what can and cannot be done with intelligence can be problematic in the complex world of liaison. Agencies may sometimes need to work with partners who do not 'adhere to the same high standards of human rights compliance'. In 2013, SIS's Sir John Sawers told MPs there 'are sometimes some fine balances to be drawn here' (ISC, 2013:n.p.). While Sawers was clear that his agency sought 'clear assurances' over how the intelligence was to be used, this is not always possible for many of the informal bilateral links quickly established following 9/11. ' … an organization which relies on information collected and shared by partners who are known for not respecting human rights in the process of interrogation could also be tainted by association', writes Manjikian (2015:706). Stopping intelligence sharing on ethical grounds may harm national security by cutting off important sources of intelligence from allies in the Middle East. It may be easier for permanent multilateral sharing such as the 'Five Eyes' community to agree, yet, even here, differing national legal definitions and policy may get in the way. Joint training and shared national policies can help put ethics at the heart of liaison arrangements, but this remains a challenging balancing act for intelligence officials and policymakers.

In worst-case scenarios, sharing can impact on security. If a partner organisation is penetrated by a hostile agency, intelligence will likely leak. Aspects of transatlantic intelligence sharing were rocked by the 'Cambridge Five' – especially by the actions of SIS's 'Kim' Philby – which saw US intelligence reach Soviet hands. In the early 1960s, France's foreign intelligence agency, the SDECE (*Service de Documentation Extérieure et de Contre-Espionnage*) was rocked by the 'Sapphire Affair' and claims by the KGB defector, Anatoly Golitsyn, of an extensive Soviet spy ring with access to NATO (and US) secrets, ultimately leading to a breakdown in CIA cooperation (Porch, 1995:410–17). Intelligence sharing inside multinational organisations can be problematic. 'We do not get everything that is releasable to the Five Eyes, but we get everything that Canada or the U.S. deem NATO should see', said former BND Director and NATO's first intelligence chief Arndt Freytag von Loringhoven in 2018 (Brewster, 2018: n.p.).

Ultimately, while modern intelligence requires liaison, it nevertheless relies on an overriding element of national self-interest. Working with intelligence partners also requires mutual trust, yet even allies, former Canadian Minister of National Defence Jean-Jacques Blais admitted, often have 'conflicting interests' (Granatstein and Stafford, 1990:194). While German Chancellor Angela Merkel claimed that 'Spying between friends, that's just not done', allies frequently spy on each other (Spillius, 2013:n.p.). In wartime, British codebreakers read the diplomatic traffic of allies and neutrals alike. One important target was General de Gaulle's Free French, with British–American interception of French communications continuing post-1945 (Aldrich, 2011:109). In 2015, the website Wikileaks revealed reports that the NSA spied on French President François Hollande and two predecessors – Jacques Chirac and Nicholas Sarkozy – despite being long-term allies, leading to a diplomatic rebuke from the French Foreign Ministry (Smith-Spark and Mullen, 2015:n.p.). For all of Angela Merkel's complaints about US spying, Germany's BND had a history of spying on the US. West

German agencies monitored cables used by US diplomatic and CIA channels, and had the capacity to intercept the signals of at least 'fourteen friendly nations' unwittingly giving East German foreign intelligence access to US secrets. 'The West Germans did the dirty work of spying on their American allies, and we stole their information', explained Marcus Wolf, the head of the foreign intelligence branch of the Stasi (Wolf and McElvoy, 1997). More recently, the BND eavesdropped on at least two US Secretaries of State – Hillary Clinton and John Kerry – as well as Turkey, a close NATO ally (*Der Spiegel*, 2014). Japan, France and South Korea have also engaged in economic espionage against the US, with a 1987 estimate of Japan's foreign intelligence claiming that around 80 per cent of its assets were focused on 'economic intelligence in the USA and Western Europe' (Alexander, 1998:13).

4.1 Best friends: the special relationship

Perhaps the most famous and wide-ranging example of intelligence liaison is the transatlantic special relationship between the United Kingdom and the United States. While foreshadowed by examples of liaison in the inter-war period, the US–British special intelligence relationship had its origins in the Second World War. The mutual threat of Nazi Germany and Imperial Japan led to informal liaison between British and American code-breakers even before the bombing of Pearl Harbor in December 1941, with cooperation formalised under the first Anglo-American SIGINT agreement (the 'Holden Agreement') of October 1942 dealing with cooperation on Axis naval traffic. By May 1943, a further agreement – the BRUSA agreement – was signed between the US War Department and British Government Code & Cipher School (GC&CS), leading to joint work on German Army and Air Force signals [Document 17]. Britain entered into this liaison agreement from a position of strength: GC&CS had years of experience of attacking the codes of her rivals. In the long term, however, American technical expertise, money and resources gradually tipped the balance in their favour. With the end of the war in Europe and the Far East, British and American officials searched for peacetime collaboration, which resulted in the 'British–US Communication Intelligence Agreement', of March 1946. Signed on the same day as Winston Churchill spoke about the post-war 'special relationship' at Fulton, Missouri, the agreement was, according the head of SIS, an 'important milestone' in transatlantic relations (HW 80/6, BRUSA Agreement:1946)

Post-1945 transatlantic intelligence sharing endured thanks to the shared threat of the Soviet Union. While the transatlantic relationship has been far from special at times, intelligence sharing has proved remarkably resilient. The Suez Crisis, sparked by the British/French attempt to retake a nationalised Suez Canal from Nassar's Egypt in 1956, showed a marked rift in US–UK diplomacy, yet intelligence remained largely untouched. In

London, **Sir Dick White**, SIS's chief, entertained the CIA's liaison officer in the immediate aftermath of the botched operation (Bower, 1995:201) and intelligence sharing was quick to resume. In August 1973, following significant differences over Britain's growing closeness to Europe, the UK was cut out of the US intelligence picture on the orders of National Security Advisor Henry Kissinger. However, both the CIA and NSA continued to share intelligence with their British counterparts, contrary to White House instructions (Aldrich, 2011:289). The strength of US–UK intelligence liaison stems from the 'compartmentalised', relatively isolated, nature of the relationship (Aldrich, 1998:337). Rather than the one, distinct 'special relationship' that many tend to think of, US–UK relations cross mutual interests in defence, foreign policy, economics, technology and others. The intelligence dimension is no different. There is no one all-encompassing intelligence agreement in place, but a set of bilateral arrangements between agencies governing the exchange of information. The UKUSA Agreement covers signals intelligence only, while SIS and the CIA have their own arrangements in place for HUMINT. Once formed, these relationships are resilient to wider political or diplomatic pressures. Diplomats generally regard intelligence as a 'slightly fenced-off mystery', writes Herman (2007:215). Despite US irritation at the lack of overt British support on the ground during the Vietnam War, the UK's regional intelligence support was important during the US bombing campaign against Hanoi (Wolf, 2016:338–67).

Long-term intelligence sharing produced important effects. For Britain's declining post-1945 global role, an important element of British foreign policy was, as Henry Kissinger explained, the attempt to retain 'great-power status' by becoming an integral part of US decision-making. Sharing intelligence was one way that Britain could exert real influence over their US ally (Herman, 2007:215). Joint work on Soviet intelligence estimates, nuclear proliferation and other common areas of interest, led, writes Herman, to an 'invisible colleague' process with each side influencing the intelligence assessments of the other. The CIA's Sherman Kent recalled 'we were privileged to read most of the British JIC papers and the British ... most of our NIEs ... I do put a great importance in this exchange of information with our cousins' (Jeffreys-Jones, 2013:117). Continued liaison has also led to commonality. Here, personalities are important. SIS's Chief Sir Maurice Oldfield was, the CIA's Ray Cline remarked, one of the best 'intelligence officers I have known' (Deacon, 1985:121). One Director of GCHQ even told his counterpart in the NSA that 'I have often felt closer to you than to most of my own staff' (Richelson and Ball, 1985:305). Strong bonds remained a feature of the relationship. In the immediate aftermath of 9/11, Britain's spy chiefs flew to console their US counterparts in CIA headquarters at Langley. 'They didn't have to do that. They could have called', recalled one CIA officer. Despite the inherent problems, liaison remains a strong and necessary activity for transatlantic intelligence. But liaison was not just restricted to the US, UK and their allies.

4.2 Comrades: the Soviet Bloc

Liaison was an important tool on both sides of the 'Iron Curtain'. From the start of the Cold War, both the KGB and GRU gradually built up partners in Soviet Bloc or pro-Soviet countries around the world. In 1984, one of the KGB's top priorities was identified as developing 'cooperation with intelligence services of countries of the socialist community and the special services of some liberated countries' (Andrew and Gordievsky, 1991:22). As in the West, intelligence sharing was beneficial. It gave access to new sources, was cost-effective and, in some cases, gave plausible deniability for KGB or GRU activity in the case of covert action. The KGB even held conferences for friendly Soviet Bloc agencies, attended by allies from Cuba, Mongolia and Vietnam. In Europe, the KGB established successful partnerships with allied agencies, most notably the East German Ministry for State Security (MfS or Stasi). In the 1950s, following Stasi's formation, cooperation became increasingly intimate. KGB self-styled 'advisors' were formalised as 'liaison officers' and an official agreement established to regulate relations between the two (Childs and Popplewell, 1999:125). In almost all areas, both services extensively cooperated. The KGB's main database – 'System for Operational and Institutional Data' or SOUD – became the mainstay for sharing information across the Warsaw Pact, with training, institutional knowledge and technology forming part of the relationship. By the early 1970s, the KGB's East German allies became increasingly important following Britain's decision to expel over 100 Soviet 'diplomats', crippling KGB operations there. The Stasi quickly filled the intelligence void, acting as a KGB surrogate. This growing importance was underlined by further agreements signed in 1973 and 1978. Both the KGB and the Stasi were allied in fighting 'ideological subversion' and 'uncovering and thwarting the hostile plans of the enemy' with extensive sharing of 'political, military, economic, and scientific-technological intelligence'. Both sides were committed to helping 'penetrate' rival governments, develop 'counterintelligence' and carry out 'active measures'. By March 1978, rules on the KGB's thirty liaison officers with the Stasi were also agreed [Document 18]. In 1981, East Germany's Erich Mielke told a meeting of KGB-Stasi officials: 'we continue to feel – and quite comfortably so – as if we are a division of the glorious Cheka ... No differences of opinion exist'. Naturally, there were differences, however. While outwardly friendly, KGB-Stasi relations were 'marked by distrust and double dealing' (Murphy, 1999:229). Moscow's increasingly high-handed attitude towards their junior partner, KGB running of 'confidential sources' in East Germany and wider diplomatic differences were a constant source of tension (Childs and Popplewell, 1999:125). The Soviets could also rely on Czech State

Security (*Statni Bezpecnost* or **StB**) at least until the crushing of the Prague Spring in 1968 and the defection of StB officer Josef Frolik a year later. In the 1960s, the StB managed to provide important information on Britain's nuclear strike force and embarrassing political information from sources inside the Labour Party (Andrew and Gordievsky, 1990:431–5). As with the Stasi, StB success owed something to Western willingness to talk more freely to Moscow's allies who played on fears of nuclear war, anti-Americanism and affinity to socialist thinking to develop 'confidential contacts' in the West (Lomas, 2018:n.p.).

KGB liaison was also important in spreading Moscow's influence around the world. In South America, the KGB were at the forefront of establishing links with Fidel Castro's communist regime in Havana, established in 1959. Exploiting the Cuban 'bridgehead' quickly became important for Moscow, with significant training and financial support given to Castro's *Dirección General de Inteligencia* (DGI). From 1962 to 1966 an estimated 650 Cuban illegals – deep undercover agents – were trained by the StB and KGB. By the 1970s, the KGB and DGI agreed to jointly run agents in the Pentagon and US military bases in Latin America and Spain, with the DGI specialising in the recruitment of Latinos (Andrew and Mitrokhin, 2006:91). The DGI even managed to recruit Ana Montes, a US Defence Intelligence Agency worker, finally arrested after a 16-year career helping the Cubans. As the true state of the Soviet Union quickly became apparent in the West, undermining the ideological walk-ins of the early Cold War, the Cubans could still appeal to idealists with the mythology of Castro (Haslam, 2015:269). The KGB also established contacts with Peru's National Intelligence Service (*Servicio de Inteligencia Nacional* or SIN), 'highly valued' by Moscow Centre, and supported **Salvador Allende's** Marxist government after its election in 1973. But liaison extended beyond HUMINT.

Soviet ground-based SIGINT also benefitted. Moscow's links to Warsaw Pact and Soviet-aligned governments around the world provided secure facilities for signals intelligence stations. The KGB's Sixteenth Directorate (responsible for SIGINT) and GRU ran a series of global intercept sites. In Cuba, the KGB's Havana station was the third most important intercept post – behind Washington and New York, while the Soviets also ran a large SIGINT site at Lourdes, Cuba (codenamed TERMIT-S) (Andrew and Mitrokhin, 2006:92), run by over 3,000 staff at its peak (Haslam, 2015:234). By the 1980s, the US government reported that 'Cuba's strategic location makes it an ideal site for an intelligence facility'. Working alongside smaller Soviet SIGINT facilities from diplomatic posts in New York, Washington and Los Angeles, the facilities at Lourdes allowed the Soviets to monitor US merchant and naval shipping, track US commercial satellites and monitor the NASA space programme, as well as 'eavesdrop on telephone conversations in the United States' (Ball, 1989:60). Cuban Defence Minister Raul Castro revealed in 1993 that Russia got an estimated

75 per cent of its 'strategic military information' from Lourdes (Aid and Wiebes, 2001:10) before the base closed in May 2002. In 2016, Russia said the base may re-open in line with Vladimir Putin's 'more assertive' foreign policy (Lawler, 2016:n.p.). The Soviets also maintained significant SIGINT sites in South Yemen at Al Adan (previously Aden) and Cam Rah Bay, Vietnam, as well as maintaining liaison arrangements with Lebanon, Syria, Libya and North Korea (Ball, 1989:37). East Germany's SIGINT organisation (Hauptverwaltung III) was an especially important ally, intercepting the calls of almost every West German politician. 'The MfS was one of the biggest ears in the world', said Germany's federal attorney (Fischer, 1998:142).

4.3 Complicity: extraordinary rendition

Western intelligence's liaison with certain global partners since the events of 9/11 has led to allegations of complicity in torture and other forms of unethical behaviour. In the aftermath of the attacks in Washington and New York, the 'gloves came off' as the CIA was permitted to fight the global 'War on Terror' by any means possible. Following a Presidential finding just days after the attacks, America's spies were authorised to conduct new paramilitary and psychological warfare, targeted assassinations and 'snatch' operations abroad to detain senior al-Qaeda operatives who posed a 'continuing, serious threat of violence or death to U.S. persons and interests' (Senate Select Committee on Intelligence, 2014:11). Those captured would be secretly flown to 'black sites' outside the US and subjected to brutal interrogations in a process that would become known as 'extraordinary rendition' – the unlawful transfer of a detainee to another country for interrogation purposes – before transfer to US detention facilities in the controversial Guantanamo Bay Naval Base, Cuba. As part of the plan, the CIA's existing relationships with spies in Egypt, Algeria and Jordan were strengthened, while new regimes like Libya and Syria were also courted to provide facilities. In all, an estimated 54 governments participated in the scheme, from hosting prison facilities, allowing CIA flights to use national airspace to refuel, to detaining or interrogating individuals across the continents of Africa, Asia, Australasia, Europe and North America (Globalizing Torture, 2013:6). As early as October 2001, the plan went into effect; several suspected al-Qaeda operatives were kidnapped and flown by US aircraft to Jordan, Pakistan and Egypt (Paglen and Thompson, 2007:20–21). By the summer of 2002, the CIA was given permission to use 'enhanced interrogation techniques' – effectively tantamount to the use of torture – by the Bush administration. A 2004 report to the Department of Justice detailed the use of physical violence, solitary confinement, sleep deprivation and starvation, sexual humiliation and waterboarding – a form of water torture – to extract information [Document 19]. Between 125 and 136 individuals were subjected to this treatment (Senate Select Committee on Intelligence, 2014:16), with the CIA's rendition programme provoking considerable controversy over its effectiveness. While former members of the Bush administration and CIA officials defended the programme, pointing to important information obtained (Killough, 2014:n.p.), human rights groups, the UN and others have roundly condemned it, pointing to the ineffectiveness of torture and the ethical dimension. A 2014 report by the Senate Intelligence Committee found the rendition programme was often ineffective. Detainees were repeatedly tortured – one was waterboarded 183 times – without providing any useful information (Senate Select Committee on Intelligence, 2014:85). As well as the CIA's own programme, individuals were also outsourced to friendly agencies for interrogation beyond US legal processes. In 2002, a Canadian engineering student suspected of terrorism, Maher Arer, was arrested in the US before being flown to Italy, Jordan and, finally, Syria where he was abused. 'Not even animals could withstand it', he said (Mayer, 2005:n.p.). A year later the CIA, helped by Italy's Military Intelligence and Security Service (*Servizio per le Informazioni e la Sicurezza Militare*), abducted and rendered radical Egyptian cleric Hasaan Mustafa Osama Nasr, also known as Abu Omar, from the streets of Milan, flying him to Egypt for questioning by the country's internal security agency, the State Security Investigations Service. The case resulted in criminal prosecutions of CIA officers and censure by the European Court of Human Rights.

In the UK, concerns about the involvement of Britain's intelligence and security agencies in the CIA's programme – and the outsourcing of torture to allies in the Middle East and elsewhere – have continued despite repeated denials by the UK government. In 2009, SIS's Chief, Sir John Scarlett, told the BBC that his agency was 'not complicit' and that officers 'are as committed to the values and the human rights values of liberal democracy as anybody else' (Corera, 2009:n.p.), while his successor, Sir John Sawers, told journalists that torture 'is illegal and abhorrent under any circumstances and we have nothing whatsoever to do with it' (Sawer, 2010:n.p.). Their former counterpart in the Security Service, Eliza Manningham-Buller, similarly denied the UK's complicity: 'Nothing, even saving lives, justifies torture' (Norton-Taylor, 2010:n.p.). Yet both agencies have had what Lord Neuberger, the Master of the Rolls, believed to be a 'dubious record' when it comes to human rights, torture and rendition (Blitz, 2010:n.p.). In July 2002, an MI5 officer reported from an interrogation facility in Afghanistan that a US official was 'getting a detainee ready' using sleep deprivation and stress positions, though 'no further action' was taken (HMSO 2005, Cm. 6469, 2005:15). Both SIS and MI5 helped US 'Renditions to Justice' after 9/11, though, as the UK's Intelligence and Security Committee noted, 'assurances on detainee treatment' were always sought, except in one 'regrettable' case (Cm. 7171, 2013:34). There is growing evidence to suggest that Britain's spies were, in fact, crossing the line when it came to complicity in rendition. In one of the most notable cases, the Ethiopian-born UK resident Binyam Mohammed claimed he was 'tortured in medieval ways' while held in Pakistan, after being detained in Afghanistan and rendered by the CIA. In Pakistan, Mohammed was questioned by an MI5 officer over a 'cup of tea', having first been softened up by Pakistani intelligence officers, shortly before he was rendered to Morocco where he was brutally tortured, and made false statements about a 'dirty bomb plot' (Cobain, 2013:228). The British government later paid compensation for his treatment – one of 17 individuals to receive out-of-court settlements. Evidence of UK involvement in rendition and torture also emerged in the case of Abdul Hakim Belhadj, a Libyan opposition leader and former head of the Libyan Islamic Fighting Group. A critic of Libyan dictator Muammar Gaddafi, Belhadj was seized in Bangkok and, along with his pregnant wife, Fatima Boudchar, was rendered to Libya by the CIA. Documents found after the collapse of Gaddafi's regime in 2011 showed that SIS provided the initial tip-off. In a letter to the head of Libya's national intelligence agency *Mukhabarat el-Jamahiriya*, SIS's Mark Allen congratulated the Libyans on Belhadj's safe arrival, pointing out that the intelligence leading to the arrest 'was British'. The claims led to the setting up of an inquiry under Sir Peter Gibson, subsequently shelved due to a criminal investigation. In 2016, Britain's Crown Prosecution Service (CPS) found there was insufficient evidence to pursue criminal prosecution, resulting in a private claim against Mark Allen and Britain's then Foreign Secretary Jack Straw (Cobain, 2017) which only ended after a government apology in May 2018 [Document 20].

Intelligence liaison is important in today's globalised world. Threats such as terrorism, other non-state actors and even foreign states, often transcend national boundaries, forcing intelligence agencies to cooperate with each other. Of course, intelligence sharing is nothing new. Throughout the twentieth century, allies have always shared information, and liaison became an important feature during the Second World War, most clearly in the growing transatlantic intelligence relationship between Great Britain and the United States, cementing post-war cooperation. The Cold War also saw extensive sharing on both sides of the 'Iron Curtain'; Moscow used intelligence to develop new allies beyond the Eastern Bloc, while Western liaison shaped the UKUSA (or 'Five Eyes') community. Intelligence sharing is a cornerstone of the global 'War on Terror' with the US and its allies moving beyond traditional partnerships into the Middle East, Asia and Africa. Liaison is certainly important. New sources of intelligence, greater resources, a second opinion on intelligence assessments and the ability to influence allies are just some of the benefits, yet liaison also carries significant risks. Sharing intelligence may compromise security if a friendly intelligence agency has been penetrated by rival organisations. Leaks can undermine trust in the long term, undermining intelligence sharing. Allies may also become too dependent on one another for information, while 'spying on friends' occur if trust continues to be undermined. Increasingly, liaison also carries with it ethical considerations. Sharing intelligence with friendly organisations that may illegally render individuals, use enhanced interrogation techniques or torture, and use intelligence to carry out targeted drone strikes or extrajudicial killings can lead to claims of 'complicity'. Liaison forms an integral part of modern-day intelligence, yet officials and policymakers need to carefully balance the pros and cons.

5 Catching spies

Counterintelligence

There are obvious advantages to be had from knowing what one's intelligence rivals are up to. With such knowledge, it is possible to take steps to interfere with their operations, or to stop them outright. An important aspect of intelligence work, therefore, is to protect it from the opposition. Referred to broadly under the heading of counterintelligence (**CI**), this work has two key components. The first is security. This involves broadly defensive measures that can be taken to ensure that details of operational activity do not leak, most of which may be considered common sense, such as ensuring the physical security of information through the use of locks on doors and filing cabinets, using safes to store sensitive information and protecting access to computer networks with passwords, while issuing ID passes to help make sure that employees are who they say they are. Security also involves carrying out detailed background checks on potential employees, to ensure there is little possibility of their actually being a 'plant' for a rival agency. The second aspect of CI work is more proactive, and involves both efforts to interfere with the operations of the rival organisation, and the search for any enemy spies who have penetrated the agency. Catching spies is challenging work; as West (2007:230) notes, 'few spies are caught as a result of the "vigilance of colleagues" or routine security screening'. Rather, they are more likely to be uncovered by being outed, either by a defector or by a current employee of a rival intelligence organisation who is willing to betray their agency. Known as counter-espionage, this area of activity – which, as this chapter will demonstrate, can become incredibly convoluted and complicated for those involved in it – displays intelligence work at its most introspective, as a game between competing sides: spy versus spy.

5.1 Agents in place

Existing employees of an intelligence agency who betray its secrets to a rival, known as 'agents in place', are perhaps the most valuable sources of information for CI purposes. Among the most well-known of such agents during the Cold War was **Oleg Penkovsky**. An officer in Soviet military intelligence, the GRU, Penkovsky led a trade delegation to London in 1961, a cover for his real mission – to operate a spy network. Disillusioned with communism, by the time of his arrival in London Penkovsky had already made contact with British intelligence, and a covert meeting was quickly arranged. It was agreed that Penkovsky would continue his work for the GRU, while at the same time reporting to Western intelligence. He proceeded to provide a mass of information 'relating to the Soviet Union's overall military aims, plans and espionage operations around the world. Identifying scores of Soviet agents, armaments, missile systems and even giving details on Soviet satellites' (Bennett, 2003:213). Penkovsky has been dubbed 'The Spy Who Saved the World', on account of the intelligence he was able to provide on Soviet ballistic missiles during the Cuban Missile Crisis. His activities were ultimately detected by the Soviets; Penkovsky was tried in May 1963, convicted and executed.

More recently, the FBI Special Agent **Robert Hanssen**, who volunteered his services to the KGB and GRU, has been described as 'the best example of an extraordinarily productive counterintelligence human source' (Redmond, 2010:551). Bridging the gap between the fall of the Soviet Union and the re-emergence of Russia, for over 20 years Hanssen informed the Soviets, later Russians, of the existence

> of human-source operations the CIA and FBI were running against the Soviet Union/Russia; some truly exquisite and productive technical and SIGINT collection operations; details of the double-agent program; and, of signal importance, full details of the FBI's counterintelligence program and operations against the Russians. This latter body of data gave the KGB/SVR an enormous advantage in acquiring and managing sources in the United States.
>
> (Redmond, 2010:551)

At around the same time, another US citizen, this time a CIA officer, was also providing information to the Soviet Union. On 21 February 1994, **Aldrich Hazen Ames** was arrested, along with his wife (Figure 5.1). Both were charged with conspiracy to commit espionage on behalf of Russia and the former Soviet Union, dating back to the mid-1980s (Senate Committee Report, 1994:1). Ames had been with the CIA for over 30 years, and was 'in a position to have done grievous harm' (Senate Committee Report, 1994:III). Ames's job meant that he knew a great deal about intelligence operations and various other activities against the Soviet Union in general, along with the identities of most of the CIA's agents there, in particular. In a statement read out in court, Ames admitted that he had compromised 'virtually all Soviet agents of the CIA and other American and foreign services known to me', alongside a 'huge quantity of information on United States foreign, defense and security policies' (Senate Committee Report, 1994:2). As Paul J. Redmond, who helped to uncover Ames, notes,

Figure 5.1 Aldrich Ames from FBI surveillance video
Source: Time Life Pictures/Fbi/The LIFE Picture Collection/Getty Images

he 'essentially ruined the CIA's ability to spy against the Soviets during the final years of the Cold War' (Johnson, 2017:124). At least in part a result of his actions, more than 200 CIA operations against the Kremlin were rolled up (Johnson, 2017:125; see also Fischer, 2016). In exchange, Ames 'received substantial payments for the information he had provided – money that he had used years earlier to purchase a new Jaguar automobile and a $540,000, home, with cash, in Arlington' (Senate Committee Report, 1994:1). Given Ames's salary of under $70,000 a year, perhaps his lifestyle should have warranted greater scrutiny [Document 21].

While it is difficult to 'plant' an individual within a rival intelligence organisation, it is not impossible, as can be seen in the case of 'Kim' Philby, a member of the notorious Cambridge Spy Ring (5.2). An agent of the KGB since the 1930s, Philby was successfully recruited into the British Secret Intelligence Service shortly after the outbreak of the Second World War. As such, he was in a position to provide much valuable information about British intelligence to the Soviet Union; later made head of the section which dealt with Soviet counterintelligence (Section IX), he was ideally placed to monitor and report on any betrayal

Figure 5.2 Kim Philby

Source: Pictorial Parade/Getty Images

on the part of Soviet intelligence to the British. Posted to Washington to act as SIS liaison with the CIA in 1949, Philby enjoyed a friendly relationship with the CIA counterintelligence officer **James Jesus Angleton.** A well-liked and effective officer within MI6, Philby was at one point actually tipped as a possible future head of the organisation! Not long after his move to America, however, Philby was recalled to London, and his double life began to unravel. Sacked from MI6, Philby fled to the Soviet Union in 1963.

5.2 Defectors

Much valuable information can also be obtained from individuals who have worked within their nation's intelligence community, but who subsequently decide, for a variety of reasons, to seek political asylum in another country, taking their knowledge with them. While Eastern European intelligence services 'proved resilient to penetration by western agencies' during the Cold War, they were less successful in avoiding 'very damaging' defections (West, 2007:230). Although their information will inevitably be limited to the point at which they left their role, and damage limitation will likely be put in place when their former employees learn of their defection, defectors tend to be 'gold mines for data in starting investigations', while West goes so far as to state that 'Defectors have changed the course of history' (West, 2007:230).

Shortly after the dropping of the first atomic bomb on Hiroshima and the end of the Second World War, in September 1945, **Igor Gouzenko**, a young cipher clerk working for Soviet military intelligence at the Soviet embassy in Canada, left work with a bundle of secret documents stuffed inside his shirt, to be used to secure his defection. These papers, alongside Gouzenko's wider knowledge of Soviet espionage activity in the West, would send a shockwave through the Western intelligence community, a harbinger of the coming Cold War. The Canadian Prime Minister, Mackenzie King, recorded his shock in his diary: 'During the period of war, while Canada has been helping Russia and doing all we can to foment Canadian-Russian friendship, there has been one branch of the Russian service that has been spying on [us]' (Andrew, 2009:342). Gouzenko revealed the existence of a large spy network operating in Canada, and numerous arrests followed. Even more alarming was the revelation that the Soviets had managed to penetrate the atomic programme, and had obtained 'documentary materials of the atomic bomb: the technological process, drawings, calculations' (cited in Andrew, 2009:342). Gouzenko's documents identified an agent codenamed ALEK; in reality, the British scientist Alan Nunn May. May was placed under surveillance upon his return to the UK, where he was expected to meet with his Soviet handler, but no such meetings took place, Soviet intelligence – and May – having been tipped off by *their* agent within British intelligence, Kim Philby (Andrew, 2009:342–6). Now working at Britain's atomic energy research centre, May was questioned by Commander Leonard Burt of Scotland Yard in February 1946 (Andrew, 2009:345), and 'signed a statement admitting he had been approached by a "Soviet agent", whom he refused to identify, and had given him a report on atomic research together with two samples of uranium' (Andrew, 2009:348). Put on trial, charged with breaching the Official Secrets Act, May was sentenced to 10 years' imprisonment with hard labour (Andrew, 2009:348).

Some years later, in December 1961, another defection came in the form of Anatoli Golitsyn. Golitsyn approached the CIA Head of Station in

Helsinki, explaining that he was in a position to identify 'hundreds' of Soviet agents currently working in the West, in exchange for asylum (Bennett, 2003:118). While some in the CIA were suspicious of Golitsyn's credentials, fearing him to be a Soviet plant, he was able to provide 'a wide range of intelligence to the CIA on the operations of most of the "Lines" (departments) at the Helsinki and other residencies, as well as KGB methods of recruiting and running agents' (Andrew and Mitrokhin, 1999:241–2).

While they can provide much valuable information, defectors can also cause complications. 'A senior French intelligence officer, the Comte de Marenches, is credited with the observation that defector information is like wine: the first pressing is best, and subsequent growths are generally inferior' (West, 2007:232). While their ability to provide valuable information is undisputed, as Redmond (2010:543–4) notes, 'once the excitement of their defection is over, they have told all that they know and attention toward them lags, they often start to make up stories'. During the investigation

> which led to Ames's identification as a spy, a defector from the then KGB's internal security component ... concocted a story for his American handler about the recruitment of a CIA officer in Moscow. It turned out that he made up the story to retain the attention of the CIA and FBI.
>
> (Redmond, 2010:543–4)

Perhaps the most notorious illustration of a defector who was capable of such behaviour was Anatoli Golitsyn. Having been thoroughly debriefed, Golitsyn 'began telling grandiose tales about Soviet strategic deception and making outlandish charges that prominent Americans and Britons were Kremlin spies' (Robarge, 2003:37).

Given that they have a finite amount of information, it is also possible for defectors to reveal their information piece by piece, carefully controlling what they provide. This can have a useful dual advantage; in addition to maintaining the interest of the agency involved in the debriefing, it allows the potential for a degree of leverage to be exerted over the home agency, should they be considering retribution; as Redmond notes, the most famous case in this regard is that of Alexander Orlov,

> a senior Bolshevik intelligence officer, who defected in Canada in 1938 because he thought he was about to be assassinated as part of the Great Purge. He knew the identities of most of the important spies working for the Soviets in the West, including the high-level penetrations of the British government; but he did not reveal this information, having sent a message to Stalin via the head of Bolshevik intelligence saying that he would tell all if anything happened to himself or his family.
>
> (Redmond, 2010:547)

5.3 Complications

There are many aspects of CI work which make it a complicated business. Great care has to be taken, for example, not to arouse suspicions in the penetrated intelligence agency that they have a 'mole'. This can be seen in the case of **George Blake** and the Berlin Tunnel. Blake was an SIS (MI6) officer stationed at Seoul who offered his services to the Soviets/Communists while a prisoner during the Korean War. Upon his return to London, while continuing to work for SIS, Blake was also reporting back to the KGB, which meant that he was in a position to reveal to his masters in Moscow not only the names of the British agents who were active in East Germany, but also details of Operation Stopwatch/Gold: a joint plan between the CIA and MI6 to dig a 500-mile long tunnel from West Berlin underneath East Berlin, thereby allowing the Western intelligence agencies to monitor certain Soviet military communications. As Stafford (2003) notes, even though they were aware of the fact that they were being bugged, the Soviets did not use this knowledge to start a deception operation:

> If the West once guessed that a deception campaign was afoot, they would immediately realize that the Soviets knew about the tunnel. This would instantly spark a mole hunt, which would inevitably lead to George Blake, one of the small handful of their operatives to know about it.
>
> (Stafford, 2003:180)

'To protect Blake', Stafford goes on, 'the KGB was ultimately ready to let the West listen in on the Red Army' (Stafford, 2003:181). Arrangements could then be made for the existence of the tunnel to be discovered, apparently accidentally, in April 1956.

CI activity can start to become complicated when agents in place or defectors provide an agency with details of the extent to which it has itself been penetrated by the opposition. Such information is obviously of great importance – in the cases of both Aldrich Ames and Robert Hanssen, detailed above, their eventual detection was due in part to information from a CIA asset within the SVR (the successor organisation to the KGB), the existence of whom neither man was aware of (Johnson, 2017:125). In other cases, matters quickly become more complicated; for example, when a defector has information about a traitor within an organisation but where that traitor themselves is involved in counterintelligence work! As we have seen, due to his inside knowledge of Gouzenko's defection in 1945, Philby was able to warn Soviet intelligence that Alan Nunn May was under suspicion, thereby avoiding any further compromising contact between May and his handler. Such knowledge can have more sinister consequences, as can be seen in the case of Konstantin Dmitrievich Volkov, an NKGB officer based in Turkey who expressed a wish to defect to the

British. In September 1945, Volkov turned up at the British embassy in Istanbul. In exchange for political asylum for both himself and his wife, along with a large amount of cash, Volkov

> offered important files and information which he had obtained while working on the British desk in the Centre. As an indication of the importance of the intelligence he had on offer, Volkov revealed that among the most highly rated British Soviet agents were two inside the Foreign Office (no doubt Burgess and Maclean) and seven 'inside the British intelligence system', including one 'fulfilling the function of head of a section of British counter-espionage in London', which was almost certainly a reference to Philby himself.
>
> (Andrew, 2009:344)

Informed of events in Istanbul, Philby arranged to take personal responsibility for the case. He was able to alert Moscow to Volkov's offer in time for preventative steps to be taken, deliberately prevaricating in travelling to Istanbul, thereby allowing time for Moscow to act. By the time Philby finally arrived, Volkov and his wife had vanished; they were bound for Moscow, where Volkov faced interrogation and execution (Andrew, 2009:344–5). As the Volkov case demonstrates, what may first appear to be a 'game' of CI one-upmanship between rival intelligence agencies can have deadly consequences – in the case of HUMINT operations, it may result in the deaths of the agents concerned. By providing the names of agents involved, a penetration agent may be considered to be effectively signing their death warrants. In the case of George Blake, all of the agents whose identities he betrayed were captured and murdered. The deaths of over 40 individuals can be considered the direct consequence of Blake's actions, while the information provided by Aldrich Ames 'led to the murder of at least ten Agency assets operating inside the government in Moscow' (Johnson, 2017:125)

Complicating matters further, counterintelligence work can also involve deception. It is possible for an intelligence agency to arrange a false defection, whereby the defector arrives with false information which is accepted as true, resulting in chaos and confusion. Alternatively, the offer to provide information on a rival organisation by one of its employees may itself be false, the source actually being a double agent; that is, an agent who pretends to provide information but is actually working for a rival, perhaps with the purpose of providing misleading details concerning their own organisation's work, or being used to specifically misdirect an agency already searching for a mole. While such 'dangle' operations are complicated, and involve passing over genuine secrets in order to establish credibility and authenticity with the target agency in the first place, they can nevertheless be effective, seemingly offering an intelligence organisation information that is simply too tempting to pass up. As Redmond notes, the countries of the Warsaw Pact enjoyed considerable success in mounting such operations against US intelligence during the Cold War. Cuban intelligence officer Florentino Aspillaga Lombard dropped a bombshell upon his defection to the CIA in 1987, when he announced that 'all of the CIA's Cuban agents – some four dozen over a 40-year period – were actually Havana's agents' (Redmond, 2010:49). Control of these agents meant that Cuban counterintelligence 'could identify the CIA case officers and monitor their activities'. The following year, Cuban television broadcast 'an eleven-part series based on clandestine footage of CIA officers engages in various operational tasks against the island nation' (Redmond, 2010:49). In his memoir published in 1997, former East German spymaster **Markus Wolf** claimed that, by the late 1980s,

> we were in the enviable position of knowing that not a single CIA agent had worked in East Germany without having been turned into a double agent or working for us from the start. On our orders they were all delivering carefully selected information and disinformation to the Americans.
>
> (Wolf and McElvoy, 1997:285)

His claim has been corroborated by comments made by former CIA officials; as one anonymous CIA officer noted: 'they dangled people in front of us ... [and] we wound up taking the bait' (Redmond, 2010:50). Such 'dangle' operations can provide a particularly useful means of deflecting a mole at work within a rival organisation, deflecting any possible suspicion for operational failures away from them through bogus information. In this way Soviet intelligence sought to protect Aldrich Ames; for years, the KGB 'used dangles and a false defector to divert, mislead, and confuse CIA investigators looking into the agent losses of 1985–1986. Moscow sent the investigators off on wild goose chases that led nowhere but always away from Ames' (Redmond, 2010:54).

5.4 Paranoid tendencies

The degree of suspicion involved in catching spies, through which one may well find that a colleague is not all that they appear to be, can have a significant psychological impact on those charged with carrying it out. As Olson (2001:n.p.) notes, 'It is hard to immerse oneself daily in the arcane and twisted world of CI without falling prey eventually to creeping paranoia, distortion, warping and overzealouness in one's thinking' (An old – likely apocryphal – joke in CI circles tells of a counterintelligence officer looking at himself in the shaving mirror in the morning, and thinking, 'I wonder what organisation he works for ...?'). Such paranoid tendencies can be particularly destructive forces, which can lead to chasing shadows; suspecting innocent individuals or misdeeds that they have not actually committed. At best, this may have an impact on the moral of the staff involved; at worst, it may lead to their removal from their job. Ironically, such disruption within an organisation can end up *aiding* the rival intelligence agency!

The most well-known case of such damaging behaviour concerns James Jesus Angleton (Figure 5.3). Angleton was a key figure in the CIA's counterintelligence division for 20 years, from 1954 until he was sacked in 1974. Angleton became concerned over the extent of Soviet penetration of Western intelligence agencies in general, and of the CIA in particular. In itself, this was not an entirely unreasonable position; in the early 1960s, a number of intelligence officers, including his British friend Kim Philby, were either arrested or defected to the USSR. The fact that Philby, with whom Angleton had worked closely during his time in America, came as a heavy psychological blow. This was exacerbated by the increasingly paranoid testimony of Golitsyn, mentioned above. Taken together, these factors fuelled Angleton's obsession with the prospect of Soviet penetration of the CIA. The combination of Philby's defection and Golitsyn's wild theories also caused trouble for British intelligence. Fears that there may have been further Soviet penetration of the intelligence and security services led to suspicions remarkably coming to fall upon both the Director General of MI5, Roger Hollis, and the Deputy Director, Graham Mitchell. In

Figure 5.3 James Jesus Angleton
Source: Bettmann/Contributor/Getty Images

November 1964, a joint MI6-MI5 working group, known as 'Fluency', was established in order to investigate such suspicions further, and continued its work – which has been described by the Authorised Historian of the British Security Service as a paranoid 'witch-hunt' which failed to stand up to critical scrutiny but nevertheless continued for several years (Andrew, 2009:515). The self-inflicted damage done by the witch-hunt, not least in terms of morale, bemused the KGB: according to Gordievsky, 'when the KGB saw the chaos caused by the allegations against Hollis, their laughter made Red Square shake' (Smith, 2004:111).

While more usually associated as a battle between rivals, counterintelligence activity can also take place between friendly intelligence agencies. Here, if uncovered, the political damage can be high. This can be seen in the case of **Jonathan Pollard**. Pollard was a US naval intelligence analyst, who passed sensitive information to Israel, a close ally of the United States. Arrested in 1985, Pollard was subsequently sentenced to life imprisonment. Israeli efforts to secure Pollard's release have caused tension in the relationship between the two countries, with the then Director of Central Intelligence, George J. Tenet, threatening to resign if a pardon was issued by President Clinton – 'whereupon Clinton dropped the issue' (Lowenthal, 2017:511). More recently, in 2010, it was reported 'that Netanyahu was willing to freeze the building of new Israeli settlements on the West Bank, a major irritant in Israel's relations with the United States, in exchange for Pollard's release' (Lowenthal, 2017:511). Ultimately, as Lowenthal notes, the case represents 'a successful penetration whose political costs may far outweigh any intelligence that was obtained' (Lowenthal, 2017:511).

Counterintelligence work may be considered to represent intelligence not only at its most introspective, but also at its most devious. One may not unreasonably think that the most appropriate thing to do when a rival is detected having penetrated an intelligence organisation is simply to apprehend them. Yet in the world of intelligence there are other, potentially more useful, ways to proceed; while quietly preventing the imposter from accessing as much secret information as possible, efforts may also be made to actually *create* false information, in the hope that the agent will report it back to their true masters. In this way, such an imposter may report back that certain officers within his real agency are themselves actually working for the rival organisation. While untrue, the fact that such information has been obtained from an agent in place, it is likely to be believed – with negative consequences for the careers of the officers involved – if not indeed for their lives! In such a manner, the agency which thinks it is doing damage to its rival may unknowingly end up being damaged itself. In short, it is not for nothing that the world of counterintelligence has been described as a 'Wilderness of Mirrors'.

6 The 'hidden hand'

Covert action

Known throughout the world by a variety of different names, including 'special activities', 'secret intervention', 'active measures', 'action operations', 'the third option', and 'dirty tricks', covert action involves the exercise of influence on a foreign audience, be that a particular leader, a government, a population, or indeed a non-state actor such as a terrorist group, with the goal of altering its policies or actions in ways that benefit the government that has initiated the action. As the name 'the third option' suggests, in this way covert action navigates the grey area between military operations and diplomacy, where diplomacy alone is insufficient but where all-out war would be excessive. While there may be some debate over what types of operation may be considered under this heading, what is clear is that it must be possible for the country responsible for masterminding the action to plausibly deny their role in it. In some cases, it may be possible for a covert operation to be carried out without anyone in the target country being any the wiser that such action is taking place – the dissemination of propaganda, for example, may be done silently and discreetly. However, in others this is more difficult; while it may appear unusual for an operation that involves, for example, the assassination of a leading political figure from a foreign country to be considered 'covert', what ultimately remains covert is the identity of the sponsor – the 'hidden hand' of the country behind the operation.

Covert action as we understand it today may be considered to be a product of the Cold War. It is therefore unsurprising that much of the writing on such activity is informed by the US experience during its fight against the expansion of communism. Details of many US covert action operations were sensationally revealed to the public during the 1970s, through both investigative journalism and subsequently a US Select Committee chaired by Senator Frank Church (the Church Committee). As Beitz (2006:206–7) notes, the United States has involved itself in a wide range of covert activity since the end of the Second World War, ranging from support for moderate political parties in Italy and France during the late 1940s, to backing *coups d'état* in Iran and Guatemala in the 1950s and plotting the assassination of foreign leaders including Fidel Castro and Patrice Lumamba in the 1960s [Document 22].

The US took as its foundation in this area the National Security Act of 1947, and a National Security Directive dated 18 June 1948. The National Security Act provided the authority for the Director of Central Intelligence and the newly formed CIA to perform 'such other functions and duties related to intelligence affecting the national security as the President or the National Security Council may direct'. The National Security Directive of the following year was more explicit; this authorised the CIA to engage in

> propaganda, economic warfare, preventive direct action, including sabotage, anti-sabotage, demolition and evacuation measures, subversion against hostile states, including assistance to underground resistance movements, guerrillas and refugee liberation groups, and support of indigenous anti-communist elements in threatened countries of the free world.

More recently, the US Congress provided a formal, statutory definition of covert action as being 'an activity or activities of the United States Government to influence political, economic, or military conditions abroad, where it is intended that the role of the United States Government will not be apparent or acknowledged publicly' (Shulsky and Schmitt, 2002:76).

6.1 Types of covert action

Covert action involves a vast array of different methods that can be employed separately or in some form of combination. As William J. Doherty, a senior retired CIA officer, has written, these stretch

> from the nearly invisible to the spectacularly public, from the almost benign to the highly provocative, from a subtle appeal to the intellect to the violent taking of lives. From an event lasting but a few minutes to a years long campaign.
>
> (Daugherty, 2007:281)

The different types of covert action can be usefully mapped against what Lowenthal refers to as a 'ladder of escalation'; here, as the level of violence increases, so too the potential for plausible deniability decreases (Lowenthal, 2017:257). Low on the ladder sits propaganda, followed a few rungs up by political action/activity and economic disruption, while paramilitary style 'special operations' sit near the top. Such operations may be initiated separately or used in some form of combination. More recently, attention has turned to the impact of technology, and the emergence of cyber covert action. While some see cyber covert action, elsewhere described as Information Warfare, as a discrete category in its own right, it could also be argued that the internet and other developments in cyber technology simply provide a new tool for the operations detailed above to be carried out (Carruthers, 2018:159)

6.1.1 Propaganda

Otherwise known as 'perception management' by the CIA, propaganda is widely considered to be the most frequently used covert action methodology, on account of a combination of its subtlety, flexibility and relatively low cost. Propaganda comes in a number of different forms. Most of it – over 90 per cent of it in the US case, according to Loch Johnson, is truthful, essentially repeating what officials are saying publicly through overt communication channels. This is classed as 'White' propaganda, whereby it simply tells the truth. For Daugherty (2007:281), this constitutes the 'best use of propaganda', which was used extensively by the US during the Cold War, which

> merely involved airing truthful accounts of events to counter the falsehoods about international and internal actions the Soviet government fed its own citizenry, to help keep alive the histories of the ethnic minorities persecuted by the Communist system, and to provide the population with desirable materials banned by Moscow

such as copies of the Bible and literature by such writers as Pasternak and Solzhenitsyn. 'Grey' propaganda tells the truth but involves an element of deception; while it tells the truth the source, the sponsor, is concealed. Finally, 'Black' propaganda involves the dissemination of information that it totally fabricated, and its source remains hidden. During the early Cold War, Britain's SIS used lies to smear Soviet officials and ran 'black' radio stations across the Middle East to promote Western interests in the region (Cormac, 2018:51). In the Vietnam War, the Americans created a fake anti-communist guerrilla movement in North Vietnam called the Sacred Sword of the Patriots League, aiming to divert resources to North Vietnamese internal security forces. The Soviet Union also engaged in such propaganda, its main purpose being to 'generate negative feelings against the United States among Third World inhabitants' (Daugherty, 2007:282). An example of such propaganda concerns the story spread by the Soviet Union/KGB (Operation INFEKTION) during the 1980s that the HIV disease had actually been created by the United States as part of a biological warfare campaign [Document 23]. According to Andrew and Mitrokhin, the operation began in 1984, and within just three years it had been covered by some 40 different countries as a major news story, undermining trust in the United States (Andrew and Mitrokhin, 2006:340, 466). In 1987, Soviet officials, worried about the story's impact of diplomatic relations with the West, officially disowned the campaign. But the KGB maintained other disinformation campaigns. A 1986 report by the US State Department concluded

> there is a massive and highly organized effort by the Soviet Union and its proxies to influence world opinion ... [It] includes a persistent, widespread program of disinformation and deception designed to discredit the US image abroad and disrupt US foreign policy objectives.
> (United States Department of State, 1986:iii)

Propaganda can be spread in a number of different ways. Authorities can pass information to journalists, for example, for inclusion in a story that will then receive a wide audience upon publication – and might even be picked up by rival news outlets, resulting in further dissemination. The CIA-backed Congress for Cultural Freedom funded over twenty journals and had a presence in over 35 countries, influencing intellectuals, trade unionists, students and other groups, countering communist influence and developing links with the US. Britain's Information Research Department (**IRD**) worked with politicians, journalists, writers and foreign governments to counter Soviet statements through unattributable propaganda before its disbandment in 1977. IRD promoted reports of Soviet prison camps, anti-communist literature and even George Orwell's work. By the 1960s, IRD had staff in 48 countries and a significant budget, moving beyond anti-communist propaganda into promoting Britain's interests in Europe, later countering IRA propaganda during 'The Troubles' in Northern Ireland.

Propaganda can also be spread via the radio, targeting an audience in another country. This was achieved during the Cold War through Radio Liberty and Radio Free Europe, which were used by the US. The former transmitted into the Soviet Union, while the latter was focussed on Soviet-controlled Eastern Europe, its stations broadcasting in Polish, Czechoslovakian, Hungarian, Roumanian and Bulgarian. Unlike the officially avowed Voice of America which broadcast official US views, both stations gave populations in the Eastern Bloc information about their countries that was unavailable through state-controlled media. Alternatively, radio stations can be established at a frequency very close to that of the target, in the hope that it will be picked up accidentally by listeners, who may continue to listen, under the mistaken belief that they are listening to the station that they were trying to find. This technique was used by the Solidarity movement in Poland during the 1980s.

One of the most successful CIA propaganda operations took place in Guatemala in 1954 as part of a wider operation against the supposedly pro-communist dictator Jacobo Árbenz Guzmán. The CIA established a radio station in the mountains of Guatemala, where 'local assets began broadcasting the [total] fiction that a full-fledged revolution was taking place and that the masses were rising up against the supposedly pro-communist dictator Jacobo Árbenz'. Árbenz was shocked by this and resigned, believing 'that a mythical people's army of 5,000 was marching toward the capital' (Johnson, 2017:91). Propaganda does not, however, always have such an immediate effect; it can take time to achieve its desired result. As Daugherty notes, it takes time for people to absorb a new concept, and longer to adopt it in the place of a previously held position. It also has its limits. In 1970, the CIA distributed news stories, leaflets and pamphlets to discredit presidential candidate Salvador Allende, showing an Allende win would destroy Chilean democracy. Allende won the election, ushering in a new wave of CIA activity.

6.1.2 Political action

More provocative than propaganda, covert political action can take a number of different forms. It can involve efforts to undermine the government of a country, leading to its removal and replacement with a more favourable regime, or an effort to make the government change its policy in a given area. It can involve the covert supply of financial support to a preferred political party, or a particular electoral candidate, in a foreign county. Throughout the Cold War the CIA was responsible for providing large sums of money to political groups and individuals overseas. In the immediate aftermath of the Second World War, for example, the US covertly provided political groups and their leaders in Italy with money, in order to counter the threat posed by the Italian Communist Party. Rositzke suggests that financial support continued to be provided until the late 1960s, and amounted to millions of dollars a year (Rositzke:187), especially by pro-Western parties and groups in, for example, West Germany, Greece, Egypt, the Philippines and Chile. In 1964, the CIA provided over two and a - half million dollars to support Eduardo Frei Montalva, a Christian Democrat candidate in the presidential election, who was running against the Marxist candidate, Salvador Allende, in Chile. The US government gave extensive support to the independent Polish trade union Solidarity in the 1980s after the communist government declared martial law, supplying financial assistance, communications equipment, computers, fax machines and printing presses to produce propaganda, and covert training, allowing Solidarity members to hide from the authorities (Daugherty, 2004).

At its most extreme, political covert action could aim at carrying out a *coup d'état*, achieving a change of government in another state by force. It has been estimated that, during the Cold War, the US tried to remove foreign governments on at least 72 occasions – 66 covert operations and six overt coups (O'Rourke, 2016:n.p.). For the CIA the 1950s and 1960s seemed to herald a 'golden age' of covert action. 1953 and 1954 marked what **DCI Allen Dulles** would call his 'best years' (Andrew, 1996:202). The Agency removed governments in Iran and Guatemala (Operation

PBSUCCESS), strengthening the CIA's role at the heart of US policymaking, yet the CIA drew dubious conclusions on the merits of regime change. 'They drew the erroneous lesson that the Agency could alter world events in the Third World at will and with minimal expense', the CIA admitted (Koch, 1998:81). For Dulles especially, covert action led to hubris; in 1961, following the botched CIA-backed Bay of Pigs invasion, he was forced to stand down as DCI.

Perhaps the most well-known example of such activity that has since come to light concerns the Anglo-American operation to remove Mohammed Mossadeq as Iran's Prime Minister in August 1953. Mossadeq's nationalisation of the Anglo-Iranian Oil Company in 1951 led British officials to plot his removal, even if their US counterparts were initially lukewarm about the idea. Growing fears of communist influence and internal instability in Iran eventually brought the CIA on side. 'Mossadeq had to go', an internal history made clear (Koch, 1998:16). SIS and CIA officials planned to use bribery, unattributable grey propaganda, and friendly groups to support the anti-Mossadeq General Fazlollah Zahedi. The Shah would appoint Zahedi as Prime Minister, legally removing Mossadeq. If that failed, a military coup would take place. Iran's religious leaders would spread their 'disapproval with Mossadeq' while anti-government propaganda would spread around the streets of Tehran. Western money would buy support for the new regime. The plan, codenamed BOOT by the British and AJAX (or TPAJAX) by the CIA, was approved by London and Washington in June with the coup planned to start in August. While the plan had a rocky start, it was ultimately successful. On 19 August 1953, a British/American inspired anti-Mossadeq protest, including religious leaders and exercise clubs (*Zuhrkhaneh*), shouting 'pro-Shah slogans', triggered a military coup with Zahedi installed as the new Prime Minister. The Shah returned in triumph a few days later. 'I owe my throne to God, my people, my army – and to you', he told the CIA's chief planner Kermit Roosevelt (Roosevelt, 1979:199).

Shortly after its success in Iran, the CIA turned its attention closer to home, to Guatemala, where communism appeared to be flourishing 'in America's backyard'. This resulted in an operation which sought to remove Jacabo Árbenz Guzmán, who had been democtratically elected President in November 1950, using what an internal CIA account by historian Nicholas Cullather describes as

> an extensive paramilitary and psychological campaign to replace a popular, elected government with a political nonentity. In method, scale, and conception it had no antecedent, and its triumph confirmed the belief of many in the Eisenhower administration that covert operations offered a safe, inexpensive substitute for armed force in resisting Communist inroads in the Third World.
>
> (Cullather, 2006:7)

6.1.3 Economic action

Undermining the economy of a country constitutes another form of covert action. This could be achieved through several means, including the destabilisation of a country's economy by introducing counterfeit currency into its money supply, aiming to cause inflation and thereby undermine the political leadership. As Daugherty notes, 'Planting the fake currency of a nation already in serious economic straits could be nothing less than ruinous for that country's leadership' (Daugherty, 2007:282). South America proved to be an important testing ground for the CIA's use of economic covert action. As part of its efforts to undermine Cuba during the 1960s (Operation MONGOOSE), the CIA planned to sabotage the sugar industry. Overseas brokers were encouraged to drive down the price of sugar, drying up a major source of income for Castro's regime, while the Americans plotted to use biological agents leading to 'crop failure'. As the US blockade of Cuba began to bite, CIA officers also arranged the delivery of defective machinery and spare parts, with plans to flood Cuba's economy with counterfeit currency to finance the thriving Cuban black market and undermine trust in the currency. Before Salvador Allende, a Marxist, became President of Chile in 1970, the US Director of Central Intelligence, **Richard Helms**, was present at a meeting in the Oval Office with President Nixon and Secretary of State Henry Kissinger. Discussing what the US could do if Allende won the presidency, Helms noted 'Make the economy scream'. The CIA subsequently used a number of schemes to harm the Chilean economy, one of which involved exploiting a series of strikes by truckers (Prados, 1996:319). Economic factors played an important role in CIA plans to destabilise the revolutionary Sandinista National Liberation Front (FSLN) in the 1980s. Using a CIA 'mother ship' a flotilla of heavily armed speed boats mined the ports of Corinto, Puerto Sandino and El Bluff, disrupting oil supplies and putting off international trade.

6.1.4 Paramilitary operations

Paramilitary, or 'special', operations may be considered to constitute covert action at its most extreme, with the highest degree of violence and greatest tendency to attract attention, likely making it difficult to maintain 'plausible deniability' for very long. Yet such risks did not prevent its use during the Cold War. As Johnson notes, from the 1950s onwards, the CIA

> mobilized its paramilitary capabilities in several secret military attacks against foreign governments, offering support (with mixed degrees of success) for anti-communist insurgents in such places as the Ukraine, Poland, Albania, Hungary, Indonesia, Oman, Malaysia, Iraq, the Dominican Republic, Venezuela, Thailand, Haiti, Greece, Turkey and Cuba.
>
> (Johnson, 2017:94)

The use of assassinations, targeted killings and 'wetwork' (from the Russian *mokroye delo* – or 'wet affairs') against foreign leaders, dissidents and rivals is the most controversial type of paramilitary covert action. Other than to remove critics or problematic leaders, targeted killings are designed to instil fear, undermine trust and enhance the all-powerful perceptions of those intelligence agencies who carry out such actions. In February 2017, the half-brother of North Korea's Kim Jong-un was murdered by state agents using a VX nerve agent at Kuala Lumpur airport. Russia's intelligence agencies have also killed; in November 2006, former FSB officer **Alexander Litvinenko** was poisoned in central London, using highly radioactive polonium-210. A public inquiry into the killing, chaired by Sir Robert Owen, concluded it was 'probably' ordered by the head of the FSB and Russia's President Vladimir Putin [Document 24]. The poisoning of another former Russian spy, Sergei Skripal and his daughter, Yulia, in Salisbury in March 2018, using a Novichok nerve agent, has also been linked to Russia. From the Cheka to the NKVD, SMERSH (drawn from the phrase *smert shpionam*, meaning 'death to spies') to the KGB and Russia's modern-day FSB and SVR there has been a tradition of 'wet affairs'. An exiled Leon Trotsky, Ukrainian nationalist Lev Rebet, and Chechen leader Zelimkhan Yandarbiyev have all been victims of assassination plots by Russia's spies [Document 25]. Most of the targets were anti-Soviet dissidents and defectors, even if Stalin reportedly ordered the MGB (the KGB's predecessor) to plan the killing of Yugoslavia's troublesome leader Tito (Haslam, 2015:173). The NKVD's Directorate of Special Tasks, formed in December 1936, and the KGB's executive action branch, the Thirteenth Department, were at the forefront of the campaigns. Poisons developed by the KGB were used against Bulgarian dissidents, most notably Georgi Markov, then working for the BBC's World Service, using an umbrella with a poisoned tip (Andrew and Gordievsky, 1990:541–2).

Israeli intelligence has a long history of targeted killing, having 'assassinated more people than any other country in the Western world' since the Second World War, according to Bergman. Before 2000, Israel's spies conducted over 500 assassination missions, killing over 1,000 people. The start of the second Palestinian uprising or Intifada in September 2000 resulted in 168 successful 'liquidations', with around 800 targeted killings against Hamas officials and Israeli opponents since then (Bergman, 2018: xxii). Israeli intelligence has been equally ingenious in the methods used. Poisoned toothpaste, drones, exploding mobile phones, letter bombs, specially shaped charges and supressed firearms are the weapons of choice. The reputation of Israel's Mossad has been shaped by this 'strike first, ask questions later approach'. The killing of 11 Israeli athletes at the 1972 Munich Games by the Palestinian militant group Black September led Prime Minister Golda Meir to approve 'Operation Wrath of God'. Those linked to Black September and the Palestine Liberation Organisation (PLO) were tracked down and killed. Recently, Israel's spies have been linked to the killing of four Iranian scientists in an attempt to disrupt Iran's nuclear programme. But for all the talk of Mossad's prowess, the agency has sometimes got things spectacularly wrong. In 1973, Mossad agents misidentified Moroccan-born waiter Ahmed Bouchiki as Black September operations chief Ali Hassan Salameh ('the Red Prince'), gunning him down in the street of Lillehammer, leading to the arrest of six Israeli spies. The 2010 killing of Hamas official Mahmoud Al-Mabhouh in a Dubai hotel room by a Mossad team using false European and Australian identities provoked a wake of criticism, leading to the expulsion of an Israeli 'diplomat' in London. As with other forms of covert action, assassination carries significant risks. Killing is no easy fix. But it also serves to underline an important message: 'Israel was perceived as a country with a very long arm and the memory of an elephant' (Raviv and Melman, 2014:139).

In the United States, evidence of the CIA's attempted use of murder first came to light in 1975, resulting in a major investigation into CIA activities led by Senator Frank Church. CIA officers used terms such as 'termination with extreme prejudice' or 'neutralisation' to refer to assassination, even setting up the 'Health Alteration Committee' to approve plans to 'incapacitate' individuals ('Alleged Assassination Plots', 1975:38, 181). Under Presidents Eisenhower, Kennedy, Johnson and Nixon, the CIA was involved in a number of plots to remove foreign leaders, most notably Cuba's Fidel Castro. The Church Committee found evidence of 'at least eight' CIA plots using a range of exotic gadgets from 'high-powered rifles to poison pills, poison pens, deadly bacterial powders, and other devices which strain the imagination' (ibid.). The CIA also tried to use 'gangster-type action' through the Mafia; contacts with mobster Johnny Roselli and others were to be exploited with plans to use a 'potent pill, that could be placed in Castro's food or drink' (CIA, 1973:00013) [Document 27]. Congo's Patrice Lumumba was another target, with 'rubber gloves, a mask and a syringe', along with 'lethal biological material', sent to CIA officers with the aim of killing him. In the end, the plan was abandoned, and Lumumba was killed by rivals in 1961. 'The Company' has also been linked to other killings: the Dominican Republic's Rafael Trujillo, South Vietnam's Ngo Diem, and Chile's René Schneider were also killed by CIA-linked assassins. CIA's Special Operations Division worked alongside the US army on the infamous Phoenix Program to identify and kill communist Viet Cong guerrillas in South Vietnam, capturing, killing or 'neutralising' 80,000 cadres. The controversy led President Gerald Ford to sign Executive Order 11905 in 1976, ruling that 'No employee of the United States Government shall engage in, or conspire to engage in, political assassination' (Executive Order 11905, 1976).

Since the end of the Cold War, the CIA, in conjunction with the US Air Force, has developed what Loch Johnson describes as 'its most deadly paramilitary weapon': UAVs – unmanned aerial vehicles – drones

(Johnson, 2017:99). Controlled remotely, these are equipped with cameras to identify targets, and missiles for use once the target has been identified. Figures show that anywhere between 2,500 and 4,000 people were killed by strikes in Pakistan from 2004 to 2018, while Afghanistan saw 3,500 to 4,778 deaths in the period from 2015 to 2018 (Bureau of Investigative Journalism, 2017:n.p.). There are, perhaps unsurprisingly, a number of serious concerns over the drone programme, the question of oversight, in terms of who gets to decide who should be added to the 'kill list', and also the ability of this drone programme to make mistakes – the 'collateral damage', as it is termed, of innocent civilians being hit by the missiles.

More recently, there has been an increased blurring of the boundaries between covert action and military special operations, the activities of Special Operations Command (SOCOM) leading to questions of whether the military are now, in fact, conducting covert operations – traditionally the remit of the CIA. This leads on to other questions, particularly concerning oversight. The 1991 Intelligence Authorization Act, which remains the governing legislation on congressional oversight of covert action, codified two requirements for such action – the first, that the President should notify congress of the intended action with a 'Finding', referred to system that was already in place. The second point in the legislation concerned those who carried out covert action, described as 'any department, agency or entity of the United States government'. The legislation, however, included some exceptions – specifically, 'traditional ... military activities or routine support to such activities' (Intelligence Authorization Act, 1991). This caused some controversy during the administration of George W. Bush – covert operations conducted by military special operations forces do not require a Finding, and do not require congress to be informed. Does this mean that they allow a President to circumvent oversight?

6.2 The pros and cons of covert action

According to Daugherty (2007), every President of the United States during the Cold War made use of covert action during their time in office. Offering them 'a policy option situated *between* purely overt diplomatic and/or economic measures ... and resort to open employment of military force' (Daugherty, 2007:280), it is not difficult to appreciate its attraction. Compared to military force, covert action can also be relatively inexpensive. Distributing negative news articles, supplying equipment to dissidents or buying influence can be cost-effective compared to higher-risk alternatives on the table. It is not, however, without a degree of risk; should a covert action operation fail, and that failure reach the public domain, then there would undoubtedly be negative consequences for policymakers. The sinking of the Greenpeace ship *Rainbow Warrior* in Auckland by France's *Direction générale de la sécurité extérieure* (**DGSE**) in July 1985 led to the capture of two French agents. This resulted in the resignation of Defence Minister Charles Hernu, the sacking of the head of the DGSE, and tense diplomatic relations with New Zealand. The French government paid compensation to the family of a photographer killed in the attack, reimbursed Greenpeace for the loss of the ship and sent a formal apology to the New Zealand government for the incident, in return for the release of the DGSE agents into French custody (Porch, 1995:455–67). The 'Iran–Contra' scandal over the illegal sale of arms to Iran to fund anti-communist Contras in Nicaragua sparked a political scandal in Washington and placed growing pressure on President Reagan, leading to a significant short-term drop in his approval rating. More recently, the alleged poisoning of Sergei Skripal led to over 20 allied countries expelling dozens of Russian diplomats and worsened diplomatic relations with Moscow. Paramilitary type operations can also be costly in human lives. Many of the American agents parachuted into Eastern Europe to 'rollback' Soviet influence were captured, tortured and executed soon after arrival.

Perhaps the main danger associated with covert action concerns its capacity for unintended consequences. Covert action does not come with a crystal ball and the ability to forecast what the long-term consequences/repercussions of the action are likely to be. This may not be a prime concern for a contemporary politician, concerned with today's problems, but it may create difficulties for a future leader. In the case of Guatemala, where Jacobo Árbenz Guzmán was removed through, in significant part, the use of black propaganda, the country was brought under a military dictatorship, which over the next 40 or so years saw the death of thousands of Guatemalans, and bolstered anti-American sentiment throughout Latin America. The overthrow of the Mossadeq government in Iran, and the re-installation of the pro-Western Shah in 1953 may have worked, but the Shah proved to be a cruel and oppressive leader, exhibiting a viciousness that sparked the creation of the revolutionary movement that ultimately caused him to flee Iran in 1979, leaving the country both with a strong anti-Western outlook in general and a vehemently anti-American one in particular. Failed operations have also worsened the situation. The efforts to assassinate Fidel Castro resulted in some 50 years of difficult relations between Cuba and the US, and further anti-American sentiment, while similar attempts to remove Indonesia's President Sukarno only strengthened the Communist Party. Arming the Mujahadeen during the Soviet occupation of Afghanistan during the 1980s would certainly have been hailed as a good idea at the time, and could be considered to have put one of the final nails in the coffin of the Soviet Union, but the withdrawal of Soviet troops and the collapse of the Najibullah government resulted in a civil war, allowing the Taliban to eventually take over and create a safe haven for Osama bin Laden's al-Qaeda and starting the road to 9/11.

6.3 Covert action: ethical considerations

Covert action is the area of intelligence activity which raises the most ethical and moral questions. While much intelligence work consists of collecting information – an activity which (for the most part) no one is immediately, directly harmed by – covert action involves, as the name indicates, action: doing things, which have consequences. As Beitz notes, covert action is 'interventionist': it aims 'at influencing the course of political life in the target state by including or preventing a change in government or policy' (Beitz, 2006:208). David L. Perry argues that providing covert financial support for foreign political leaders or other figures 'can plausibly be considered a form of humanitarian intervention', offering the example of 'CIA aid to centrist political parties in postwar France, Italy, and Japan', which 'helped to counter covert Soviet aid to communist parties there, while CIA assistance to Christian Democrats in El Salvador was intended to prevent an election victory by right-wing candidates tied to death squads' (Perry, 2006:233). 'Almost certainly', Perry argues, 'the political consequences in those countries would have been grave had no aid been provided by [*sic*] CIA' (Perry, 2006:233), a sentiment reflected by William Colby, the Director of the CIA who oversaw such support to politicians in Italy during the 1950s. The problem is that there is no set moral compass for covert action. What may be acceptable in one country may be unacceptable to others. Britain's Intelligence and Security Act allows SIS to carry out 'other tasks' though officers are not allowed to do anything abroad that would be illegal in the UK, with such activities as theft and bribery signed off by the Foreign Secretary. Another issue is secrecy. American Presidents are required by law to issue presidential findings on special operations to the House and Senate Intelligence Committees. Elsewhere, there is no such oversight. 'The major moral principle we would set for the conduct of covert action is that it should be the sort of thing that would be acceptable to the American people, if its details were revealed', writes Jan Goldman (2006:124). But what is acceptable? *New York Times* columnist Tom Wicker argued 'a democratic nation, supposedly devoted to the rule of law and the self-determination of peoples, has no right to destabilize or subvert even governments we disapprove, or to try to change – much less kill or kidnap – even undesirable leaders' (Wicker, 1988:n.p.). Former Defence and State Department official Lincoln Bloomfield Jnr. argues the contrary: 'Covert action has an anomalous but necessary role in the functioning of an open democracy ... What might surprise disillusioned citizens is how much the system is receptive to their values' (Bloomfield, 2006:195). In short, covert action is a moral minefield which raises more questions than answers.

Assessment

It isn't all James Bond

John Ferris, the official historian of British signals intelligence, once observed that 'Students of intelligence should aim not just to astonish their audience, but to bore them' (Ferris, 2002:55). While this may at first appear to be somewhat odd advice – we certainly hope not to have bored anyone with our introduction to the world of intelligence and espionage – Ferris makes a valid point, in terms of how these matters tend to be understood by the general public. Long-standing traditions of official secrecy have for many years provided a vacuum, which has been filled to a considerable degree by works of fiction, which have certainly long astonished their audience – it has been claimed that around half the population *of the entire world* has heard of James Bond! Having read the previous chapters, our readers hopefully now have a greater degree of scepticism over the role of such a secret agent within the wider intelligence process. Certainly, there is a considerable non-fiction literature on covert action – the intelligence 'mission' which perhaps most comfortably encapsulates Bond's antics – and we have been happy to discuss it here, but the sheer volume of literature is surely disproportionate to the extent to which intelligence agencies engage in such activity. Writing in the 1990s, Urban cited an anonymous source who estimated that some 96 per cent of SIS's time was spent 'gathering information' (Urban, 1996:35), which really leaves very little room for James Bond-style adventures. Even in the United States, with its greater focus on covert action programmes, the CIA's paramilitary operations, drone operations and secret influence activities absorbed just $2.6 billion of the Agency's estimated $14.7 billion budget for 2013.

The overwhelming bulk of intelligence work does not involve assassinations, explosions and the like. The heroics constitute the bravery (or treachery, depending upon one's national perspective) of those lone individuals who offer up secrets to a different nation. For those on the frontline of HUMINT, this can certainly be dangerous work. The former SIS officer Anthony Cavendish experienced first hand the risks agents took behind the Iron Curtain to provide information to the West, and was haunted by the fate of his agent, Frieda: 'I never saw her again. Shortly afterwards she was caught, tried and shot. She was nineteen. I was twenty-three ... I reflect now on how ruthless I was at twenty-three' (Cavendish, 1990:9). But for all the attention given to the human dimension of espionage, most *secret* intelligence is actually derived from technical sources – SIGINT and IMINT – while even more information, likely higher than 80 per cent, comes from open sources. Stories of SIGINT analysts would likely do little to spark the public's imagination – and even less so stories of OSINT collectors, poring over newspapers, online chatrooms, library books and the like as the basis of their reports. Pouring the coldest of water on the mythology that surrounds intelligence, diplomat and former chair of the JIC Sir Roderic Braithwaite once compared it to the work of the Inland Revenue, which is also a collecting body – albeit collecting taxes, rather than intelligence: 'both are legitimate and essentially humdrum functions of government. To glamorise or mystify intelligence, or to exaggerate what it is capable of doing is not in anyone's real interests' (Braithwaite, 2003).

Failures are public, successes are secret

When intelligence does hit the headlines, this has tended to be on account of something having gone wrong; in the contemporary world, likely due to a terrorist atrocity which the intelligence and security agencies have failed to prevent. 'The secret of our success is the secret of our success', says the CIA. While we know about Penkovsky, Gordievsky and Mitrokhin, SIS ran an estimated 40 to 60 agents across the Eastern Bloc – as such, many other stories remain unknown, as their identities are fiercely protected by SIS. The organisation's use of a fake rock containing a transmitter to receive information from agents was only revealed thanks to covert surveillance by Russia's internal security agency, the FSB. More recently, perceived intelligence failures around the 2017 terrorist attacks at Westminster, the Manchester Arena and London Bridge, killing a total of 35 people, led to criticism of MI5's work against jihadist groups in the UK. Speaking to allied intelligence officials in May 2018, MI5's Director General Andrew Parker refuted claims of failure; since March 2017 the Security Service thwarted 12 serious Islamist plots and disrupted 25 since 2013 (Parker, 2018) – successful cases we know little about. Here, academics who study intelligence are themselves, perhaps, part of the problem. Intelligence failures are often well documented in post-mortem inquiries. 9/11 and Iraq resulted in thousands of hours of testimony, the declassification of a mass of documents and generated much material for scholars to look at. In contrast, successes continue to remain hidden.

Playing down expectations

Intelligence communities will always be taken by surprise, however much money and effort goes into intelligence collection and analysis. 'There is too often an exaggerated idea of what it can achieve and a corresponding readiness to criticise anything short of omniscience', writes Cradock (2002:290). Claims of 'intelligence failure' are often simplistic, relying on knowledge after the event to piece together what should have been done. What was a complex issue for analysts suddenly becomes easier to interpret with all the evidence at our fingertips. Vague information that was ignored as it failed at the time to fit the intelligence jigsaw quickly becomes important. 'Hindsight can sometimes see the past clearly – with 20/20 vision', concluded the 9/11 Commission report after stating that intelligence before an event is 'obscure and pregnant with conflicting' messages. Predicting what might happen in future is extremely difficult and intelligence professionals are no better at it than 'journalists, academics, diplomats, or ordinary people with common sense' (Braithwaite, 2003). US Secretary of State for Defence Donald Rumsfeld summed up the difficulties of predicting future events through talk of 'known unknowns' and 'unknown unknowns': 'We know there are known unknowns; that is to say we know there are some things we do not know. But there are also unknown unknowns – the ones we don't know we don't know'. In other words, some intelligence may never be known – analysts are prisoners to the information they have access to. By the 1980s, Western analysts were proficient in building up the Red Army's order of battle. Analysts could locate Soviet units and judge the effectiveness of their equipment thanks to a range of sources, including IMINT and SIGINT. For Herman, the West were 'better at producing hard and semi-hard facts, but many important "soft" ones were still derived from analysis and open to question' (Herman, 2011:888). In particular, very little was known about Soviet decision-making at the top. 'One of the things that kept the Cold War scary', recalled DCI Robert Gates, 'was the lack of understanding on each side of the mentality of the other' (Barrass, 2009:379). Judging how the Soviet leadership would respond to Western policy remained hard for analysts to gauge, thanks, in part, to the lack of sources. Speeches, academia and diplomatic reports helped fill a void, yet there was room for error. The reality is that intelligence organisations are far from the all-seeing, all-knowing entities of public imagination. They will often get things wrong, inevitably leading to claims of 'intelligence failure', but perhaps this says more about our inflated expectations than what happens behind closed doors.

Part II

Documents

Document 1

Spies are motivated by several factors. Money, ideology, jealously and sex are just some of the reasons why individuals chose to become human intelligence (HUMINT) sources.

Soviet atom bomb spy Klaus Fuchs was arrested in 1950 following a joint British–US investigation into leaks from the wartime Manhattan Project that produced the atomic bombs dropped in August 1945. Fuchs gave the Soviets information on the production of the atomic bomb helping Moscow detonate an atomic bomb in 1949 – years earlier than expected. In January 1950 Fuchs finally gave MI5 a confession giving details on his motivation for passing atomic secrets to Soviet intelligence.

I was asked to help Professor Peierls in Birmingham, on some war work. I accepted it and I started work without knowing at first what the work was. I doubt whether it would have made any difference to my subsequent actions if I had known the nature of the work beforehand. When I learned about the purpose of the work I decided to inform Russia and I established contact through another member of the Communist Party. Since that time I have had continuous contact with persons who were completely unknown to me, except that I knew that they would hand whatever information I gave them to the Russian authorities. At this time I had complete confidence in Russian policy and I believed that the Western Allies deliberately allowed Russia and Germany to fight each other to the death. I had therefore no hesitation in giving all the information I had, even though occasionally I tried to concentrate mainly on giving information about the results of my own work.

In the course of this work I began naturally to form bonds of personal friendship and I have to conceal them from my inner thoughts. I used my Marxist philosophy to establish in my mind two separate compartments. One compartment in which I allowed myself to make friendships, to have personal relations, to help people and to be in all personal ways the kind of man I wanted to be and the kind of man which, in a personal way, I have been before with my friends in or near the Communist Party. I could be free and easy and happy with other people without fear of disclosing myself because I knew that the other compartment would step in if I approached the danger point …

In the post war period I began … to have my doubts about Russian policy. It is impossible to give definite incidents because now the control mechanism acted against me also in keeping away from me facts which I could not look in the face but they did penetrate and eventually I came to a point where I knew I disapproved of many actions of the Russian Government and of the Communist Party, but I still believed that they would build a new world and that one day I would take part in it and that on that day I would have to stand up and say to them that there are things which they are doing wrongly. During this time I was not sure that

I could give all the information that I had. However it became more and more evident that the time when Russia would expand her influence over Europe was far away and that therefore I had to decide myself whether I could go on for many years to continue handing over information without being sure in my own mind whether I was doing right ...

KV 2/1250, Statement of Emil Julius Klaus FUCHS, 27 January 1950

Document 2

KGB officer Oleg Gordievsky became one of the most important agents recruited by Britain's Secret Intelligence Service (SIS). Gordievsky provided significant insights into Soviet political attitudes towards the West, helping shape Cold War policy before defecting to the West in July 1985. Gordievsky recalls in his memoirs his conversion from KGB officer to Western agent.

Until the early 1970s I clung to the hope that the Soviet Union might still reject the Communist yoke and progress to freedom and democracy. Until then I had continued to meet people who had grown up before the revolution or during the 1920s, when the Soviet system was still not omnipotent. They were nice, normal Russians – like some distant relatives of my father who were engineers: not intellectuals or ideologues, but practical, decent people ...

My belief at the time was the nation would never recover, but that at least something ought to be done to protect democracy in the West against the huge concentration of military power and the deluge of propaganda. In practical terms, this meant that I must try and help Western Europe and North America to protect their security, their independence and their freedom, by whatever means I could devise.

Those means were limited. All I could do was to pass information, to show what the KGB leadership in the Kremlin were doing. Of course, in the sum of things, I knew little, but I reckoned that even fragments of knowledge would be better than nothing. I was naïve enough to suppose that, since in the KGB every little fact and statistic was secret, or at least classified, *any* disclosure would be potentially valuable ...

Looking back now, I find it extraordinary that I was driven so hard by ideological compulsion. Yet my feelings were immensely strong because I was living and working on the frontier between the totalitarian world and the West, seeing both sides, and constantly angered by the contrast between the two. The totalitarian world was blinded by prejudice, poisoned by hared, riddled by lies. It was ugly, yet pretending to be beautiful; it was stupid, without vision, and yet claiming to lead the way and pioneer a path into the future for the rest of mankind. Anything I could do to damage this monster, I gladly would.

Oleg Gordievsky, *Next Stop Execution: The Autobiography of Oleg Gordievsky* (London: Macmillan, 1995), pp. 197–198

Document 3

In 2009 a former Rockwell and Boeing engineer ***Dongfan 'Greg' Chung*** *was found guilty of passing sensitive aerospace and military information to agents of the People's Republic of China (PRC).*

Chung was sentenced to over 15 years in prison for economic espionage a year later.

The United States of America (the 'Government') charged Defendant Dongfan 'Greg' Chung with one count of acting as a foreign agent, one count of conspiring to violate the Economic Espionage Act of 1996 ('EEA'), six counts of violating the EEA, one count of making a false statement to the Federal Bureau of Investigation ('FBI'), and one count of obstructing justice. After conducting a ten-day bench trial in this matter, the Court finds Mr. Chung guilty on all counts except for the count of obstructing justice.

Mr. Chung has been an agent of the People's Republic of China ('PRC') for over thirty years. Under the direction and control of the PRC, Mr. Chung misappropriated sensitive aerospace and military information belonging to his employer, The Boeing Company ('Boeing'), to assist the PRC in developing its own programs. To accomplish his mission, Mr. Chung kept over 300,000 pages of documents reflecting Boeing's trade secret and proprietary information in his home. Mr. Chung sent information that he misappropriated to the PRC through the mail, sea freight, a Chinese agent named Chi Mak, and even the Chinese consulate. On several occasions, Mr. Chung also used the information that he misappropriated from Boeing to prepare detailed briefings that he later presented to Chinese officials in the PRC. The trust Boeing placed in Mr. Chung to safeguard its proprietary and trade secret information obviously meant very little to Mr. Chung. He cast it aside to serve the PRC, which he proudly proclaimed as his 'motherland'. The Court now must hold Mr. Chung accountable for his crimes.

...

Federal agents first suspected that Mr. Chung was spying for the PRC during its 2005 investigation of another engineer named Chi Mak, who worked for a naval defense contractor. Mr. Chung had significant contact with Chi Mak over the years, and the federal agents were concerned that their relationship was more than purely social. Federal agents knew that Chi Mak was using his position and security clearance to pass sensitive naval technology to the PRC. In 2007, a jury convicted Chi Mak of conspiring to export defense articles, attempting to export defense articles, acting as an unregistered agent of a foreign government, and making a false statement. This Court sentenced Chi Mak to approximately twenty-four years in prison for his crimes.

During a search of Chi Mak's home in October 2005, federal agents found address books containing contact information for Mr. Chung ... As part of the investigation in the Chi Mak case, Mr. Chung was interviewed on 24 April 2006. Mr. Chung told federal agents he first met Chi Mak in 1992 through a mutual friend 'Mr. Gu' (later identified as Gu Weihao of the Chinese Ministry of Aviation), whom he described as an exchange scholar from China. In June 2006, during a second search of Chi Mak's home, federal agents discovered letters to Mr. Chung from Gu Weihao. In one letter, dated 2 May 1987, Gu Weihao asked Mr. Chung to provide information on airplanes and the Space Shuttle and referred to information that Mr. Chung had previously provided to the PRC ...

Following the discovery of the letter to Mr. Chung from Gu Weihao, federal agents conducted surveillance and trash searches at Mr. Chung's home. In August and September 2006, federal agents discovered that Mr. Chung had disposed of technical documents taken from work by secreting them within the pages of newspapers ... The documents included design drawings and diagrams, structural and material specifications, project management data, and engineering modification reports for the Space Shuttle and the International Space Station. Exs. 170–173.

Based on the information found in Mr. Chung's trash, federal agents believed that it was necessary to take a closer look at him and his activities. On 11 September 2006, federal agents interviewed Mr. Chung and searched his home. Federal agents were astonished at what they found. Mr. Chung had over 300,000 pages of sensitive and proprietary documents belonging to Boeing. More specifically, federal agents found a veritable treasure trove of Boeing's documents relating to the Space Shuttle, Delta IV Rocket, F-15 fighter, B-52 bomber, CH-46/47 Chinook helicopter, and other proprietary aerospace and military technologies. Federal agents also found numerous letters, tasking lists, and journals detailing Mr. Chung's communications with officials in the PRC. As federal agents sifted through the hundreds of thousands of pages of documents in Mr. Chung's home, the story of Mr. Chung's secret life became clear. He was a spy for the PRC.

United States of America v. Dongfan 'Greg' Chung, Memorandum of Decision, 16 July 2009

Document 4

CIA-officer-turned-KGB-agent Aldrich Ames was arrested and imprisoned in 1994. Ames spied for money, being paid a total of $2.5 million for selling US secrets to Moscow. Despite a modest CIA salary of less than $70,000 a year, Ames was able to buy a new $50,000 Jaguar car and pay for a $540,000 house in cash.

Ames has admitted that his motivation to commit treason changed over time. Because of his perception of his growing financial problems, Ames say he initially planned a one-time 'con game' to provide the Soviets with the identities of their own double agent operatives, in return for a one-time payment of $50,000 to cover his debts. He guessed the KGB would pay him the $50,000 and thought this would solve most of his outstanding financial problems.

...Ames received, in addition to the initial payment of $50,000, regular payments during his subsequent luncheons with [Sergei] Chuvakin, in amounts ranging from $20,000 and $50,000 (Transcript, 7/18/94, p. 56). At some point between October and December 1985, the Soviets told him he would be paid an additional $2 million, above and beyond the recurring cash payments. He was advised the Soviets would hold the money for him. Ames has said he did not solicit this money and never made any additional request for money beyond his first meeting, but that the KGB promise of $2 million 'sealed his cooperation' ...

Ames maintained several local bank accounts in his name, as well as in his new wife's name, where he would regularly deposit the cash he received from the Soviets. When Ames received a payment from the KGB, he generally broke it down into smaller cash deposits – in increments under $10,000 – in order to avoid bank reporting requirements which might have led to inquiries by banking regulators.

An assessment of the Aldrich H. Ames espionage case and its implications for US intelligence (November 1994), pp. 13–19

Document 5

British civil servant John Vassall was the victim of a KGB 'honeytrap' and blackmailed into spying for the Soviets in the 1950s. A homosexual when it was illegal in Britain, Vassall was targeted while working at the British Embassy in Moscow and, after returning to London, fearing being removed from his post, handed over to Soviet intelligence information on British naval technology, before being arrested in 1962. Vassall served ten years in prison. Here Vassall recalls being confronted with evidence of the 'honeytrap' after meeting Russian officials at a party.

When I was in the Embassy my work took me to the administration section where an official, who was employed locally, was very helpful. He was known as MIKHAILSKY and he was a Pole. He invited me, not long after I got back to Moscow from leave in England in April, 1955, to dinner in a restaurant. In the course of this social contact other people were introduced to me – I dined on several occasions with MIKHAILSKY and met a number of educated Russians.

This normal social contact lasted for about three months and then, one evening, the Pole introduced me to three of his friends whom I had not met before. One of them suggested that I should go and have dinner with them at another restaurant. When we arrived at the restaurant ... we were taken to the first floor where I first thought was a dining room, but they invited me into a private room. We had drinks, a large dinner and

I was plied with very strong brandy and after half-an-hour I remember everybody taking off their jackets and somebody assisted me to take off mine. I remember the lighting was very strong, and gradually most of my clothes were removed ... I remember two or three people getting on to the bed with me, all in a state of undress. Then certain compromising sexual actions took place. I remember someone in the party taking photographs. After a short while, we all got up and undressed, and left the restaurant ...

At a subsequent meeting with MIKHAILSKY I met a military officer who invited me to a flat. I cannot remember the name of the officer, but the flat was in Central Moscow. Very shortly afterwards he disappeared and two officials in plain clothes confronted me and asked me who I was. They asked me questions where I worked, whether I had a diplomatic passport, and where I went in Moscow. Suddenly, one of these officials produced photographs showing me in various forms of compromising sexual acts. They asked me if this was myself and I replied that it was. They told me that I had committed a serious offence and that I could be kept in Russia ... They then started to question me about my position at the Embassy; what I did. I said that I worked in the Naval Attachés Office. They then threatened to show the compromising photographs to various senior members of the Embassy Staff, including the Ambassador's wife, Lady Hayter.

CRIM 1/4003, Statement of William John Christopher Vassall

Document 6

In January 1917 codebreakers in the British Admiralty's Room 40 intercepted and deciphered a telegram from Germany's Foreign Minister Arthur Zimmerman to the German Minister in Mexico. Zimmerman proposed a German–Mexican alliance if the United States were drawn into the First World War, promising to return Mexican lost territory in Texas, New Mexico and Arizona. The message was shared with Washington, resulting in US entry to the First World War on the side of Britain, France and their allies.

From: – Washington

To: – Mexico

The Foreign Office telegraphs on Jan. 16.

We intend to begin on the first of February unrestricted submarine warfare. We shall endeavour in spite of this to keep the U.S.A. neutral. In the event of this not succeeding we make Mexico a proposal of alliance on the following basis: –

MAKE WAR TOGETHER

MAKE PEACE TOGETHER

General financial support and an understanding on our part that Mexico is to reconquer the lost territory in Texas, New Mexico and Arizona. The settlement in detail is left to you. You will inform the President of the above most secretly, as soon as the outbreak of war with the U.S.A. is certain and add the suggestion that he should on his own initiative invite Japan to immediate adherence and at the same time mediate between Japan and ourselves.

Please call the President's attention to the fact that the ruthless employment of our submarines now offers the prospect of compelling England in a few months to make peace.

Acknowledge receipt.

ZIMMERMAN.

HW 7/8

Document 7

In May 1944, codebreakers in Britain's Government Code & Cipher School intercepted and decrypted a message from the Japanese Ambassador to Berlin providing details of a recent discussion with Adolf Hitler. The decrypt provided British intelligence with Hitler's views – a rare insight for the British – on the upcoming Allied invasion of Europe.

31 May 1944

From: Japanese Ambassador, BERLIN

To: Minister for Foreign Affairs, TOKYO

DATE: 28 May, 1944

On the 27th I called on Foreign Minister RIBBENTROP at FUSCHL and lunched with him, having about two hours' conversation; and during the afternoon of the same day I have about two hours' conversation with HITLER at BERGHOF ...

He said that he thought about eighty divisions had already been assembled in ENGLAND (of these divisions about eight had had actual experience of fighting and were very good troops). I accordingly asked the Fuehrer if he thought that these British and American troops had completed their preparations for landing operations, and he replied in the affirmative.

I then asked him what [corrupt passage: ? form he thought the second front would materialised] and he told me that at the moment what he himself thought was most probable was that after having carried out diversionary operations (Ablenkungsoperation [in German]) in NORWAY, DENMARK, the southern part of the west [coast] of FRANCE and the French Mediterranean coast, they would establish a bridge-head in NORMANDY or BRITTANY and, after seeing how things went, would then embark upon the establishment of a real second front in the Channel. GERMANY would like nothing better, he said, than to be given an opportunity of coming to blows with large forces of the enemy as soon as possible ...

TNA, HW 1/2866

Document 8

This internal National Security Agency document, leaked by US whistle-blower Edward Snowden, provides information on GCHQ's TEMPORA programme. TEMPORA provided 'big access to big data' and resulted from GCHQ's ability to access fibre-optic cables carrying internet traffic in and out of the UK, rivalling similar NSA programmes and underlining GCHQ's continued importance to the US. Both GCHQ and NSA were able to collect mass data from the cables carrying the world's phone calls and internet traffic, storing huge volumes of data so it can be processed and analysed through the XKeyscore search engine interface used by the NSA.

(C//REL) TEMPORA – 'The World's Largest XKEYSCORE' – Is Now Available to Qualified NSA Users

From: (U//FOUO)

NSA Integree at GCHQ

Run Date: 09/19/2012

(U//FOU) SIGINT analysts: We have all heard about Big Data: now you can get **Big Access** to Big Data.

(TS//SI//REL) What happens when one site contains more data than all other XKEYSCORE combined? At more than 10 times larger than the next biggest XKEYSCORE,* **TEMPORA** at GCHQ is the world's largest XKEYSCORE and the NSA workforce is now getting greater access to it. This massive site uses over 1000 machines to process and make available to analysts more than 40 billion pieces of content a day. And starting today skilled NSA XKEYSTROKE uses can get access to the TEMPORA database ...

(TS//SI//REL) **What is TEMPORA?** TEMPORA is GCHQ's XKEY-SCORE 'Internet Buffer' which exploits the most valuable Internet links available to GCHQ. TEMPORA provides a powerful discovery capability against the Middle East, North African and European target sets (among others). Analysts who have benefitted from GCHQ Special Source access like INCESTER or MUSCULAR will almost certainly benefit from TEMPORA.

(TS//SI//REL) **How valuable is TEMPORA?** The value and utility of TEMPORA were proven early into a 5-month evaluation that began this past March. With a limited user base of 300 analysts, TEMPORA became the second most valuable XKEYSCORE access for discovery. Additionally, this small group of analysts produced over 200 end-product reports and provided critical support to SIGINT, defensive, and cyber mission elements.

(TS//SI//REL) **Why TEMPORA?** TEMPORA provides the ability to do content-based discovery and development across a large array of high-priority signals. Similar to other XKEYSCORE deployments, TEMPORA effectively 'slows down' a large chunk on Internet data, providing analysts with three working days to use the surgical toolkit of the GENESIS language to discover data that otherwise would have been missed. This tradecraft of ***content-based discovery*** using the GENESIS language is a critical tool in the analyst's discovery tool kit, and nicely complements the existing and well-known tradecrafts of strong selection targeting and bulk meta-data analysis.

Report on NSA's access to TEMPORA, 19 September 2012

Document 9

The VENONA programme was one of the great SIGINT successes of the Cold War. This joint American–British program to intercept, read and exploit Soviet messages gave the West an important insight into intelligence operations, allowing Western counterintelligence to break up some of the most important Soviet spy rings, some inside the Allied atomic bomb project (codenamed ENORMOUS by the Soviets). The VENONA secret was revealed in 1995. This document provides details on a meeting between Soviet agents 'Gus' and 'Rest' in February 1944. 'Gus' was later identified as chemist Harry Gold, sentenced to thirty years imprisonment in 1951, and 'Rest' was identified as the German-born physicist Klaus Fuchs. Fuchs admitted to spying for the Soviet Union and received a fourteen year sentence.

While the VENONA story presents a significant breakthrough for the West, only a fraction of the intercepted messages were ever decrypted; almost half of the NKVD cables from 1944 were decrypted, while only 15 per cent were ever read for 1943. Just over 1 per cent of messages for 1942 and 1945 were available. Many of the messages, as the below example shows, were often incomplete. Even today, many parts of the messages are 'unrecoverable'. SIGINT is rarely a 'smoking gun', one senior US official was quoted as saying. SIGINT is often 'fragmentary', as the VENONA decrypts show, leaving analysts with significant gaps to fill.

From: NEW YORK

To: MOSCOW

No: 195

9 February 1944

Personal to VIKTOR[i].

In reply to No. 302[ii].

On 5th February a meeting took place between 'GUS'[iii] and 'REST'[iv]. Beforehand GUS' was given a detailed briefing by us. REST greeted him pleasantly but was rather cautious at first, [1 group unrecovered] the discussion GUS' satisfied himself that REST was aware of whom he was working with. R. [iv] arrived in the COUNTRY[STRANA] [v] in September as a member of the ISLAND [OSTROV] [vi] mission on ENORMOUS [ENORMOZ] [vii]. According to him the work on ENORMOUS in the COUNTRY is being carried out under the direct control of the COUNTRY's army represented by General SOMERVELL[SOMERVILL] [viii] and STIMSON [ix]: at the head of the group of ISLANDERS[OSTROVITYaNE[[vi] is a Labour Member of Parliament, Ben SMITH[x].

The whole operation amounts to the working out of the process for the separation of isotopes of ENORMOUS. The work is proceeding in two directions: the electron method developed by LAWRENCE[LAURENS] [xi]

[71 groups unrecoverable]

Separation of isotopes by the combined method, using the diffusion method for preliminary and the electron method for final separation. The work

[46 groups unrecovered]

18th February, we shall report the results.

No. 92		ANTON[xii]
Footnotes:	[i] VIKTOR:	Lt. Gen. P.M. FITIN
	[ii] Not available.	
	[iii] GUS':	i.e. "GOOSE"; Harry GOLD
	[iv] REST/R.:	Dr. Emil Julius Klaus FUCHS.
	[v] COUNTRY:	U.S.A.
	[vi] ISLAND, ISLANDERS:	GREAT BRITAIN, British.
	[vii] ENORMOUS:	a) U.S. Atomic Energy Project.
		b) Uranium

[viii] General SOMERVELL:	Lt. General Brehan Burke SOMERVELL, Commanding General Army Service Forces, War Department.
[ix] STIMSON:	Henry Lewis STIMSON, Secretary of War.
[x] Ben SMITH:	Rt. Hon. Ben SMITH, Minister Resident in WASHINGTON for Supply from 1943.
[xi] LAWRENCE:	Professor Ernest Orlando LAWRENCE.
[xii] ANTON:	Leonid Romanovich KVASNIKOV.

Venona decrypt: New York to Moscow, 9 February 1944

Document 10

The Butler report reviewed the intelligence available to the British government before the 2003 invasion of Iraq. Chapter 2 discusses the nature and use of intelligence. Here Butler's report discusses one of the major weaknesses of secret information: its incompleteness. Contrary to popular imagination, intelligence rarely gives the full picture. Often, when received, intelligence is piecemeal with analysts needed to add their expert interpretation for policymakers.

Governmental decisions and actions, at home and abroad, are based on many types of information. Most is openly available or compiled, much is published, and some is consciously provided by individuals, organisations or other governments in confidence. A great deal of such information may be accurate, or accurate enough in its own terms. But equally much is at best uninformed, while some is positively intended to mislead. To supplement their knowledge in areas of concern where information is for one reason or another inadequate, governments turn to secret sources. Information acquired against the wishes and (generally) without the knowledge of its originators or possessors is processed by collation with other material, validation, analysis and assessment and finally disseminated as 'intelligence'.

The most important limitation on intelligence is its incompleteness. Much ingenuity and effort is spent on making secret information difficult to acquire and hard to analyse. Although the intelligence process may overcome such barriers, intelligence seldom acquires the full story. In fact, it is often, when first acquired, sporadic and patchy, and even after analysis may still be at best inferential.

Extract from Review of Intelligence on Weapons of Mass Destruction (Butler Report), July 2004

Document 11

The Presidential Daily Brief (PDB) is an all-source intelligence report submitted to the President of the United States in a variety of formats since 1961. The document provides a summary of the latest intelligence that may impact policymaking. The following is an extract from the PDB sent to President George Bush Jnr. in August 2001 warning that al-Qaeda wanted to attack targets in the US. The next month, **AQ** *terrorists using hijacked aircraft struck the World Trade Centre in New York and Pentagon in Washington killing almost 3,000 people.*

Bin Laden determined to strike in US (6 August 2001)

Clandestine, foreign government, and media reports indicate bin Laden since 1997 has wanted to conduct terrorist attacks in the US. Bin Laden implied in U.S. television interviews in 1997 and 1998 that his followers would follow the example of World Trade Center bomber Ramzi Yousef and 'bring the fighting to America'.

After U.S. missile strikes on his base in Afghanistan in 1998, bin Laden told followers he wanted to retaliate in Washington, according to a [REDACTED] service.

An Egyptian Islamic Jihad (EIJ) operative told [REDACTED] service at the same time that bin Laden was planning to exploit the operative's access to the U.S. to mount a terrorist strike.

The millennium plotting in Canada in 1999 may have been part of bin Laden's first serious attempt to implement a terrorist strike in the U.S. Convicted plotter Ahmed Ressam has told the FBI that he conceived the idea to attack Los Angeles International Airport himself, but that in bin Laden lieutenant Abu Zubaydah encouraged him and helped facilitate the operation. Ressam also said that in 1998 Abu Zubaydah was planning his own U.S. attack.

Ressam says bin Laden was aware of the Los Angeles operation.

Although bin Laden has not succeeded, his attacks against the U.S. Embassies in Kenya and Tanzania in 1998 demonstrate that he prepares operations years in advance and is not deterred by setbacks. Bin Laden associates surveyed our embassies in Nairobi and Dar es Salaam as early as 1993, and some members of the Nairobi cell planning the bombings were arrested and deported in 1997.

Al-Qaeda members – including some who are U.S. citizens – have resided in or traveled to the U.S. for years, and the group apparently maintains a support structure that could aid attacks. Two al-Qaeda members found guilty in the conspiracy to bomb our embassies in East Africa were U.S. citizens, and a senior EIJ member lived in California in the mid-1990s.

A clandestine source said in 1998 that a bin Laden cell in New York was recruiting Muslim-American youth for attacks.

We have not been able to corroborate some of the more sensational threat reporting, such as that from a [REDACTED] *service in 1998 saying that Bin Laden wanted to hijack a U.S. aircraft to gain the release of 'Blind Sheikh' Omar Abdel Rahman and other U.S.-held extremists.*

Nevertheless, FBI information since that time indicates patterns of suspicious activity in this country consistent with preparations for hijackings or other types of attacks, including recent surveillance of federal buildings in New York.

The FBI is conducting approximately 70 full-field investigations throughout the U.S. that it considers bin Laden-related. CIA and the FBI are investigating a call to our embassy in the UAE in May saying that a group or bin Laden supporters was in the U.S. planning attacks with explosives.

The Presidential Daily Brief: 'Bin Laden determined to strike in US (6 August 2001)'

Document 12

In the run-up to the 2003 invasion of Iraq, Britain's assessments staff in the Joint Intelligence Committee (JIC) were responsible for giving policymakers reports on the development of Iraqi weapons of mass destruction (WMD). In subsequent inquiries, the assessments of the JIC came under scrutiny for failing to restrain the views of policymakers that Iraq had WMD – despite the reverse being the truth. The 2016 Chilcot report criticised the JIC's chairman John Scarlett for getting too close to policymakers. This JIC assessment from September 2002 formed the basis of advice given to MPs.

JIC Assessment, 9 September 2002

Iraqi use of chemical and biological weapons – possible scenarios

Key judgements

I. Iraq has a chemical and biological weapons capability and Saddam is prepared to use it.
II. Faced with the likelihood of military defeat and being removed from power, Saddam is unlikely to be deterred from using chemical and biological weapons by any diplomatic or military means.
III. The use of chemical and biological weapons prior to any military attack would boost support for US-led action and is unlikely.
IV. Saddam is prepared to order missile strikes against Israel, with chemical or biological warheads, in order to widen the war once hostilities begin.
V. Saddam could order the use of CBW weapons in order to deny space and territory to Coalition forces, or to cause casualties, slow any advance, and sap US morale.

VI. If not previously employed, Saddam will order the indiscriminate use of whatever CBW weapons remain available late in a ground campaign or as a final act of vengeance. But such an order would depend of the availability of delivery means and the willingness of commanders to obey.

Iraqi WMD: Extract from JIC Assessment, 9 September 2002

Document 13

In October 1962 the deployment of Soviet nuclear missiles to Cuba sparked a Cold War confrontation in the Caribbean. Despite the initial failure to foresee such a provocative Soviet move, US intelligence analysts quickly gave policymakers the evidence they needed, giving President Kennedy an accurate insight into Soviet thinking during the crisis.

SUBJECT: SNIE 11–19-62: MAJOR CONSEQUENCES OF CERTAIN US COURSES OF ACTION IN CUBA

THE ESTIMATE

STATUS OF SOVIET MILITARY BUILDUP IN CUBA

1. Firm evidence indicates the presence in Cuba of four MEBM and two IRBM launch sites in various stages of construction and organized into at least three regiments. Of these, two regiments of right launchers each are mobile and designed to launch MRBMs with a range of about 1,100 n.m., while one regiment of eight fixed launchers may be designed for IRBMs with a range of about 2,000 n.m.
2. The 16 launchers for 1,100 n.m. MRBMs must be considered operational now. Four of the fixed launchers for the 2,200 n.m. IRBMs could probably become operational within the next six weeks. The other four would become operational in 8 to 10 weeks. We have no direct evidence that nuclear weapons are now present in Cuba, and it is unlikely that we would be able to obtain such evidence. However, the construction of at least one probable nuclear storage facility is a strong indication of the Soviet intent to provide nuclear warheads. In any case, it is prudent to assume that when the missiles are otherwise operational, nuclear warheads will be available. These could be brought in by air, submarine, or surface ship ...
5. The inventory of other major Soviet weapons now identified in Cuba includes:

   a. 22 IL-28 jet light bombers, of which one is assembled and three others have been uncrated;
   b. 39 MIG-21 jet fighters, of which 35 are assembled and fur are still in crates, and 62 other jet fighters of less advanced types;
   c. 24 SA-2 sites, of which 16 are believed to be individually operational with some missiles on launcher;

d. 3 cruise missile sites for coastal defence, of which 2 are now operational;
e. 12 Komar cruise missile patrol boats, all probably operational or nearly so.

6. Cuban-based MRBMs and IRBMs with nuclear warheads would suggest the present limited Soviet ICBM capability by virtue of their ability to strike at similar types of targets with warheads of generally similar yields. In the near future, therefore, Soviet gross capabilities for initial attack on US military and civilian targets can be increased considerably by Cuban-based missiles. However, the deployment of these missiles in Cuba will probably not, in the Soviet judgement, insure destruction of the US second strike capability to a degree which would eliminate an unacceptably heavy retaliatory attack on the USSR. If the missile buildup in Cuba continues, the Soviet capability to blunt a retaliatory attack will be progressively enhanced.

PURPOSE OF SOVIET BUILDUP

7. A major Soviet objective in their military buildup in Cuba is to demonstrate that the world balance of forces has shifted so far in their favour that the US can no longer prevent the advance of Soviet offensive power even into its own hemisphere. In this connection they assume, of course, that these deployments sooner or later will become publicly known. At the same time, they expect their missile forces in Cuba to make an important contribution to their total strategic capability vis-à-vis the US.
8. Consequently, it is unlikely that the USSR is installing these missiles primarily in order to use them in bargaining for US concessions elsewhere. Moreover, the public withdrawal of Soviet missiles from Cuba would create serious problems in the USSR's relations with Castro; it would cast doubt on the firmness of the Soviet intention to protect the Castro regime and perhaps on their commitments elsewhere.
9. If the US acquiesces to the presence of strategic missiles in Cuba, we believe that the Soviets will continue the buildup. We have no basis for estimating the force level which they wish to reach, but it seems entirely clear now that they are going well beyond a token capability ...

A US BLOCKADE

14. Two basis modes of blockade could be considered: total and selective. We believe that even under a total blockade individual aircraft and submarines might get through to deliver vital military items, e.g. nuclear warheads. Even the most severe blockade would not deprive

the Soviets of the use of missiles already in Cuba for a nuclear strike on the US …

15. Under any form of blockade, the Soviets would concentrate on political exploitation, especially in the UN. They might risk violent encounters in an attempt to penetrate the blockade, but they would not resort to major force in the area of Cuba or forceful retaliations elsewhere, at least initially. If US enforcement of the blockade involved use of force by the US, the Soviets might respond on an equivalent level, but would seek to avoid escalation.
16. This any blockade situation would place the Soviets under no immediate pressure to choose a response with force. They could reply on political means to compel the US to desist, and reserve a resort to force until the US has actually used force. They would estimate that the inherent difficulties of enforcing the blockade and the generally adverse reactions, including those of US allies to it, would result in enormous pressures on the US to desist …

SOVIET REACTION TO THE USE OF MILITARY FORCE

18. In the case of US use of force against Cuban territory, the likelihood of a Soviet response by force, either locally or for retaliation elsewhere, would be greater than in the case of blockade. The Soviets could be placed automatically under great pressure to respond in ways which, if they could not save Cuba, would inflict an offsetting injury to US interests. This would be true whether the action was limited to an effort to neutralise the strategic missiles, or these missiles plus airfields, surface-to-air missile sites, or cruise missile sites, or in fact an outright invasion designed to destroy the Castro regime.
23. Finally, we believe that … the Soviet leaders would not deliberately initiate general war or take military measures, which in their calculation, would run grave risks of general war.

Extract from Special National Intelligence Estimate,
20 October 1962

Document 14

British Prime Minister Winston Churchill had a lifelong interest in spies and secrets, using intelligence to shape British policy. Churchill enjoyed unrivalled access to intelligence from an early age and, during the Second World War, had an insatiable appetite signals intelligence from the decryption of Germany's Enigma machine and encouraged the Special Operations Executive to famously set Nazi-occupied 'Europe ablaze'. Churchill maintained this thirst or intelligence during his second term as Prime Minister, as shown by this extract from the CIA history of Operation

TPAJAX – a joint US and British coup in Iran in 1953 – when CIA officer Kermit Roosevelt met the Prime Minister after the successful operation.

At 1400 hours Roosevelt was received by the Prime Minister who was in bed at 10 Downing Street. This was a most touching occasion. The Prime Minister seemed to be in bad shape physically. He had great difficulty in hearing: occasional difficulty in articulating; and apparent difficulty in seeing to his left. In spite of this he could not have been more kind personally nor more enthusiastic about the operation. He was good enough to express envy of Roosevelt's role and a wish that he had been 'some years' younger and might have served under his command. He repeated the statement that he had already made to Sinclair, that if the success of this operation could be maintained it would be the finest operation since the end of the war ... Our operation had given us a wonderful and unexpected opportunity which might change the whole picture in the Middle East ...

The Prime Minister made several references which indicated that he regarded SIS as <u>his</u> service, and that is was very close to his heart. Perhaps due to his physical condition at the time, however, he appeared a bit hazy as to its jurisdiction and the distinction between MI-5 and MI-6. He was definitely hazy on Sinclair and upon the American setup. The initials CIA meant nothing to him, but he had a vague idea that Roosevelt must be connected in some way with his old friend Bedell Smith.

Extract from CIA Clandestine Service History: Overthrow of Premier Mossadeq of Iran, November 1952 – August 1953

Document 15

Allegations that British Prime Minister Tony Blair and his inner circle politicised intelligence during debates before the 2003 invasion of Iraq continue to be a source of controversy. In September 2002, the British government published a document, based on the JIC's assessments, on Iraq's WMD programme. Speaking to MPs, Blair said the intelligence was 'extensive, detailed and authoritative' and that Iraqi dictator Saddam Hussein had an active WMD programme, with weapons deployable in '45 minutes' – a claim that captured public and media attention. In fact, the intelligence on Iraq's WMD – as several post-war inquiries have made clear – was far from extensive with more weight placed on the information than it could bear. In reality, the JIC's assessments came with caveats. The intelligence was 'limited' with the JIC relying on 'judgement and assessment' to fill in the blanks – a message not repeated in Blair's statement to the House of Commons.

I set out the history in some detail because occasionally debate on this issue seems to treat it almost as if it had suddenly arisen, coming out of nowhere on a whim in the last few months of 2002. It is actually an 11-year history:

a history of UN will flouted, of lies told by Saddam about the existence of his chemical, biological and nuclear weapons programmes, and of obstruction, defiance and denial.

There is one common, consistent theme, however: the total determination of Saddam to maintain that programme; to risk war, international ostracism, sanctions and the isolation of the Iraqi economy to keep it. At any time, he could have let the inspectors back in and put the world to proof. At any time, he could have co-operated with the United Nations. Ten days ago, he made the offer unconditionally under threat of war. He could have done it at any time in the last 11 years, but he did not. Why?

The dossier that we publish gives the answer. The reason is that his chemical, biological and nuclear weapons programme is not an historic left-over from 1998. The inspectors are not needed to clean up the old remains. His weapons of mass destruction programme is active, detailed and growing. The policy of containment is not working. The weapons of mass destruction programme is not shut down; it is up and running now.

The dossier is based on the work of the British Joint Intelligence Committee. For over 60 years, beginning just before world war two, the JIC has provided intelligence assessments to British Prime Ministers. Normally, its work is obviously secret. Unusually, because it is important that we explain our concerns about Saddam to the British people, we have decided to disclose its assessments.

I am aware, of course, that people will have to take elements of this on the good faith of our intelligence services, but this is what they are telling me, the British Prime Minister, and my senior colleagues. The intelligence picture that they paint is one accumulated over the last four years. It is extensive, detailed and authoritative. It concludes that Iraq has chemical and biological weapons, that Saddam has continued to produce them, that he has existing and active military plans for the use of chemical and biological weapons, which could be activated within 45 minutes, including against his own Shia population, and that he is actively trying to acquire nuclear weapons capability.

On chemical weapons, the dossier shows that Iraq continues to produce chemical agents for chemical weapons; has rebuilt previously destroyed production plants across Iraq; has bought dual-use chemical facilities; has retained the key personnel formerly engaged in the chemical weapons programme; and has a serious ongoing research programme into weapons production, all of it well funded.

Hansard: Parliamentary Debates, sixth series, vol. 390, Tuesday 22 September 2002

Document 16

In January 2017 the US intelligence community released its assessment of Russian involvement in the Presidential election. The report was based on a still-classified document that argued Russia had used a sophisticated campaign using official agencies, state media and online trolls to influence the election in favour of President Trump.

Russian efforts to influence the 2016 US presidential election represent the most recent expression of Moscow's longstanding desire to undermine the US-led liberal democratic order, but these activities demonstrated a significant escalation in directness, level of activity, and scope of effort compared to previous operations.

We assess Russian President Vladimir Putin ordered an influence campaign in 2016 aimed at the US presidential election. Russia's goals were to undermine public faith in the US democratic process, denigrate Secretary Clinton, and harm her electability and potential presidency. We further assess Putin and the Russian Government developed a clear preference for President-elect Trump. We have high confidence in these judgments.

- We also assess Putin and the Russian Government aspired to help President-elect Trump's election chances when possible by discrediting Secretary Clinton and publicly contrasting her unfavorably to him. All three agencies agree with this judgment. CIA and FBI have high confidence in this judgment; NSA has moderate confidence.
- Moscow's approach evolved over the course of the campaign based on Russia's understanding of the electoral prospects of the two main candidates. When it appeared to Moscow that Secretary Clinton was likely to win the election, the Russian influence campaign began to focus more on undermining her future presidency.
- Further information has come to light since Election Day that, when combined with Russian behavior since early November 2016, increases our confidence in our assessments of Russian motivations and goals.

Moscow's influence campaign followed a Russian messaging strategy that blends covert intelligence operations – such as cyber activity – with overt efforts by Russian Government agencies, state-funded media, third-party intermediaries, and paid social media users or 'trolls'. Russia, like its Soviet predecessor, has a history of conducting covert influence campaigns focused on US presidential elections that have used intelligence officers and agents and press placements to disparage candidates perceived as hostile to the Kremlin.

- Russia's intelligence services conducted cyber operations against targets associated with the 2016 US presidential election, including targets associated with both major US political parties.
- We assess with high confidence that Russian military intelligence (General Staff Main Intelligence Directorate or GRU) used the

Guccifer 2.0 persona and DCLeaks.com to release US victim data obtained in cyber operations publicly and in exclusives to media outlets and relayed material to WikiLeaks.

- Russian intelligence obtained and maintained access to elements of multiple US state or local electoral boards. **DHS assesses that the types of systems Russian actors targeted or compromised were not involved in vote tallying.**
- Russia's state-run propaganda machine contributed to the influence campaign by serving as a platform for Kremlin messaging to Russian and international audiences.

We assess Moscow will apply lessons learned from its Putin-ordered campaign aimed at the US presidential election to future influence efforts worldwide, including against US allies and their election processes.

Intelligence Community Assessment: Russian influence on the 2016 US Presidential Election, January 2017

Document 17

In March 1946 British and US intelligence officials signed the 'British–U.S. Communications Intelligence Agreement' in Washington. The agreement continued wartime Anglo-American signals intelligence cooperation and would form the cornerstone of the future UKUSA or 'Five Eyes' Agreement that includes the SIGINT organisations of the United States, United Kingdom, Canada, Australia and New Zealand.

British–U.S. communication intelligence agreement

1. Parties to the Agreement

The following agreement is made between the State-Army-Navy Communication Intelligence Board (STANCIB) (representing the U.S. State, Navy, and War Departments and all other U.S. Communication Intelligence authorities which may function) and the London Signal Intelligence (SIGINT) Board (representing the Foreign Office, Admiralty, War Office, Air Ministry, and all other British Empire Communication Intelligence Authorities which may function).

2. Scope of the Agreement

The agreement governments the relations of the abovementioned parties in Communication Intelligence matters only. However, the exchange of such collateral material as is applicable for technical purposes and is not prejudicial to national interests will be effected between the Communication Intelligence agencies in both countries.

3. Extent of the Agreement – Products

(a) The parties agree to the exchange of the products of the following operations relating to foreign communications:

 (1) collection of traffic
 (2) acquisition of communication documents and equipment
 (3) traffic analysis
 (4) cryptanalysis
 (5) decryption and translation
 (6) acquisition of information regarding communication organizations, practices, procedures, and equipment

(b) Such exchange will be unrestricted on all work undertaken except when specifically excluded from the agreement at the request of either party and with the agreement of the other. It is the intention of each party to limit such exceptions to the absolute minimum and to exercise no restrictions other than those reported and mutually agreed upon.

4. Extent of the Agreement – Methods and Techniques

(a) The parties agree to the exchange of information regarding methods and techniques involved in the operations outlined in paragraph 3(a).
(b) Such exchange will be unrestricted on all work undertaken, except that upon notification of the other party when its special interests so require. Such notification will include a description of the information being withheld, sufficient in the opinion of the withholding party, to convey its significance. It is the intention of each party to limit such exceptions to the absolute minimum.

5. Third Parties to the Agreement

Both parties will regard this agreement as precluding action with third parties on any subject appertaining to Communication Intelligence except in accordance with the following understanding:

(a) It will be contrary to this agreement to reveal its existence to any third party whatever.
(b) Each party will seek the agreement of the other to any action with third parties, and will take no such action until its advisability is agreed upon.
(c) The agreement of the other having been obtained, it will be left to the party concerned to carry out the agreed action in the most appropriate way, without obligation to disclose precisely the channels through which action is taken.

(d) Each party will ensure that the results of any action are made available to the other.

6. The Dominions

(a) While the Dominions are not parties to this agreement, they will not be regarded as third parties.
(b) The London SIGINT Board will, however, keep the U.S. informed of any arrangements or proposed arrangements with any Dominion agencies.
(c) STANCIB will make no arrangements with any Dominion agency other than Canadian except through, or with the prior approval of, the London SIGINT Board.
(d) As regards Canada, STANCIB will complete no arrangements with any agency therein without first obtaining the views of the London SIGINT Board.
(e) It will be conditional on any Dominion agencies with whom collaboration takes place that they abide by the terms of paragraphs 5, 8, and 9 of this agreement ...

...

8. Dissemination and Security

Communication Intelligence and Secret or above technical matters connected therewith will be disseminated in accordance with identical security regulations to be drawn up and kept under review by STANCIB and the London SIGINT Board in collaboration. Within the terms of these regulations dissemination by either party will be made to U.S. recipients other than Canadian only as approved by the London SIGINT Board; to Canadian recipients only as approved by either STANCIB or the London SIGINT Board; and to third party recipients only as jointly approved by STANCIB and the London SIGINT Board.

...

10. Previous Agreements

This agreement supersedes all previous agreements between British and U.S. authorities in the Communication Intelligence field.

11. Amendment and Termination of Agreement

This agreement may be amended or terminated completely or in part at any time by mutual agreement. It may be terminated completely at any time on notice by either party, should either consider its interests best served by such action.

12. Activation and Implementation of the Agreement

This agreement becomes effective by signature of duly authorized representatives of the London SIGINT Board and STANCIB. Thereafter, its implementation will be arranged between the Communication Intelligence authorities concerned, subject to the approval of the London SIGINT Board and STANCIB.

TNA: HW 80/4, BRITISH-U.S. COMMUNICATION INTELLIGENCE AGREEMENT, 5 March 1946

Document 18

During the Cold War the Soviet KGB enjoyed close relationships with allied organisations. The East German Ministry for State Security (the MfS or Stasi) was formed under the influence of the Soviet intelligence services and went on to have a long relationship with the KGB. In 1978 the MfS and KGB negotiated an agreement of cooperation, including the sharing of liaison officers.

Article I

The resolution of general issues of cooperation between the MfS of the GDR and the KGB with the Council of Ministers of the USSR ... is conducted by the leadership of the Ministry of State Security of the GDR and the leadership of the Representation of the KGB with the MfS of the GDR.

Article II

The resolution of general issues of cooperation between the MfS of the GDR and the KGB with the Council of Ministers of the USSR, ... is to be conducted through the leaders of units in the MfS of the GDR, ... and the liaison officers with these units from the Representation of the KGB with the MfS of the GDR.

Article III

In order to ensure close cooperation between units of the MfS of the GDR and the KGB with the Council of Ministers of the USSR ... the Representation of the KGB with the MfS of the GDR will designate liaison officers to maintain permanent working contacts ...

[...]

Article V

Liaison officers from the Representation of the KGB with the MfS of the GDR, as well as other employees from the Representation of the KGB with the MfS of the GDR designated to maintain contacts with directors of units in the MfS of the GDR, will be provided with official documents from the MfS of the GDR. They will allow them to enter office buildings of the MfS of the GDR …

Article VII

The receipt of research of material from the archives of the MfS of the GDR and the KGB with the Council of Ministers of the USSR is handled on the basis of requests by respective liaison officers from the Representation of the KGB with the MfS of the GDR, according to procedures established by the MfS of the GDR and the KGB ….

Article VIII

The Ministry for State Security of the GDR and the Representation of the KGB with the MfS of the GDR will implement measures required to ensure, within the framework of cooperation of the MfS of the GDR and the KGB with the Council of Ministers of the USSR, the secrecy of all mutually provided information, data and insights, in particular with regard to individuals recruited for a secret collaboration. They will ensure that such information, data and insights will not become known to people who have no authority in this regard.

Protocol Guiding Cooperation between the Ministry for State Security of the GDR and the Representation of the Committee for State Security, March 1978. Source: Office of the Federal Commissioner for the Stasi Records (BStU), MfS, BdL/Dok. Nr. 001862. Translated from German for CWIHP by Bernd Schaefer. The Cold War International History Project, Wilson Center Digital Archive, https://digitalarchive.wilsoncenter.org/document/115716

Document 19

Following the 9/11 attacks American spies were authorised by the White House to fight the 'war on terror' by any means possible. Paramilitary and psychological warfare, targeted assassinations and 'snatch' operations were allowed, with captured al-Qaeda *operatives being flown to 'black sites' for interrogation. The process became known as 'extraordinary rendition'. Detainees would be subjected to 'enhanced interrogation' methods by the CIA and allied intelligence agencies to extract intelligence. The following extract provides an overview of some of the techniques used.*

Extract 1

The purpose of interrogation is to persuade High-Value Detainees (HVD) to provide threat information and terrorist intelligence in a timely manner, to allow the US government to identify and disrupt terrorist plots …

... Effective interrogation is based on the concept of using both physical and psychological pressures in a comprehensive, systematic, and cumulative manner to influence HVD behaviour, to overcome a detainee's resistance posture. The goal of interrogation is to create a state of learned helplessness and dependence conductive to the collection of intelligence in a predictable, reliable, and sustainable manner. For the purpose of this paper, the interrogation process can be broken into these phases: Initial Conditions; Transition to Interrogation; and Interrogation.

Interrogation

[...]

2. Conditioning Techniques. The HVD is typically reduced to a baseline, dependent state using the three interrogation techniques discussed below in combination. Establishing this baseline state is important to demonstrate to the HVD that he has no control over basic human needs. The baseline state also creates in the detainee a mindset in which he learns to perceive and value his personal welfare, comfort, and immediate needs more than the information he is protecting. The use of these conditioning techniques do not generally being immediate results; rather, it is the cumulative effect of these techniques, used over time and in combination with other interrogation techniques and intelligence exploitation methods, which achieve interrogation objectives. These conditioning techniques require little to no physical interaction between the detainee and the interrogator. The specific conditioning interrogation techniques are:
   a. Nudity. The HVD's clothes are taken and he remains nude until the interrogators provide clothes to him.
   b. Sleep Deprivation. The HVD is placed in the vertical shackling position to begin sleep deprivation. Other shacking procedures may be used during interrogations. The detainee is diapered for sanitary purposes, although the diaper is not used at all times.
   c. Dietary manipulation. The HVD is fed Ensure Plus or other food at regular intervals. The HVD receives a target of 1500 calories per day per OMS guidelines.
3. Corrective Techniques. Techniques that require physical interaction between the interrogator and detainee are used principally to correct, startle, or to achieve another enabling objective with the detainee. These techniques – the insult slap, abdominal slap, facial hold and attention grasp – are not used simultaneously but are often used interchangeably during an individual interrogation session. These techniques generally are used while the detainee is subjected to the conditioning techniques outlined above (nudity, sleep deprivation, and dietary manipulation...)

Background Paper on CIA's Combined Use of Interrogation Technique, December 2004

Extract 2

The Committee finds, based on a review of CIA interrogation records, that the use of the CIA's enhanced interrogation techniques was not an effective means of obtaining accurate information or gaining detainee cooperation.

For example, according to CIA records, seven of the 39 CIA detainees known to have been subjected to the CIA's enhanced interrogation techniques produced no intelligence while in CIA custody. CIA detainees who were subjected to the CIA's enhanced interrogation techniques were usually subjected to the techniques immediately after being rendered to CIA custody. Other detainees provided significant accurate intelligence prior to, or without having been subjected to these techniques.

While being subjected to the CIA's enhanced interrogation techniques and afterwards, multiple CIA detainees fabricated information, resulting in faulty intelligence. Detainees provided fabricated information on critical intelligence issues, including the terrorist threats which the CIA identified as its highest priorities.

At numerous times throughout the CIA's Detention and Interrogation Program, CIA personnel assessed that the most effective method for acquiring intelligence from detainees, including from detainees the CIA considered to be the most 'high-value,' was to confront the detainees with information already acquired by the Intelligence Community. CIA officers regularly called into question whether the CIA's enhanced interrogation techniques were effective, assessing that the use of the techniques failed to elicit detainee cooperation or produce accurate intelligence.

Extract from Senate Select Committee report on the CIA's detention and interrogation programme

Document 20

MI5 and SIS have also supported their US counterparts and allies elsewhere in rendition, leading to claims that the UK is 'complicit' in torture. Intelligence supplied by UK agencies was used by allies to detain and render terror suspects to 'black sites'. The Court of Appeal ruled in 2010 that MI5 was complicit in the abuse of ***Binyam Mohamed****, an Ethiopian national resident in the UK, having interviewed him while being detained by Pakistan's ISI. In a number of cases, the UK government has paid compensation. In 2018 the British government reached an out-of-court settlement with Libyan national* ***Abdel Hakim Belhaj*** *with Prime Minister Theresa May issuing an unprecedented public apology for their 'appalling treatment'. The following extracts look at Britain's role.*

Extract 1

Binyam Mohamed was detained by the US as an enemy combatant in the US government prison facility at Guantánamo Bay in Cuba. Mohamed was captured in Pakistan in 2002 while trying to return to the UK under a false passport and brutally interrogated at facilities in Pakistan, Morocco and Afghanistan before being transferred to Cuba. During his incarceration, Mohamed claims he was questioned by officials from Britain's MI5. He was released in 2009 and received significant compensation from the UK government.

I hope you will understand that after everything I have been through I am neither physically nor mentally capable of facing the media on the moment of my arrival back to Britain. Please forgive me if I make a simple statement through my lawyer. I hope to be able to do better in days to come, when I am on the road to recovery.

I have been through an experience that I never thought to encounter in my darkest nightmares. Before this ordeal, 'torture' was an abstract word to me. I could never have imagined that I would be its victim. It is still difficult for me to believe that I was abducted, hauled from one country to the next, and tortured in medieval ways – all orchestrated by the United States government.

While I want to recover, and put it all as far in my past as I can, I also know I have an obligation to the people who still remain in those torture chambers. My own despair was greatest when I thought that everyone had abandoned me. I have a duty to make sure that nobody else is forgotten.

I am grateful that in the end I was not simply left to my fate. I am grateful to my lawyers and other staff at Reprieve, and to Lt. Col. Yvonne Bradley, who fought for my freedom. I am grateful to the members of the British Foreign Office who worked for my release. And I want to thank people around Britain who wrote to me in Guantánamo Bay to keep my spirits up, as well as to the members of the media who tried to make sure that the world knew what was going on. I know I would not be home in Britain today if it were not for everyone's support. Indeed, I might not be alive at all.

I wish I could say that it is all over, but it is not. There are still 241 Muslim prisoners in Guantánamo. Many have long since been cleared even by the US military, yet cannot go anywhere as they face persecution. For example, Ahmed bel Bacha lived here in Britain, and desperately needs a home. Then there are thousands of other prisoners held by the US elsewhere around the world, with no charges, and without access to their families.

And I have to say, more in sadness than in anger, that many have been complicit in my own horrors over the past seven years. For myself, the very worst moment came when I realised in Morocco that the people who were torturing me were receiving questions and materials from British intelligence. I had met with British intelligence in Pakistan. I had been open with them. Yet the very people who I had hoped would come to my rescue, I later realised, had allied themselves with my abusers.

I am not asking for vengeance; only that the truth should be made known, so that nobody in the future should have to endure what I have endured.

Thank you.

Binyam Mohamed

Statement from Binyam Mohammed, February 2009

Extract 2

Secret documents found in the ruins of the Libyan capital Tripoli after the collapse of the Colonel Gaddafi's regime in 2011 provided for the first time evidence of Britain's links with Libya's national intelligence agency, Mukhabarat el-Jamahiriya. The documents provided new information on the CIA rendition of Libyan dissident Abdel Hakim Belhaj and his pregnant wife Fatima Boudchar from the Far East in 2004. Both were detailed after an SIS tip-off, as admitted by SIS's Director of Counter-Terrorism Mark Allen in a letter shortly after Belhaj and Boudchar's arrival in Libya.

Most importantly, I congratulate you on the safe arrival of Abu Abd Allah Sadiq. This was the least we could do for you and for Libya to demonstrate the remarkable relationship we have built over the years. I am so glad. I was grateful to you for helping the officer we sent out last week. Abu 'Abd Allah's information on the situation in this country is of urgent importance to us. Amusingly, we got a request from the Americans to channel requests for information from Abu 'Abd Allah through the Americans. I have no intention of doing any such thing. The intelligence on Abu 'Abd Allah was British. I know I did not pay for the air cargo. But I feel I have the right to deal with your direct on this and am very grateful for the help you are giving us.

Letter by Sir Mark Allen, 18 March 2004

Extract 3

In May 2018, the UK government formally apologised to Belhaj and Boudchar following a lengthy legal battle. Details of the statement were released to Parliament by the UK Attorney General.

THE PRIME MINISTER

10 May 2018

Dear Mr Belhaj and Mrs Boudchar

The attorney general and senior UK government officials have heard directly form you both about your detention, rendition and the harrowing experiences you suffered.

Your accounts were moving and what happened to you is deeply troubling.

It is clear that you were both subjected to appalling treatment and that you suffered greatly, not least the affront to the dignity of Mrs Boudchar who was pregnant at the time.

The UK government believes your accounts. Neither of you should have been treated in this way.

The UK government's actions contributed to your detention, rendition and suffering.

The UK government shared information about you with its international partners.

We should have done more to reduce the risk that you would be mistreated. We accept this was a failing on our part.

Later, during your detention in Libya, we sought information about and from you. We wrongly missed opportunities to alleviate your plight. This should not have happened.

On behalf of Her Majesty's Government, I apologise unreservedly. We are profoundly sorry for the ordeal that you both suffered and our role in it.

The UK government has learned many lessons from this period. We should have understood much sooner the unacceptable practices of some of our international partners and we sincerely regret our failures.

Yours sincerely

Theresa May

Document 21

With the money he received from the Soviet Union (and subsequently from Russia) in exchange for information about American intelligence activities, Aldrich Ames was able to enjoy something of a lavish lifestyle, which by 1990 had started to attract attention within the CIA.

5 December 1990.

Memorandum for: [Deleted.] Office of Security

From: [Deleted.] Counterintelligence Center

1. In connection with our investigation into the compromise of a number of SE Division operations during the mid-1980's, we request that the Office of Security open a reinvestigation on Aldrich H. Ames and review the records of his account at Northwest Federal Credit Union. Our request is based on our receipt of information concerning Ames' lavish spending habits over the past five years. Ames is an SE Division Operations Officer currently assigned to the Counterintelligence Center. While serving in SE Division, he had access to a number of operations that were later compromised. He was favorably polygraphed on 2 May 1986.

2. The Counterintelligence Center has learned the following information about Aldrich Ames and his spouse, Rosario C. Ames:

   On 6 September 1989, Ames and his spouse purchased a home located at 2312 N. Randolph St., Arlington, VA. The home was purchased for $540,000. There is no record of a mortgage or lien filed with Arlington County. A credit check conducted in September 1990 also failed to disclose a mortgage. Ames and his spouse lived in an apartment prior to the purchase of the above home.

   In November 1989, [Deleted] Ames was renovating the kitchen of his new home and redecorating. [Deleted], Ames was sparing no expense.

   Upon his return from Rome (July 89), Ames purchased a white Jaguar, Virginia license number QHI319. The automobile is valued at approximately $49,500. Purchased price and place of purchase are unknown.

   [Deleted], on 1 August 1989, Ames exchanged $22,107 worth of Italian Lira at First Virginia Bank, Arlington, VA (that's approximately 28,363,281 Lira).

   [Deleted], on 18 February 1986, Ames deposited $13,500 into checking account number 183–40-150 at Dominion Federal Bank, Vienna, VA.

   [Deleted], on 18 October 1983, Ames deposited $15,660 in checking account 183–40-150 at Dominion Federal Bank, Vienna, VA.
3. While we are certainly concerned with the above information, there may be a logical explanation for Ames's spending habits. Between 1985 and 1990, Ames mother died. We do not know if Ames received any money or property via insurance or inheritance. A review of public records in the country where his mother lived could answer the question of inheritance. Unfortunately, we do not know the location of his mother's last residence. We have been informed that Ames's mother obituary was listed in the Washington Post. She was formerly employed as a teacher in Fairfax County. [Deleted] she lived in North Carolina.
4. The money could also have come from his in-laws. Ames's in-laws were well connected politically in Colombia. Rasario was formerly the Protocol Officer for the Colombian Embassy in Mexico City. She was directly appointed to that position by the President of Colombia.
5. The deposits made into Ames's checking account could be explained by loans he may have received from Northwest Federal Credit Union. [Deleted.]
6. There is a degree of urgency involved in our request. Since Ames has been assigned to CIC, his access has been limited to a degree. Unfortunately, we are quickly running out of things for him to do without granting him greater access. It is our hope to at least get Ames through polygraph before we are forced to take such action.

7. If you have any questions regarding this investigation, please contact [deleted]. We appreciate your assistance in this matter. [Deleted.]

APPENDIX 2 of US Senate, Select Committee on Intelligence, 'An assessment of the Aldrich H. Ames espionage case and its implications for U.S. intelligence' (1994): memorandum from Counterintelligence Center to Office of Security, 5 December 1990

Document 22

The CIA's use of covert action to shape US foreign policy was laid bare by the findings of the Senate Select Committee to Study Governmental Operations with Respect to Intelligence Activities, popularly known as the 'Church Committee'. Chaired by Senator Frank Church, the committee was part of a wider series of investigations into US intelligence activity, reporting in 1975. The final report detailed CIA links to assassinations and coups around the world.

No activity of the Central Intelligence Agency has engendered more controversy and concern than 'covert action,' the secret use of power and persuasion. The contemporary definition of covert action as used by the CIA – 'any clandestine operation or activity designed to influence foreign governments, organizations, persons or events in support of United States foreign policy' – suggests an all-purpose policy tool. By definition, covert action should be one of the CIA's least visible activities, yet it has attracted more attention in recent years than any other United States foreign intelligence activity. The CIA has been accused of interfering in the internal political affairs of nations ranging from Iran to Chile, from Tibet to Guatemala, from Libya to Laos, from Greece to Indonesia. Assassinations, coups d'etat, vote buying, economic warfare – all have been laid at the doorstep of the CIA. Few political crises take place in the world today in which CIA involvement is not alleged.

Extract: The Church Committee Report

Document 23

The spread of disinformation or 'fake news' is not new and was extensively used during the Cold War. In the 1980s, the KGB developed Operation INFEKTION, a campaign to spread disinformation that the HIV/AIDS virus had been developed by the US in Maryland. The campaign aimed to undermine US credibility around the world and cause tensions with allies, resulting in wild conspiracies on US covert operations. As late as 2005, a report by the RAND Corporation found that nearly 50 per cent of African Americans believed AIDS was man-made. Here the US State Department provides more information on the campaign.

In October 1985, the Soviet Union mounted an extensive campaign to convince the world that the AIDS virus (acquired immunodeficiency syndrome virus, or HIV-I) had been 'manufactured' as a result of genetic engineering experiments conducted at Fort Detrick, Maryland, allegedly to develop new biological weapons. The charge that the AIDS virus could have been created artificially has been rejected by internationally renowned medical and scientific experts. This paper outlines the Soviet disinformation campaign and discusses the technical reasons why the Soviet accusations are false.

One of the most striking aspects of the campaign is the fact that eminent members of the Soviet health community consistently have supplied factual information on AIDS, stressing the natural origins of the disease and attempting to inform the Soviet public about its dangers. This stands in stark contrast to the distortions appearing elsewhere in Soviet media and indicates that Soviet statements on AIDS are being handled at two different official levels, each with differing objectives.

Disinformation alleging the 'manufacture' of the Al DS virus first appeared in mid-1983 in a publication established by the Soviets in India for propaganda purposes (see Appendix A). It has since been published in or broadcast by Soviet media – on at least 32 occasions between January and June 1987 – as part of Moscow's broader efforts to:

- Discredit the United States and generate anti-American sentiment abroad;
- Reinforce longstanding false Soviet propaganda charges of U.S. biological warfare activities and counter U.S. reports of Soviet violations of the 1925 Geneva Protocol on Chemical Weapons and the 1972 Biological Weapons Convention;
- Undermine U.S. defense arrangements with allied countries and create pressures for the removal of U.S. military facilities overseas by inking the spread of AIDS to the presence of U.S. Armed Forces personnel stationed abroad; and
- Discourage contacts with Americans (including tourists, diplomats, and businesspeople) by demonstrating to Soviet citizens that 'American imperialism' is responsible for a frightening disease that has made its way into the U.S.S.R. and Eastern Europe.

United States Department of State: Soviet Influence Activities: A Report on Active Measures and Propaganda, 1986–1987 (August 1987), p. 33

Document 24

In November 2006, former Russian FSB officer Alexander Litvinenko was poisoned in central London using the poison polonium-210 ingested after drinking tea. Litvinenko died twenty-two days later, leading to an extensive police investigation. In 2014, the British government set up an inquiry under Sir Robert Owen, publishing a 300-page report in January 2016. The report concluded that Litvinenko's murder had been likely sanctioned by the Russian President Vladimir Putin. Here Owen summarises the report's findings.

Alexander Litvinenko was born on 4 December 1962, a citizen of the Soviet Union. He died aged 44 on 23 November 2006 in University College Hospital London, by then a British citizen. Post-mortem examination revealed that his death had been caused by an ingestion of a fatal dose of the radioactive isotope polonium-210. The circumstances of his death attracted worldwide interest and concern. They were referred to by the foreign affairs select committee as '... a miniature nuclear attack on the streets of London'. In July 2007 the then Foreign Secretary observed that 'the manner of Litvinenko's death put many hundreds of other people at risk'. A motion of the United States House of Representatives dated 1 April 2008 noted that polonium-210 'could be used to kill large numbers of people, or spread general panic and hysteria among the public'.

In the course of the inquest hearings, it was submitted on behalf of media organisations that the issues to which it gave rise '... include allegations of state-sponsored assassination by radioactive poisoning ...' of a British citizen in London, issues of the greatest public concern.

Over nine years have elapsed since his death ... The inquest into his death was opened by Her Majesty's Coroner for Inner North London on 30 November 2006 but was adjourned pending the police investigation into his death and any ensuing criminal proceedings. The police investigation led to the conclusion that the fatal dose of polonium-210 was probably consumed by Mr Litvinenko on 1 November 2006 when in the company of Mr Andrei Lugovoy and Mr Dmitri Kovtun, Russian nationals, at a hotel in London. Warrants were in due course issued for their arrest, and the Crown Prosecution Service sought unsuccessfully to extradite them from the Russian Federation to stand trial for murder.

...The evidence establishes that Mr Litvinenko ingested the fatal dose whilst drinking tea from a teapot contaminated with polonium-210 in the Pine Bar of the Millennium Hotel in the West End of London in the afternoon of 1 November in the company of Andrei Lugovoy and Dmitri Kovtun. I am sure that Mr Lugovoy and Mr Kovtun placed the polonium-210 into the teapot at the Pine Bar and did so with the intention of poisoning Mr Litvinenko.

I am also sure that the two men made the earlier attempt to poison Mr Litvinenko, also using polonium-210, at a meeting on 16 October 2006. I am sure that Mr Lugovoy and Mr Kovtun knew that they were using a deadly poison and that they intended to kill Mr Litvinenko. I do not, however, believe that they knew precisely what the chemical that they were handling was or the nature of all its properties.

There is no evidence to suggest that either had any personal reason to kill Mr Litvinenko. All the evidence points in one direction, namely that when they killed Mr Litvinenko, they were acting on behalf of someone else. I have concluded that there is a strong probability that when Mr Lugovoy poisoned Mr Litvinenko, he did so under the direction of the FSB, the Federal Security Service of the Russian Federation. I have further concluded that Mr Kovtun was also acting under FSB direction, possibly indirectly through Mr Lugovoy, but probably in the knowledge that that was the body for which he was acting. I have further concluded that the FSB operation to kill Mr Litvinenko was probably approved by Mr Patrushev, then head of the FSB, and also by President Putin.

Statement by Sir Robert Owen, 21 January 2016

Document 25

KGB officer Bohdan Stashynsky fled to West Germany in August 1961 claiming to have assassinated anti-communist Ukrainian dissidents Lev Rebet and Stepan Bandera. Rebet and Bandera's deaths had previously been ruled as natural, with Stashynsky finally revealing that he had used a spray gun firing poison cyanide gas into the faces of his victims. Stashynsky was sentenced to eight years for the killings and released early in 1966, before being given a new identity and moving to South Africa. This CIA document provides insight into KGB assassination plots.

4. ...On 15 October 1959 Stefan Bandera (aka Stefan Popel), Ukranian Chief of the Foreign Section of the Organization of Ukranian Nationalists (Zch/OUN), was assassinated in Munich. Results of the autopsy on Bandera's body showed traces of potassium cyanide poisoning, but it was never established that the cyanide was the cause of death. The autopsy also produced a fragment of gelatinous material which the examining doctors thought might have been the remains of a capsule. There was no proof, however, that the capsule originally contained poison. According to those close to him, Bandera had been taking various pills for a cold ...

5. On 12 August 1961 Bogdan Nikolayevich Stashinskiy (aka Josef Lehman, Siegfried Draeger, Hans Joachim Budeit), Ukrainian, born 4 November 1931, in Borshevitsy, USSR (then in Poland), defected with his wife from East Berlin to West Berlin and told American authorities that, under orders from the KGB, he had assassinated Bandera, as well as Lev Rebet, a leading Ukrainian émigré who had died in 1957 apparently of a heart attack. Stashinskiy, a KGB non-staff agent employee since 1951, said that in both assassinations he had used a weapon which fired a poisonous liquid into the victim's face. This liquid gave off vapors [sic] which were fatal when inhaled by the victim but which left no trace. He

said the weapon used against Rebet had a single barrel, whereas the weapon used against Bandera was double-barrelled.

Memorandum for the Record – Subject: Assassination of Stefan Bandera, 22 April 1976

Document 26

The CIA was involved in several plots to assassinate Cuba's Fidel Castro as early as 1959. Castro and the regime in Havana was seen as a thorn in the side of US policy with plans to kill Castro part of a wider campaign to destabilise Cuba's communist system and return a pro-US government, initially known as 'The Cuba Project' and later 'Operation Mongoose'. One plan discussed CIA files reveal involved the use of Mafia contacts to kill Castro.

1. In August 1960, Mr. Richard M. Bissell approached Colonel Sheffield Edwards to determine if the Office of Security had assets that may assist in a sensitive mission requiring gangster-type action. The mission target was Fidel Castro.
2. Because of its extreme sensitivity, only a small group was made privy to the project. The DCI was briefed and gave his approval ...
3. Robert A. Maheu, a cleared source of the Office of Security, was contacted, briefed generally on the project, and requested to ascertain if he could develop an entree into the gangster elements as the final first step toward accomplishing the desired goal.
4. Mr. Maheu advised that he had met one Johnny Roselli on several occasions while visiting Las Vegas. He only knew him casually through clients, but was given to understand that he was a high-ranking member of the 'syndicate' and controlled all of the ice-cream making machines on the Strip. Maheu reasoned that, if Roselli was in fact a member of the clan, he undoubtedly had connections leading into the Cuban gambling interests.
5. Maheu was asked to approach Roselli, who knew Maheu ... and tell him that he had recently been retained by a client who represented several international business firms which were suffering heavy financial losses in Cuba as a result of Castro's action. They were convinced that Castro's removal was the answer to their problem and were willing to pay a price of $150,000 for its successful accomplishment. It was to be made clear to Roselli that the United States Government was not, and should not, become aware of the operation.
6. The pitch was made to Roselli on 14 September 1960 ... His initial reaction was to avoid getting involved, but through Maheu's persuasion, he agreed to introduce him to a friend, Sam Gold, who knew the 'Cuban crowd'. Roselli made it clear he did not want any money for

his part and believed that Sam would feel the same way. Neither of these individuals were ever paid out of agency funds.

7. During the week of 25 September, Maheu was introduced to Sam ... It was several weeks after his meeting with Sam and Joe, who was identified to him as a courier operating between Havana and Miami, that he saw photographs of both of these individuals ... They were identified as Momo Salvatore Giancana and Santos Trafficant ... Both were on a list of the Attorney General's ten most-wanted men ...
8. In discussing the possible methods of accomplishing this mission, Sam suggested that they not resort to firearms but, if he could be furnished with some type of potent pill, that could be placed in Castro's food or drink, it would be a much more effective operation. Sam indicated that he had a prospective nominee in the person of Juan Orta, a Cuban official who had been receiving kick-back payments from the gambling interests, who still had access to Castro ...
9. TSD was requested to produce six pills of high lethal content.
10. Joe delivered the pills to Orta. After several weeks of reported attempts, Orta apparently got cold feet and asked out of the assignment. He suggested another candidate who made several attempts without success.
11. Joe then indicated that Dr. Anthony Verona, one of the principal officers in the Cuban Exile Junta, had become disaffected with the apparent ineffectual progress of the Junta and was willing to handle the mission through his own resources.
12. He asked, as a prerequisite to the deal, that he be given $10,000 for organisational expenses and requested $1,000 worth of communications equipment.
13. Dr. Verona's potential was never fully exploited, as the project was canceled [sic] shortly after the Bay of Pigs episode. Verona was advised that the offer was withdrawn, and the pills were returned.

Extract from CIA 'Family Jewels' report (May 1973)

References

9/11 Commission Report (2004) London: W.W. Norton.

Aid, Matthew M. (2009a) *The Secret Sentry: The Untold History of the National Security Agency*, New York: Bloomsbury.

Aid, Matthew M. (2009b) 'All Glory Is Fleeting: SIGINT and the Fight against International Terrorism' in Christopher Andrew, Richard J. Aldrich, and Wesley K. Wark (eds.), *Secret Intelligence: A Reader*, Oxon: Routledge, pp. 40–7.

Aid, Matthew M. (2012) *Intel Wars: The Secret History of the Fight against Terror*, New York: Bloomsbury.

Aid, Matthew M. and Wiebes, Cees (2001) 'Introduction: The Importance of Signals Intelligence in the Cold War', *Intelligence and National Security* 16(1), pp. 1–26.

Aldrich, Richard J. (1998) 'British Intelligence and the Anglo-American "Special Relationship" during the Cold War', *Review of International Studies* 24, pp. 331–51.

Aldrich, Richard J. (2009) 'Beyond the Vigilant State', *Review of International Studies* 35(4), pp. 889–902.

Aldrich, Richard J. (2010) 'Allied Code-Breakers Co-Operate – But Not Always', *The Guardian*, 24 June. Available online at www.theguardian.com/world/2010/jun/24/intelligence-sharing-codebreakers-agreement-ukusa

Aldrich, Richard J. (2011) *GCHQ: The Uncensored Story of Britain's Most Secret Intelligence Agency*, London: Harper Press.

Aldrich, Richard J., Cormac, Rory and Goodman, Michael S. (eds.) (2014) *Spying on the World: The Declassified Documents of the Joint Intelligence Committee, 1936–2013*, Edinburgh: Edinburgh University Press.

Alexander, Martin S. (ed.) (1998) *Knowing Your Friends: Intelligence inside Alliances and Coalitions from 1914 to the Cold War*, Oxon: Routledge.

Alford, Stephen (2012) *The Watchers: A Secret History of the Reign of Elizabeth I*, London: Allen Lane.

'Alleged Assassination Plots Involving Foreign Leaders: An Interim Report of the Select Committee to Study Governmental Operations with Respect To Intelligence Activities' (1975) United States Senate, November.

Andrew, Christopher (1985) *Secret Service: The Making of the British Intelligence Community*, London: Heinemann.

Andrew, Christopher (1996) *For the Presidents Eyes Only: Secret Intelligence and the American Presidency from Washington to Bush*, London: HarperCollins.

Andrew, Christopher (2004) 'Intelligence, International Relations and "Under-Theorisation"', *Intelligence & National Security* 19(2), pp. 170–84.

Andrew, Christopher (2009) *The Defence of the Realm: The Authorized History of MI5*, London: Penguin.

Andrew, Christopher and Gordievsky, Oleg (1990) *KGB: The Inside Story of its Foreign Operations from Lenin to Gorbachev*, London: Hodder & Stoughton.

Andrew, Christopher and Gordievsky, Oleg (1991) *Instructions from the Centre: Top Secret Files on KGB Foreign Operations, 1975–1985*, London: Sceptre.

Andrew, Christopher and Elkner, Julie (2003) 'Stalin and Foreign Intelligence', *Totalitarian Movements and Politics Religions* 4(1), pp. 69–94.

Andrew, Christopher and Mitrokhin, Vasili (1999) *The Mitrokhin Archive: The KGB in Europe and the West*, London: Penguin.

Andrew, Christopher and Mitrokhin, Vasili (2006) *The KGB and the World: The Mitrokhin Archive II*, London: Penguin.

'Assessing Russian Activities and Intentions in Recent US Elections' (2017), Intelligence Community Assessment, January.

Ball, Desmond (1989) *Soviet Signals Intelligence (SIGINT)*, Canberra, Australia: Strategic and Defence Studies Centre.

Ball, Desmond (2002) 'Desperately Seeking Bin Laden: The Intelligence Dimension of the War against Terrorism' in Ken Booth and Tim Dunne (eds.), *Worlds in Collision: Terror and the Future of the Global Order*, Basingstoke: Palgrave, pp. 60–73.

Bar-Joseph, Uri (1995) *Intelligence Intervention in the Politics of Democratic States*, University Park, PA: Pennsylvania State University Press.

Bar-Joseph, Uri (2005) *The Watchman Fell Asleep: The Surprise of Yom Kippur and Its Sources*, New York: State University of New York Press.

Barnes, Julian E. (2001) 'P. & G. Said to Agree to Pay Unilever $10 Million in Spying Case', *The New York Times*, 7 September. Available online at www.nytimes.com/2001/09/07/business/p-g-said-to-agree-to-pay-unilever-10-million-in-spying-case.html

Barrass, Gordon S. (2009) *The Great Cold War: A Journey Through the Hall of Mirrors*, Stanford, CA: Stanford Security Studies.

Beitz, Charles R. (2006) 'Covert Intervention as a Moral Problem' in Jan Goldman (ed.), *Ethics of Spying: A Reader for the Intelligence Professional*, Oxford: Scarecrow, pp. 206–20.

Bellaby, Ross (2010) 'What's the Harm? The Ethics of Intelligence Collection', *Intelligence and National Security* 27(1), pp. 93–117.

Bennett, Richard (2003) *Espionage: Spies and Secrets*, London: Virgin Books.

Bergman, Ronen (2018) *Rise and Kill First: The Secret History of Israel's Targeted Assassinations*, London: John Murray.

Betts, Richard (2004) 'The New Politics of Intelligence: Will It Work This Time?', *Foreign Affairs* 83(3). Available online at www.foreignaffairs.com/articles/2004-05-01/new-politics-intelligence-will-reforms-work-time

Bhattacharjee, Yudhijit (2014) 'A New Kind of Spy: How China Obtains American Technological Secrets', *The New Yorker*, 5 May. Available online at www.newyorker.com/magazine/2014/05/05/a-new-kind-of-spy

Black, Ian and Morris, Benny (1991) *Israel's Secret War: Untold History of Israeli Intelligence*, London: Hamish Hamilton.

Blitz, James (2010) 'Brown Defends MI5 after Court Censure', *Financial Times*, 26 February. Available online at www.ft.com/content/08e5e864-2311-11df-a25f-00144feab49a

Bloomfield Jr., Lincoln P. (2006) 'Legitimacy of Covert Action: Sorting out the Moral Responsibilities' in Jan Goldman (ed.), *Ethics of Spying: A Reader for the Intelligence Professional*, Oxford: Scarecrow, pp. 193–205.

Borger, Julian (2017) 'White House "Pressuring" Intelligence Officials to Find Iran in Violation of Nuclear Deal', *The Guardian*, 28 August. Available online at www.theguardian.com/world/2017/aug/28/iran-nuclear-deal-violations-white-house-search-intelligence

Bower, Tom (1995) *The Perfect English Spy: Sir Dick White and the Secret War 1935–90*, New York: St. Martin's Press.

Braithwaite, Sir Roderick (2003) 'Defending British Spies: The Uses and Abuses of Intelligence'. Speech given to The Royal Institute of International Affairs, Chatham House, on 5 December.

Braithwaite, Sir Roderick (2004) Cited in BBC *Panorama*, 'A Failure of Intelligence', July. Available online at http://news.bbc.co.uk/nol/shared/spl/hi/programmes/panorama/transcripts/afailureofintelligence.txt

Bregman, Ahron (2016) *Israel's Wars: A History since 1947*, Oxon: Routledge.

Brewster, Murray (2018) 'NATO Intelligence Chiefs Admit Sharing Secrets Is a "Challenge" within the Alliance', 24 May. Available online at www.cbc.ca/news/politics/nato-intelligence-chiefs-meeting-1.4677045

Bruce, James and George, Roger (eds.) (2014) *Analysing Intelligence: National Security Practitioners Perspectives*, Georgetown; Washington, DC: Georgetown University Press.

Bureau of Investigative Journalism (2017) 'Drone Wars: The Full Data', 1 January. Available online at www.thebureauinvestigates.com/stories/2017-01-01/drone-wars-the-full-data

Campbell, Duncan (2014) 'Revealed: GCHQ's Beyond Top Secret Middle Eastern Spy Base', *The Register*, 3 June.

Carruthers, William Robert (2018) 'Covert Action and Cyber Offensive Operations: Revisiting Traditional Approaches in Light of New Technology', University of Salford PhD thesis (unpublished).

Cullather, Nick (2006) *Secret History: The CIA's Classified Account of Its Operations in Guatemala, 1952–1954* (2nd Edition), Stanford, CA: Stanford University Press.

Cavendish, Anthony (1990) *Inside Intelligence*, London: Collins.

Chambers, David I. (2012) 'The past and present state of Chinese intelligence historiography', *Studies in Intelligence* 56(3), pp. 31–46.

Chaudhuri, Rudra (2013) 'India' in Robert Dover, Michael S. Goodman and Claudia Hillebrand (eds.), *Routledge Companion to Intelligence Studies*, Oxon: Routledge, pp. 182–90.

Childs, David and Popplewell, Richard (1999) *The Stasi: The East German Intelligence and Security Service*, Basingstoke: Macmillan.

CIA (1973) 'Family Jewels' Document. Available online at www.cia.gov/library/readingroom/collection/family-jewels

Cobain, Ian (2013) *Cruel Britannia: A Secret History of Torture*, London: Portobello.

Cobain, Ian (2017) 'How Britain Did Gaddafi's Dirty Work', 9 November. Available online at www.theguardian.com/news/2017/nov/09/how-britain-did-gaddafis-dirty-work-libya

Comey, James (2018) *A Higher Loyalty: Truth, Lies and Leadership*, London: Macmillan.

Cook, Robin (1998) 'Security and Intelligence Agencies', Hansard Col. 583 (2 November). Available online at https://publications.parliament.uk/pa/cm199798/cmhansrd/vo981102/debtext/81102-11.htm#81102-11_spmin0

Corera, Gordon (2009) 'MI6 "Is Not Complicit" in Torture', *BBC News*, 10 August. Available online at http://news.bbc.co.uk/1/hi/uk/8188307.stm

Corera, Gordon (2016) *Intercept: The Secret History of Computers and Spies*, London: Weidenfeld & Nicholson.

Cormac, Rory (2018) *Disrupt and Deny: Spies, Special Forces and the Secret Pursuit of British Foreign Policy*, Oxford: Oxford University Press.

Cradock, Percy (2002) *Know Your Enemy: How the Joint Intelligence Committee Saw the World*, London: John Murray.

Daugherty, William J. (2004) *Executive Secrets: Covert Action and the Presidency*, Lexington, KY: University of Kentucky Press.

Daugherty, William J. (2007) 'The Role of Covert Action' in Loch Johnson (ed.), *Handbook of Intelligence Studies*, Oxon: Routledge, pp. 279–88.

Davies, Huw (2007) 'The Influence of Intelligence on Wellington's Art of Command', *Intelligence and National Security* 22(5), pp. 619–43.

Davies, Philip H.J. (2002) 'Ideas of Intelligence: Divergent National Concepts and Institutions', *Harvard International Review*, Fall, pp. 62–6.

Deacon, Richard (1985) *'C': Biography of Sir Maurice Oldfield*, Colchester, Essex: The Book Service Ltd.

Dorling, Philip (2014) 'Australian Intelligence 'Feeding Data' Used for Deadly US Drone Strikes', 26 May. Available online at www.smh.com.au/politics/federal/australian-intelligence-feeding-data-used-for-deadly-us-drone-strikes-20140526-38ywk.html

Downing Street Memo (2002) Available online at https://nsarchive2.gwu.edu/NSAEBB/NSAEBB328/II-Doc14.pdf

Eftimiades, Nicholas (1994) *Chinese Intelligence Operations*, Ilford: Frank Cass.

Eftimiades, Nicholas (2014) 'China' in Robert Dover, Michael S. Goodman and Claudia Hillebrand (eds.), *Routledge Companion to Intelligence Studies*, Oxon: Routledge, pp. 191–200.

European Parliament, Committee on Civil Liberties, Justice and Home Affairs (2013) 'Draft Report on the US NSA Surveillance Programme, Surveillance Bodies in Various Member States and their Impact on EU Citizens' Fundamental Rights and on Transatlantic Cooperation in Justice and Home Affairs' (2013/2188(INI)).

Ferris, John (2002) 'The Road to Bletchley Park: The British Experience with Signals Intelligence', *Intelligence and National Security* 17(1), pp. 53–84.

Fischer, Benjamin B. (1998) '"One of the Biggest Ears in the World": East German SIGINT Operations', *International Journal of Intelligence and Counter Intelligence* 11(2), pp. 142–53.

Fischer, Benjamin B. (2016) 'Doubles Troubles: The CIA and Double Agents during the Cold War', *International Journal of Intelligence and Counterintelligence* 29(1), pp. 48–74.

Ford, Douglas (2010) 'Realistic Caution and Ambivalent Optimism: United States Intelligence Assessments and War Preparations against Japan, 1918–1941', *Diplomacy & Statecraft* 21(2), pp. 175–201.

Fox, Lauren (2017) 'Ryan on Trump's Meeting with Comey: "He's New to This"', 9 June 2017. Available online at http://edition.cnn.com/2017/06/08/politics/paul-ryan-donald-trump-new-to-this/index.html

Fox News (2016) 'Exclusive: Donald Trump on Cabinet Picks, Transition Process', 11 December. Available online at www.foxnews.com/transcript/2016/12/11/exclusive-donald-trump-on-cabinet-picks-transition-process.html
'Full Text: James Comey Testimony Transcript on Trump and Russia', 8 June. Available online at www.politico.com/story/2017/06/08/full-text-james-comey-trump-russia-testimony-239295
Gaddis, John Lewis (2007) *The Cold War*, London: Penguin.
Gass, Nick (2016) 'Trump: I Don't Trust U.S. Intelligence Information', 17 August. Available online at www.politico.com/story/2016/08/trump-us-intelligence-briefing-227109
Gentry, John A. (2018) 'Favourite INTs: How They Develop, Why They Matter', *Intelligence and National Security*, 33(6), pp. 822–38. DOI: 10.1080/02684527.2018.1449371
Gill, Peter and Phythian, Mark (2012) *Intelligence in an Insecure World* (2nd Edition), Cambridge: Polity Press.
Globalizing Torture (2013) *CIA Secret Detention and Extraordinary Rendition*, New York: Open Society Foundations. Available online at www.opensocietyfoundations.org/sites/default/files/globalizing-torture-20120205.pdf
Goldman, Jan (2006) *Ethics of Spying: A Reader for the Intelligence Professional, Volume 1*, Lanham, MD: Scarecrow Press.
Goodman, Michael S. (2007) 'The Dog That Didn't Bark: The Joint Intelligence Committee and Warning of Aggression', *Cold War History* 7(2), pp. 529–51.
Gorodetsky, Gabriel (1999) *Grand Delusion: Stalin and the German Invasion of Russia*, New Haven, CT: Yale University Press.
Granatstein, J. L. and Stafford, David (1990) *Spy Wars: Espionage and Canada from Gouzenko to Glasnost*, Toronto: Key Porter Books.
Greenwald, Glen (2015) *No Place to Hide: Edward Snowden, the NSA and the Surveillance State*, London: Penguin.
Guo, Xuezhi (2014) *China's Security State: Philosophy, Evolution, and Politics*, Cambridge: Cambridge University Press.
Handel, Michael I. (2004) *Leaders and Intelligence*, Oxon: Routledge.
Hartmann, Christian (2013) *Operation Barbarossa: Nazi Germany's War in the East, 1941–1945*, Oxford: Oxford University Press.
Haslam, Jonathan (2015) *Near and Distant Neighbours: A New History of Soviet Intelligence*, New York: Farrar, Straus and Giroux.
HC 898 (2004) 'Review of Weapons of Mass Destruction' (Butler Report), London: The Stationary Office.
Hennessy, Peter (2001) *The Prime Minister: The Office and Its Holders since 1945*, London: Penguin.
Herman, Michael (1996) *Intelligence Power in Peace and War*, Cambridge: Cambridge University Press.
Herman, Michael (2001) *Intelligence Services in the Information Age*, London: Frank Cass.
Herman, Michael (2004) 'Ethics and Intelligence after September 2001', *Intelligence and National Security* 19(2), pp. 342–58.
Herman, Michael (2011) 'What Difference Did It Make?', *Intelligence and National Security* 26(6), pp. 886–901.
Heuer, Richards J. (1999) *The Psychology of Intelligence Analysis*, Centre for the Study of Intelligence.

Heuer, Richards J. (2005) 'Limits of Intelligence Analysis', *Orbis* 49(1), pp. 75–94.

Hinsley, F.H. (1993) 'Churchill and the Use of Special Intelligence' in Robert Blake and Wm. Roger Louis (eds.), *Churchill*, Oxford: Oxford University Press, pp. 407–26.

HMSO (2005) 'The Handling of Detainees by UK Intelligence Personnel in Afghanistan, Guantanamo Bay and Iraq', Cm. 6469.

HMSO (2013) 'Rendition: Report by the Intelligence and Security Committee', Cm. 7171.

Hopkins, Nick and Borger, Julian (2013) 'Exclusive: NSA Pays £100 Million in Secret Funding for GCHQ', 1 August. Available online at www.theguardian.com /uk-news/2013/aug/01/nsa-paid-gchq-spying-edward-snowden

Horner, David (2014) *The Spy Catchers: The Official History of ASIO, Vol. 1*, Sydney, New South Wales: Allen & Unwin.

'How Germany Spies on Its Friends' (2014) *Spiegel Online*, 18 August. Available online at www.spiegel.de/international/germany/german-considers-turkey-to-be-official-target-for-spying-a-986656.html

Hribar, Gašper, Podbregar, Iztok and Ivanuša, Teodora (2014) 'OSINT: A "Grey Zone"?', *International Journal of Intellligence and CounterIntelligence* 27(3), pp. 529–49.

Hulnick, Arthur S. (2002) 'The Downside of Open Source Intelligence', *International Journal of Intelligence and Counter Intelligence* 15(4), pp. 565–79.

Intelligence Authorization Act (1991) Accessed online at www.congress.gov/bill/ 102nd-congress/house-bill/1455/text

ISC (2013) 'Transcript of Evidence Given to the ISC', 21 July 2014. Available online at http://isc.independent.gov.uk/public-evidence/7november2013

Jeffreys-Jones, Rhodri (2013) *In Spies We Trust: The Story of Western Intelligence*, Oxford: Oxford University Press.

JIC (2002) 'JIC Assessment: Iraqi Use of Chemical and Biological Weapons – Possible Scenarios', 9 September.

JIC (2013) 'Syria: Reported Chemical Weapons Use – Joint Intelligence Committee Letter', 29 August. Available online at www.gov.uk/government/publications/ syria-reported-chemical-weapons-use-joint-intelligence-committee-letter

Johnson, Loch K. (2007) 'Introduction', in Loch K. Johnson (ed.), *Handbook of Intelligence Studies*, Oxon: Routledge.

Johnson, Loch K. (2010a) 'Evaluating Humint: The Role of Foreign Agents in US Security', *Comparative Strategy* 29(4), pp. 308–32.

Johnson, Loch K. (2014) 'The Development of Intelligence Studies' in Robert Dover, Michael S. Goodman and Claudia Hillebrand (eds.), *Routledge Companion to Intelligence Studies*, Abingdon: Routledge.

Johnson, Loch K. (2017) *National Security Intelligence* (2nd Edition), Cambridge, UK: Polity Press.

Johnson, Loch K and Scheid, Kevin J. (1997) 'Spending for Spies: Intelligence Budgeting in the Aftermath of the Cold War', *Public Budgeting and Financing* 17(4), pp. 7–27.

Kahana, Ephraim (2002) 'Early Warnings versus Concept: The Case of the Yom Kippur War 1973', *Intelligence and National Security* 17(2), pp. 81–104.

Kahn, David (1980) *Hitler's Spies*, London: Arrow Books.

Kahn, David (1991) 'The Intelligence Failure of Pearl Harbor', *Foreign Affairs* 70(5), pp. 138–52. Available online at www.foreignaffairs.com/articles/japan/1991-12-01/intelligence-failure-pearl-harbor

Kahn, David (2001) 'An Historical Theory of Intelligence', *Intelligence and National Security* 16(3), pp. 79–92.

Kaleta, Philip (2017) 'Germany Rejects Creating European Intelligence Agency', 5 October. Available online at www.politico.eu/article/germany-rejects-creating-european-intelligence-agency

Kent, Sherman (1966) *Strategic Intelligence for American World Policy*, Princeton, NJ: Princeton University Press.

Kershaw, Ian (2009) *Hitler*, London: Penguin.

Khlevniuk, Oleg V. (2015) *Stalin: New Biography of a Dictator*, New Haven, CT: Yale University Press.

Killough, Ashley (2014) 'Former CIA Chief Michael Hayden slams Feinstein, Torture Report Response', 12 December. Available online at http://edition.cnn.com/2014/12/10/politics/hayden-torture-report-response/index.html

Knightley, Phillip (1986) *The Second Oldest Profession*, London: Andre Deutsch.

Koch, Scott A. (1998) *'Zendebad Shah!': The Central Intelligence Agency and the Fall of Iranian Prime Minister Mohammed Mossadeq, August 1953*, Washington, DC: Central Intelligence Agency.

Lander, Sir Stephen (2004) 'International Intelligence Cooperation: An Inside Perspective', *Cambridge Review of International Affairs* 17(3), pp. 481–93.

Laurent, Sebastien (2013) 'Is There Something Wrong with Intelligence in France? The Birth of the Modern Secret State', *Intelligence and National Security* 28(3), pp. 299–312.

Lawler, David (2016) 'Russia Says it May Reopen Soviet-era Bases in Cuba and Vietnam', *The Telegraph*, 7 October.

Lefebvre, Stephane (2004) 'A Look at Intelligence Analysis', *International Journal of Intelligence and Counter Intelligence* 17(2), pp. 231–64.

Leigh, David (2009) 'Review: The Defence of the Realm', *The Guardian*, 10 October. Available online at www.theguardian.com/books/2009/oct/10/defence-of-the-realm-mi5

Lomas, Dan (2016), *Intelligence, Security and the Attlee Governments, 1945–1951: An Uneasy Relationship?* Manchester, UK: Manchester University Press.

Lomas, Dan (2017) 'Trump versus the Intelligence Agencies – We've Seen It All Before', *The Conversation*. Available online at https://theconversation.com/trump-versus-the-intelligence-agencies-weve-seen-it-all-before-73803#comment_1233354

Lomas, Dan (2018) '"The Most Vulnerable Targets": Why the Soviet Union Loved Both Labour and Tory MPs', *The New Statesman*, 28 February. Available online at www.newstatesman.com/2018/02/most-vulnerable-targets-why-soviet-union-loved-both-labour-and-tory-mps

Lowenthal, Mark (2009) *Intelligence: From Secrets to Policy* (4th Edition), Washington, DC: CQ Press.

Lowenthal, Mark (2017) *Intelligence: From Secrets to Policy* (7th Edition), London: Sage.

Manjikian, Mary (2015) 'But My Hands Are Clean: The Ethics of Intelligence Sharing and the Problem of Complicity', *International Journal of Intelligence and Counter Intelligence*, 28(4), pp. 692–709.

Marks, Paul (2013) 'Submarine Internet Cables Are a Gift for Spooks', *New Scientist*, 25 June.

Matei, Florina Cristiana (2007) 'Romania's Intelligence Community: From an Instrument of Dictatorship to Serving Democracy', *International Journal of Intelligence and CounterIntelligence* 20(4), pp. 629–60.
Matei, Florina Cristiana and Garcia, Andres de Castro (2017) 'Chilean Intelligence after Pinochet; Painstaking Reform of an Inauspicious Legacy', *International Journal of Intelligence and Counter Intelligence* 30(2), pp. 340–67.
Mawdsley, Evan (2007) *Thunder in the East: The Nazi-Soviet War 1941–1945*, London: Bloomsbury.
Mawdsley, Evan (2009) *World War II: A New History*, Cambridge, UK: Cambridge University Press.
Mayer, Jane (2005) 'Outsourcing Torture: The Secret History of America's "Extraordinary Rendition" Programme', *The New Yorker*, 14 February. Available online at www.newyorker.com/magazine/2005/02/14/outsourcing-torture
McAuliffe, Mary S. (ed.) (1992) *CIA Documents on the Cuban Missile Crisis*, Washington, DC: CIA History Staff.
Mercardo, Stephen (2009) 'A Venerable Source in a New Era: Sailing the Sea of OSINT in the Information Age' in Christopher Andrew, Richard J. Aldrich and Wesley K. Wark (eds.), *Secret Intelligence: A Readerw*, Oxon: Routledge, pp. 78–90.
Miller, Greg (2009) 'CIA Pays for Support in Pakistan', 15 November. Available online at http://articles.latimes.com/2009/nov/15/world/fg-cia-pakistan15
Montefoire, Simon Sebag (2004) *Stalin: The Court of the Red Tsar*, London: Phoenix.
Murphy, David E. (1999) 'KGB and MfS: Friendly Enemies', *Intelligence & National Security* 14(3), pp. 228–34.
Murphy, Philip (2002) 'Creating a Commonwealth Intelligence Culture: The View from Central Africa 1945–1965', *Intelligence and National Security* 17(3), pp. 131–62.
Noakes, Jeremy and Pridham, G. (eds.) (1998), *Nazism, 1919–1945: Vol. 3 Foreign Policy, War and Racial Extermination*, Exeter: University of Exeter Press.
Norton-Taylor, Richard (1999) 'Zinoviev Letter Was Dirty Trick by MI6', *The Guardian*, 4 February. Available online at www.theguardian.com/politics/1999/feb/04/uk.politicalnews6
Norton-Taylor, Richard (2010) 'UK Complained to US about Terror Suspect Abuse, Says Ex-MI5 Boss', *The Guardian*, 10 March. Available online at www.theguardian.com/uk/2010/mar/10/manningham-buller-torture
Observer (2013) 'Genoa Coach Dressed "Like Rambo" Caught Spying on Rivals Sampdoria', 14 September. Available online at www.theguardian.com/football/2013/sep/14/genoa-coach-spying-sampdoria-rambo
Olcott, Anthony (2012) *Open Source Intelligence in a Networked World*, New York: Continuum.
Olson, James M. (2001) 'The Ten Commandments of Counterintelligence', *Studies in Intelligence* 11 (Fall–Winter). Available online at www.cia.gov/library/center-for-the-study-of-intelligence/csi-publications/csi-studies/studies/fall_winter_2001/article08.html
Open Society Foundations (2013) *Globalizing Torture: CIA Secret Detention and Extraordinary Rendition*, New York: Open Society Foundations. Available online at www.opensocietyfoundations.org/reports/globalizing-torture-cia-secret-detention-and-extraordinary-rendition

O'Rourke, Lindsey A. (2016) 'The U.S. Tried to Change Other Countries' Governments 72 Times during the Cold War', 23 December. Available online at www.washingtonpost.com/news/monkey-cage/wp/2016/12/23/the-cia-says-russia-hacked-the-u-s-election-here-are-6-things-to-learn-from-cold-war-attempts-to-change-regimes/?noredirect=on&utm_term=.4881365f2fa8

Paglen, Trevor and Thompson, A.C. (2007) *Torture Taxi: On the Trail of the CIA's Rendition Flights*, Cambridge, UK: Icon Books.

Parker, Andrew (2018) 'Director General Andrew Parker Speech to BFV Symposium', 14 May. Available online at www.mi5.gov.uk/news/director-general-andrew-parker-speech-to-bfv-symposium.

Pedlow, Gregory W. and Welzenbach, Donald E. (1998) *The CIA and the U-2 Program, 1954–1974*, Washington, DC: Centre for the Study of Intelligence.

Penrose, Barrie and Courtiour, Roger (1978) *The Pencourt File*, London: Martin Secker & Warburg Ltd.

Perry, David L. (2006) '"Repugnant Philosophy": Ethics, Espionage and Covert Action' in Jan Goldman (ed.), *Ethics of Spying: A Reader for the Intelligence Professional*, Oxford: Scarecrow, pp. 206–20.

Phythian, Mark (2008) 'The British Road to War: Decisionmaking, Intelligence, and the Case for War in Iraq' in James P. Pfiffner and Mark Phythian (eds.), *Intelligence and National Security Policymaking in Iraq*, Manchester, UK: Manchester University Press, pp. 85–105.

Pimlott, Ben (1992) *Harold Wilson*, London: HarperCollins.

Porch, Douglas (1995) *The French Secret Services: From the Dreyfus Affair to the Gulf War*, London: Macmillan.

Prados, John (1996) *Presidents' Secret Wars: CIA and Pentagon Covert Operations from World War II Through to the Persian Gulf*, Chicago, IL: Ivan R. Dee.

Raviv, Dan and Melman, Yossi (2014) *Spies against Armageddon: Inside Israel's Secret Wars*, New York: Levant Books.

Redmond, Paul J. (2010) 'The Challenges of Counterintelligence' in Loch K. Johnson (ed.), *The Oxford Handbook of National Security Intelligence*, Oxford: Oxford University Press, pp. 537–54.

Reinharz, Jehuda and Rabinovich, Itamar (eds.) (2008) *Israel in the Middle East: Documents and Readings on Society, Politics and Foreign Relations, Pre-1948 to the Present*, Lebanon, NH: Brandeis University Press.

Richelson, Jeffrey T. (2012) *The US Intelligence Community* (6th Edition), Boulder, CO: Westview Press.

Richelson, Jeffrey T. and Ball, Desmond (1985) *The Ties that Bind: Intelligence Sharing between the UKUSA Countries*, Boston, MA: Allen & Unwin.

Rimington, Stella (2002) *Open Secret: The Autobiography of the Former Director-General of MI5*, London: Arrow.

Riste, Olav (1999) *The Norwegian Intelligence Service, 1945-1970*, Oxon: Routledge.

Robarge, David (2003) 'Moles, Defectors, and Deceptions: James Angleton and CIA Counterintelligence', *Journal of Intelligence History* 3(2), pp. 21–49.

Roosevelt, Kermit (1979) *Countercoup*. New York: McGraw Hill.

Ruffner, Kevin C. (ed.) (1995) 'CORONA: America's First Satellite Program', Washington, DC: CIA History Staff, Centre for the Study of Intelligence.

Rusbridger, James and Nave, Eric (1991) *Betrayal at Pearl Harbor: How Churchill Lured Roosevelt into War*, New York: Simon & Schuster.

Sawer, Sir John (2010) Speech – Full Text, *The Guardian*, 28 October. Available online at www.theguardian.com/uk/2010/oct/28/sir-john-sawers-speech-full-text

Schaffer, Ryan (2018) 'Indian Intelligence Revealed: An Examination of Operations, Failures and Transformations', *Intelligence and National Security* 33(4), pp. 598–610

Shulsky, Abram N. and Schmitt, Gary J. (2002) *Silent Warfare: Understanding the World of Intelligence* (3rd Edition) Washington, DC: Potomac Books.

Security Intelligence Review Committee (Canada) (2006) *SIRC Annual Report 2005–2006*. Available online at www.sirc-csars.gc.ca/anrran/2005-2006/index-eng.html

Schlesinger Report (1971) 'A Review of the Intelligence Community'. Available online at https://fas.org/irp/cia/product/review1971.pdf

Senate Committe Report (1994) 'An Assessment of the Aldrich H. Ames Espionage Case and its Implications for U.S. intelligence'. Report prepared by the staff of the Select Committee on Intelligence United States Senate, One Hundred Third Congress Second Session. Washington, DC: US Government Printing Office.

Senate Select Committee on Intelligence (2014) Committee Study of the Central Intelligence Agency's Detention and Interrogation Program, December. Available online at www.amnestyusa.org/pdfs/sscistudy1.pdf

Sheffy, Yigal (2006) 'Overcoming Strategic Weakness: The Egyptian Deception and the Yom Kippur War', *Intelligence and National Security* 21(5), pp. 809–28.

Short, Philip (1999) *Mao: A Life*, London: Hodder & Stoughton.

Shpiro, Shlomo (2001) 'Intelligence, Media, and Terrorism: Imperial Germany and the Middle East', *Journal of Intelligence History* 1(1), pp. 21–35.

Sims, Jennifer E. (2006) 'Foreign Intelligence Liaison: Devils, Deals, and Details', *International Journal of Intelligence and Counterintelligence*, 19(2), pp. 195–217.

Sirrs, Owen L. (2010) *A History of the Egyptian Intelligence Service*, Oxon: Routledge.

SIS-5 (2010) Chilcot Inquiry Witness. Available online at webarchive.nationalarchives.gov.uk/20171123124129/ www.iraqinquiry.org.uk/the-evidence/transcripts-videos-of-hearings/hearings-2010-xx-xx-private-3webarchive.nationalarchives.gov.uk/20171123124129/ www.iraqinquiry.org.uk/the-evidence/transcripts-videos-of-hearings/hearings-2010-xx-xx-private-3

Smith, Michael (2004) *The Spying Game: The Secret History of British Espionage*, London: Politicos.

Smith, Michael (2017) *The Anatomy of a Traitor: A History of Espionage and Betrayal*, London: Aurum Press.

Smith-Spark, Laura and Mullen, Jethro (2015) 'France Summons US Ambassador after Reports US Spied on President', *CNN*, 24 June. Available online at http://edition.cnn.com/2015/06/24/europe/france-wikileaks-nsa-spying-claims/index.html

Spillius, Alex (2013) 'Angela Merkel: Spying between Friends Is Unacceptable', *The Telegraph*, 24 October. Available online at www.telegraph.co.uk/news/worldnews/europe/germany/10402570/Angela-Merkel-spying-between-friends-is-unacceptable.html

Stafford, David (2003) *Spies Beneath Berlin*, New York: Overlook.

Suwaed, Muhammad Youssef and Kahana, Ephraim (2018) 'Intelligence in the First Muslim State: 610–632 AD', *International Journal of Intelligence and Counter-Intelligence* 31(1), pp. 169–84.

Taylor, Stan A. and Snow, Daniel (1997) 'Cold War Spies: Why They Spied and How They Got Caught', *Intelligence and National Security* 12(2), pp. 101–25.

Turner, Stansfield (2005) *Burn before Reading: Presidents, CIA Directors and Secret Intelligence*, New York: Hyperion.

United States Congress, Select Committee on Intelligence (1994) 'An Assessment of the Aldrich H Ames Espionage Case and Its Implications for US Intelligence', 1 November. Available online at www.intelligence.senate.gov/sites/default/files/publications/10390.pdf

United States Department of State (1986) *Active Measures: A Report on the Substance and Process of Anti-US Disinformation and Propaganda Campaigns*, United States Department of State Publication 9630, Washington, DC: State Department.

Urban, Mark (1996) *UK Eyes Alpha: The Inside Story of British Intelligence*, London: Faber & Faber.

Vinograd, Samantha (2018) 'Trump Should Be Reading This Every Day', 1 April. Available online at https://edition.cnn.com/2018/02/19/opinions/the-intelligence-brief-trump-should-be-reading-opinion-vinograd/index.html

Walton, Timothy (2010) *Challenges in Intelligence Analysis: Lessons from 1300 BCE to the Present*, Cambridge, UK: Cambridge University Press.

Warner, Michael (2002) 'Wanted: A Definition of "Intelligence"', *Studies in Intelligence* 46(3). Available online at www.cia.gov/library/center-for-the-study-of-intelligence/csi-publications/csi-studies/studies/vol46no3/article02.html

West, Nigel (2007) 'Cold War Intelligence Defectors' in Loch K. Johnson (ed.), *Handbook of Intelligence Studies*, Oxon: Routledge, pp. 237–52.

Westad, Odd Arne (2017) *The Cold War: A World History*, London: Allen Lane, 2017.

Westerfield, H. Bradford (1996) 'America and the World of Intelligence Liaison', *Intelligence and National Security* 11(3), pp. 523–60.

Wicker, Tom (1988) 'Not Covert, Not Smart, Not Right'. Available online at www.nytimes.com/1988/08/02/opinion/in-the-nation-not-covert-not-smart-not-right.html

Wohlstetter, Roberta (1962) *Pearl Harbor: Warning and Decision*, Stanford, CA: Stanford University Press.

Wolf, Marcus and McElvoy, Anne (1997) *Man without A Face: The Autobiography of Communism's Greatest Spymaster*, New York: Random House.

Wolf, Nikita (2016) '"This Secret Town": British Intelligence, the Special Relationship, and the Vietnam War', *The International History Review*, 39(2), pp. 338–67.

Wright, Peter (1987) *Spycatcher: The Candid Autobiography of a Senior Intelligence Officer*, Richmond, Victoria: William Heinemann.

Zegart, Amy (2012) 'The Cuban Missile Crisis as Intelligence Failure', 2 October. Available online at www.hoover.org/research/cuban-missile-crisis-intelligence-failure

Ziegler, Philip (1993) *Wilson: The Authorised Life*, London: Weidenfeld & Nicholson.

Glossary

ABIN *Agência Brasileira de Inteligência* (Brazilian Intelligence Agency)
ABW *Agencja Bezpieczeństwa Wewnętrznego* (Polish Internal Security Agency)
AFI *Agencia Federal de Inteligencia* (Argentinian Federal Intelligence Agency)
AQ al-Qaeda
AISE *Agenzia Informazioni e Sicurezza Esterna* (Italian External Intelligence and Security Agency)
ASD Australian Signals Directorate
ASIO Australian Security Intelligence Organisation
ASIS Australian Secret Intelligence Service
AW Agencja Wywiadu (Polish Foreign Intelligence Agency)
BfV *Bundesamt für Verfassungsschutz* (German Federal Office for the Protection of the Constitution)
BIN Badan Intelijen Negara (Indonesian State Intelligence Agency)
BND *Bundesnachrichtendienst* (German Federal Intelligence Service)
BOSS Bureau of State Security (South Africa)
CBI Central Bureau of Investigation (India)
CI counterintelligence
CIA Central Intelligence Agency (US)
CNI *Centro Nacional de Inteligencia* (Spanish National Intelligence Centre)
COMINT communications intelligence
CSE Communications Security Establishment (Canada)
CSIS Canadian Security Intelligence Service
DCI Director of Central Intelligence
DGSE *Direction générale de la sécurité extérieure* (French General Directorate for External Security)
DGSI *Direction générale de la sécurité intérieure* (French General Directorate for Internal Security)
DI *Dirección de Inteligencia* (Cuban Intelligence Directorate)
DIS Defence Intelligence Staff (UK)
DIS *Dipartimento delle Informazioni per la Sicurezza* (Italian Department of Information Security)

FBI Federal Bureau of Investigation (US)
FO Foreign Office (UK); later Foreign & Commonwealth Office (FCO)
FSB *Federal'naya sluzhba bezopasnosti Rossiyskoy Federatsii* (Russian Federal Security Service)
GC&CS Government Code and Cipher School (UK)
GCHQ Government Communications Headquarters (UK)
GCSB Government Communications Security Bureau (New Zealand)
GID General Intelligence Directorate (Egypt)
GIP General Intelligence Presidency (Saudi Arabia)
HUMINT human intelligence
IMINT imagery intelligence
IRD Information Research Department (UK)
IS Islamic State
ISA Israel Security Agency (Shabak or Shin Bet)
ISI Inter-Services Intelligence (Pakistan)
ISNU Israeli SIGINT National Unit or Unit 8200
JIC Joint Intelligence Committee (UK)
KGB Komitet gosudarstvennoy bezopasnosti (Soviet Union Committee for State Security)
MfS *Ministerium für Staatssicherheit* or Stasi (East German Ministry for State Security)
MI5 Security Service (UK)
MI6 Secret Intelligence Service (SIS) (UK)
Mossad *HaMossad leModi'in uleTafkidim Meyuḥadim* (Israel's Foreign Intelligence Service)
MSS Ministry of State Security (China)
NIS National Intelligence Service (South Korea)
NRO National Reconnaissance Office (US)
NSA National Security Agency (US)
NZSIS New Zealand Security Intelligence Service
OSINT open source intelligence
PDB Presidential Daily Brief
RAW Research and Analysis Wing (India)
RGB Reconnaissance General Bureau (North Korea)
SIED *Serviço de Informações Estratégicas de Defesa* (Defence Strategic Information Service) (Portugal)
SIGINT signals intelligence
SSA State Security Agency (South Africa)
SSD State Security Department (North Korea)
StB *Státní bezpečnost* (Czechoslovakian State Security)
SVR *Sluzhba vneshney razvedki* (Russian Foreign Intelligence Service)
TECHINT technical intelligence
VAJA Ministry of Intelligence of the Islamic Republic of Iran
VSSE State Security Service (Belgium)
WMD weapons of mass destruction

Further reading

General works on intelligence

The field of intelligence studies has expanded rapidly, at least in the 'Anglosphere', and there are numerous works that take a detailed historical approach to the subject. A good example is Jeffrey Richelson's, *A Century of Spies: Intelligence in the Twentieth Century* (Oxford University Press, 1997), a major review of intelligence from Tsarist Russia and the formation of Britain's Secret Service Bureau to beyond the end of the Cold War. Michael Warner's, *Rise and Fall of Intelligence: An International Security History* (Georgetown University Press, 2014) covers the gradual professionalisation of intelligence and the challenge of new technology to the traditional state monopoly on such activity, while Christopher Andrew takes a long-view of the history of spying in *The Secret World: A History of Intelligence* (Allen Lane, 2018), from the ancient world to today's digital revolution. The theoretical study of intelligence has also gained prominence, even if the literature remains largely US focused. Two excellent introductions are Loch K. Johnson, *National Security Intelligence* (2nd edn) (Polity Press, 2017) and Mark Lowenthal, *Intelligence: From Secrets to Policy* (7th edn) (CQ Press, 2016). A classic British study is provided by former JIC secretary Michael Herman, *Intelligence Power in Peace and War* (Cambridge University Press, 1996) who explores the nature, role and effects of intelligence. Edited collections by Christopher Andrew, Richard J. Aldrich and Wesley K. Wark, *Secret Intelligence: A Reader* (2nd edn) (Routledge, 2018) and Loch Johnson, *The Oxford Handbook of National Security Intelligence* (Oxford University Press, 2010) offer valuable insights into intelligence theory and practice. An important study on the current state of intelligence studies in the transatlantic sphere is offered by Christopher Moran and Christopher J. Murphy, *Intelligence Studies in Britain and the US: Historiography since 1945* (Edinburgh University Press, 2013). The thriving nature of intelligence studies is reflected in the growth of content-specific journals such as *Intelligence and National Security*, *Studies in Intelligence*, the *International Journal of Intelligence and Counterintelligence* and *Journal of Intelligence History*.

Global intelligence

The study of intelligence remains largely focused on the traditional powers of the United States and United Kingdom, although a global approach is slowly starting to emerge. Philip H.J. Davies and Kristian C. Gustafson offer an important starting point in their edited collection *Intelligence Elsewhere: Spies and Espionage Outside the Anglosphere* (Georgetown University Press, 2013) as do chapters on Japan, India, China and Spain in Robert Dover, Michael S. Goodman and Claudia Hillebrand (eds.), *Routledge Companion to Intelligence Studies* (Routledge, 2015). Another accessible, if slightly dated, study is Jonathan Bloch and Paul Todd's, *Global Intelligence: The World's Secret Services Today* (Zed Books, 2003). Paul Maddrell, Chris Moran, Ioanna Iordanou and Mark Stout's, *Spy Chiefs, Vol. 2* (Georgetown University Press, 2018) also offers new interpretations of intelligence leadership in Europe, Asia and the Middle East. On individual communities, Jeffrey T. Richelson's updated *The US Intelligence Community* (7th edn) (Westview Press, 2015) offers a useful overview of the complex maze of organisations that make up US intelligence. The literature on British intelligence is rich. Michael Smith, *The Spying Game: The Secret History of British Espionage* (Politico's, 2004), provides a concise history, while the officially sponsored histories by the late Keith Jeffrey, *MI6: The History of the Secret Intelligence Service, 1909–1949* (Bloomsbury, 2010); Andrew, *The Defence of the Realm: The Authorised History of MI5* (Allen Lane, 2009) and Michael Goodman's *The Official History of the Joint Intelligence Community, Vol. 1* (Routledge, 2015) provide more detail. The following works are also recommended for intelligence beyond the UK–US. On Europe, Douglas Porch, *The French Secret Services: From the Dreyfus Affair to the Gulf War* (Macmillan, 1996), while Wolfgang Kreiger's chapter 'The German Bundesnachrichtendienst (BND): Evolution and Current Policy Issues' in Johnson (ed.), *The Oxford Handbook of National Security Intelligence* provides a summary of German foreign intelligence. An excellent study of East Germany's Stasi is David Childs and Richard Popplewell, *The Stasi: The East German Intelligence and Security Service* (Palgrave Macmillan, 1996). On the Soviet Union: Andrew and Oleg Gordievsky, *KGB: The Inside Story* (Hodder & Stoughton, 1990) and Andrew and Vasili Mitrokhin, *The Mitrokhin Archive: The KGB in Europe and the West* (Penguin, 2000). Mark Galeotti's briefing paper 'Putin's Hydra: Inside Russia's Intelligence Services' published by the *European Council on Foreign Relations* is an excellent introduction to the Russian Federations post-Cold War community. The emergence of post-communist agencies in Eastern Europe is documented by Kieran Williams and Dennis Deletant, *Security Intelligence Services in New Democracies: The Czech Republic, Slovakia and Romania* (Palgrave Macmillan, 2001). On Israel, see Dan Raviv and Yossi Melman, *Spies Against Armageddon: Inside Israel's Secret Wars* (Levant Books,

2014) or Ian Black and Benny Morris' *Israeli's Secret Wars: A History of Israel's Intelligence Services* (Warner Books, 1995). On Egypt, read Owen L. Sirrs, *The Egyptian Intelligence Service* (Routledge, 2011), while Kenneth Pollack's classic study *Arabs at War: Military Effectiveness, 1948–1991* (Bison, 2004) provides useful observations of intelligence in the Middle East. The growth of China's intelligence community is covered by Nicholas Eftimiades, *Chinese Intelligence Operations* (Naval Institute Press, 2011) and Xuezhi Guo's, *China's State Security: Philosophy, Evolution and Politics* (Cambridge University Press, 2012). David Horner's, *The Spy Catchers: The Official History of ASIO, 1949–1963* (Allen & Unwin, 2014), John Blaxland, *The Protest Years: The Official History of ASIO, 1963–1975* (Allen & Unwin, 2015) and Blaxland and Rhys Crawley's, *The Secret Cold War: The Official History of ASIO, 1975–1989* (Allen & Unwin, 2016) offer a comprehensive history of the Australian Security Intelligence Organisation. On Canada, read J.L. Granatstein and David Stafford, *Spy Wars: Espionage and Canada from Gouzenko to Glasnost* (Key Porter Books, 1990) while the history of South Africa's controversial intelligence services is addressed by Kevin O'Brien's, *The South African Intelligence Services* (Routledge, 2012).

What is intelligence?

Finding definitions for intelligence is an ongoing area of academic debate. Michael Warner's article, 'Wanted: A definition of "intelligence"', *Studies in Intelligence* 46(3) (2002), is a useful starting point, even if others such as David Kahn question the need to have an agreed definition in 'An historical theory of intelligence', *Intelligence and National Security* 16(3) (2001). Lowenthal (2016) and Johnson (2017) are another useful starting point, as is Peter Gill and Mark Phythian's, *Intelligence in an Insecure World* (2nd edn) (Polity Press, 2012) and Herman's *Intelligence Power in Peace and War*. Comparative studies of intelligence are provided by Davies and Gustafson's edited *Intelligence Elsewhere* and Davies own *Intelligence and Government in Britain and the United States, Vol. 1: Evolution of the U.S. Intelligence Community* (Praeger, 2012).

Intelligence collection

The interest in intelligence collection has resulted in a significant number of books. On HUMINT, a useful introduction is presented by Stan Taylor and Daniel Snow, 'Cold War Spies: Why they spied and how they got caught', *Intelligence and National Security* 12(2) (1997), as is Michael Smith's more recent *The Anatomy of a Traitor: A History of Espionage and Betrayal* (Aurum Press, 2017). The literature on individual spy cases is vast and still growing thanks to a vociferous appetite for scandal. On the 'Cambridge Five' see Andrew and Gordievsky, *KGB* with Soviet intelligence in the United States covered by John Earl Haynes and Harvey Klehr, *Spies: The Rise and Fall of the KGB in America* (Yale University Press, 2010). Jeremy Duns tells the story of CIA/SIS agent Oleg Penkovsky in *Dead Drop: The True Story of Oleg Penkovsky* (Simon and Schuster, 2014) and former KGB officer Oleg Gordievsky reveals his own life as an SIS agent in *Next Stop Execution* (Macmillan, 1995). A useful introduction to SIGINT is Matthew M. Aid and Cees Wiebes (eds.), *Secrets of Signals Intelligence During the Cold War: From Cold War to Globalisation* (Frank Cass, 2001) while Aid's own history of the NSA, *The Secret Sentry: The Untold History of the National Security Agency* (Bloomsbury, 2009) gives an agency-focused study. The early development of British SIGINT and work of Bletchley Park is told by Ralph Erskine and Michael Smith (eds.), *The Bletchley Park Codebreakers* (Biteback, 2011), while Richard J. Aldrich's, *GCHQ: The Uncensored Story of Britain's Most Secret Intelligence Agency* (Harper-Collins, 2011) explores British SIGINT after 1945. BBC security correspondent Gordon Corera provides an introduction to intelligence in the digital age in *Intercept: The Secret History of Computers and Spies* (Weidenfeld & Nicholson, 2015). There is also a growing literature on other forms of intelligence. US/UK Cold War overflights of the Soviet Union are covered by Paul Lashmar's, *Spy Flights in the Cold War* (Naval Institute Press, 1997), while Kevin Ruffner, *Corona: America's First Satellite Program* (Morgan James, 2005) documents the CIA's use of satellite technology. On OSINT, read Anthony Olcott, *Open Source Intelligence in a Networked World* (Continuum, 2012) and David Omand, Jamie Bartlett and Carl Miller's report *#Intelligence* (Demos, 2012) on the interrelated subject of social media intelligence (SOCMINT). An excellent introduction to prisoner interrogation can be found in Andrew and Simona Tobia (eds.), *Interrogation in War and Conflict: A Comparative and Interdisciplinary Analysis* (Routledge, 2014).

Intelligence analysis

Intelligence analysis has often been overlooked but there is now an increasing body of work on the subject. Lowenthal (2016) and Johnson (2017) provide an overview of analysis, while a more detailed study of the discipline comes from James Bruce and Roger George, *Analyzing Intelligence: National Security Practitioners Perspectives* (2nd edn) (Georgetown University Press, 2014) and Julian Richards, *The Art and Science of Intelligence Analysis* (Oxford University Press, 2010). CIA veteran Richards Heuer Jnr. provides an invaluable study of the problems facing analysts in *Psychology of Intelligence Analysis* (CIA, 1999) and 'Limits of Intelligence Analysis' *Orbis* 49(1) (2004), with the subject of intelligence failure dealt with by Robert Jervis in *Why Intelligence Fails: Lessons from the Iranian Revolution and the Iraq War* (Cornell University Press, 2011). Timothy Walton provides individual case studies of failure in *Challenges in*

Intelligence Analysis: Lessons from 1300 BCE to the Present (Cambridge University Press, 2011). On the Yom Kippur War, read Uri Bar-Joseph's *The Watchman Fell Asleep: The Surprise of Yom Kippur and Its Sources* (State University of New York Press, 2005). The 9/11 Commission Report is an invaluable resource in understanding US intelligence before the terror attacks in Washington and New York in September 2001. The controversy over intelligence assessments of Iraqi WMD has also generated a significant amount of material on analysis. In the UK, Lord Butler's Review *of Intelligence on Weapons of Mass Destruction* (The Stationary Office, 2004) provides a detailed post-mortem of the JIC, while, in the US, the Senate Intelligence Committee report on The US Intelligence Community's Prewar Intelligence Assessments on Iraq (2004) provided evidence of groupthink, flawed assumptions and the pressures placed on analysts. The CIA's *Documents on the Cuban Missile Crisis 1962* (CIA History Staff, 1992) edited by Mary McAuliffe provides readers with a window into agency assessments during the crisis, with examples of British intelligence assessments found in Richard J. Aldrich, Rory Cormac and Michael S. Goodman (eds.), *Spying on the World: The Declassified Documents of the Joint Intelligence Committee, 1936–2013* (Edinburgh University Press, 2014).

Intelligence and policy

For a general approach to the complex relationship between intelligence officials and policymakers see Michael Handel, *Leaders and Intelligence* (Frank Cass, 2004). Israeli academic Uri Bar-Joseph delivers a detailed look at policymakers in the United States, Israel and Britain with *Intelligence Intervention in the Politics of Democratic States* (The Pennsylvania Press, 1995). JIC Secretary Percy Cradock's *Know Your Enemy: How the Joint Intelligence Committee Saw the World* (John Murray, 2002) remains a classic for its theory of intelligence–policy relations. For a detailed study of intelligence relations with the US White House, read Christopher Andrew's *For the President's Eyes Only: Secret Intelligence and the American Presidency from Washington to Bush* (HarperCollins, 1996) and former DCI Stansfield Turner, *Burn Before Reading: Presidents, CIA Directors and Secret Intelligence* (Hyperion, 2006). A critical look at Trump's relationship with the US intelligence community can be found in former DCI Michael Hayden's *The Assault on Intelligence: American National Security in an Age of Lies* (Penguin, 2018), while former FBI James Comey gives an equally scathing first-hand assessment in *A Higher Loyalty: Truth, Lies, and Leadership* (Macmillan, 2018). On British Prime Ministers and intelligence, Peter Hennessy's *The Prime Minister: The Office And Its Holders Since 1945* (Penguin, 2001) gives a useful introduction, with Richard J. Aldrich and Rory Cormac offering more detail in *The Black Door: Spies, Secret Intelligence and British Prime Ministers* (William

Collins, 2017). Examples of individual Prime Ministers can be found in David Stafford, *Churchill and Secret Service* (Thistle, 2013) and Daniel Lomas, *Intelligence, Security and the Attlee Governments, 1945–1951: An Uneasy Relationship?* (Manchester University Press, 2016). Andrew and Julie Elkner's article 'Stalin and Foreign Intelligence', *Totalitarian Movements and Political Religions* 4(1) (2003), highlights Stalin's paranoia over intelligence, while Jonathan Haslam's comprehensive history *Near and Distant Neighbours: A New History of Soviet Intelligence* (Farrar, Straus and Giroux, 2016) contains numerous examples of intelligence politicisation, as do Andrew and Mitrokhin in *The Mitrokhin Archive* parts 1 and 2. Intelligence and Nazi policymaking in Hitler's Germany is covered by David Kahn's classic *Hitler's Spies: German Military Intelligence in World War II* (Da Capo Press, 2000) and David Jablonsky's chapter, 'The paradox of duality: Adolf Hitler and the concept of military surprise', in Handel's *Leaders and Intelligence*.

Intelligence liaison

Stephen Lander's 'Cambridge intelligence cooperation: an inside perspective', *Cambridge Review of International Affairs* 17(3) (2004) and Herman's *Intelligence Power in Peace and War* offer valuable UK practitioner-based insights into intelligence liaison. While the merits of liaison are well documented, H. Bradford Westerfield's 'America and the World of Intelligence Liaison', *Intelligence and National Security* 11(3) (1996) suggests US reliance on liaison has been negative for US national security, especially because of the US reliance on allies for HUMINT. On the history of liaison, Jeffrey T. Richelson and Desmond Ball give an important (if a little dated) overview of the UKUSA community in *The Ties That Bind: Intelligence Cooperation between the UKUSA Countries* (Allen & Unwin, 1985). The history of transatlantic intelligence and security cooperation is documented in Rhodri Jeffreys-Jones, *In Spies We Trust: The Story of Western Intelligence* (Oxford University Press, 2015) and Jeffreys-Jones and David Stafford's *American-British-Canadian Intelligence Relations, 1939–2000* (Routledge, 2000), while US–UK liaison and the war on terror has been studied by Adam Svendsen's *Intelligence Cooperation and the War on Terror: Anglo-American Security Relations after 9/11* (Routledge, 2012). In the Cold War, Norway's proximity to the Soviet Union made her spies a valuable ally for British and American intelligence, as Olav Riste's *The Norwegian Intelligence Service, 1945–1951* (Frank Cass, 1999) discusses, while details of Cold War liaison in the Eastern Bloc can be found in Andrew and Mitrokhin in *The Mitrokhin Archive* parts 1 and 2, as they can in Haslam's single volume of Soviet intelligence *Near and Distant Neighbours*. The issue of 'spying on friends' is covered by Martin Alexander's edited collection *Knowing Your Friends: Intelligence Inside Alliances and Coalitions from 1914 to the Cold War* (Frank Cass, 1998). Matthew Aid's *Intel Wars: The*

Secret History of the Fight Against Terror (Bloomsbury Press, 2012) includes details of the strained relationship between the CIA and Pakistani ISI, while the darker aspects of liaison post-9/11 and claims of complicity in torture are examined in Trevor Paglen and A.C. Thompson's investigative *Torture Taxi: On the Trail of the CIA's Rendition Flights* (Icon Books, 2007). The contemporary impact of Brexit on UK and European security is dealt with in a special edition of the *Journal of Intelligence History*, 16, no. 2 (2017).

Counterintelligence

Counterintelligence's 'wilderness of mirrors' is the subject of numerous books, chapters and articles. Chapters in Shulsky and Gary Schmitt (2002), Lowenthal (2016) and Johnson (2017) provide a general overview as do chapters in Johnson's edited *Oxford Handbook of National Security Intelligence* (2010). Former CIA officer Frederick Wettering's article 'Counterintelligence: The broken triad', *Journal of Intelligence and CounterIntelligence*, 13, 265–300, highlights some of the generic problems of counterintelligence, looking at US examples, while the 1994 report by the US Senate Select Committee on Intelligence, 'An assessment of the Aldrich H. Ames espionage case and its implications for U.S. intelligence' (Washington, 1994), provides an important case study. Taylor and Snow's article 'Cold War Spies: Why they spied and how they got caught' and John Earl Haynes and Harvey Klehr provide a useful introduction to Cold War espionage in their book *Early Cold War Spies: The Espionage Trials that Shaped American Politics* (Cambridge University Press, 2006). On the VENONA programme, John Earl Haynes and Harvey Klehr's book *VENONA: Decoding Soviet Espionage in America* (Yale University Press, 2000) highlights the importance of the project to Western counterintelligence, with declassified examples found in the CIA-edited collection *Venona: Soviet Espionage and the American Response, 1939–1957* (1996). The following works are recommended for information on individual spy cases: on members of the Cambridge Five, Ben Macintyre, *A Spy Among Friends: Philby and the Great Betrayal* (Bloomsbury, 2015) and Andrew Lownie's, *Stalin's Englishman: The Lives of Guy Burgess* (Hodder, 2016) are useful. A first-hand account of counterintelligence is provided by FBI officer Robert J. Lamphere's, *FBI-KGB War: A Special Agents Story* (W.H. Allen, 1988).

Covert action

Tales of wartime special operations, assassinations and dirty tricks have resulted in a large number of books on the subject. Lowenthal (2016) and Johnson (2017) contain general introductions, as do chapters in the edited collections by Andrew, et al. (2018) and Johnson (2010). Another good introduction is Abram Shulsky and Gary Schmitt, *Silent Warfare: Understanding the World of Intelligence* (Brassey's, 2002). On country-by-country studies, Israeli use of targeted killing is documented by Ronen Bergman's, *Rise and Kill First: The Secret History of Israel's Targeted Assassinations* (John Murray, 2018) while Dan Raviv and Yossi Melman provide further detail on Israeli operations. Britain's post-1945 use of covert action and special operations are provided by Rory Cormac's, *Disrupt and Deny: Spies, Special Forces, and the Secret Pursuit of British Foreign Policy* (Oxford University Press, 2018). As expected, the CIA's long relationship with special action has resulted in a rich literature. Tim Weiner's, *Legacy of Ashes: The History of the CIA* (Allen Lane, 2007) is a readable, if sensationalised, account of the Agency, with John Parados exploring CIA activity from Eastern Europe to the Persian Gulf in *Presidents' Secret Wars* (2nd edn) (Ivan R Dee, 1996). Andrew and Gordievsky, and Haslam provide details on KGB 'wet operations'. On Iran, read Mark Gasiorowski and Malcolm Byrne (eds.), *Mohammad Mossadeq and the 1953 Coup in Iran* (Syracuse University Press, 2017) with the CIA having declassified documents on the Guatemalan coup which can be found on their website. A Cuban view of CIA operations against Fidel Castro is given by Fabian Escalante's, *Executive Action: 638 Ways to Kill Fidel Castro* (Ocean, 2007). The importance of propaganda is underlined by Philip Taylor in *Munitions of the Mind: A History of Propaganda* (3rd edn) (Manchester University Press, 2003).

Index